MANCHESTER MEDIEVAL LITERATURE

GREENERY

Manchester University Press

MANCHESTER MEDIEVAL LITERATURE

J.J. ANDERSON, GAIL ASHTON *series editors*

This series is broad in scope and receptive to innovation, bringing together a variety of approaches. It is intended to include monographs, collections of commissioned essays, and editions and/or translations of texts, with a focus on English and English-related literature and culture. It embraces medieval writings of many different kinds (imaginative, historical, political, scientific, religious) as well as post-medieval treatments of medieval material. An important aim of the series is that contributions to it should be written in a style which is accessible to a wide range of readers.

already published

Language and imagination in the Gawain-poems
J.J. Anderson

Water and fire: The myth of the Flood in Anglo-Saxon England
Daniel Anlezark

The Parlement of Foulys (by Geoffrey Chaucer)
D.S. Brewer (ed.)

Greenery

Ecocritical readings of late medieval English literature

GILLIAN RUDD

Manchester University Press
MANCHESTER AND NEW YORK

distributed exclusively in the USA by Palgrave

Copyright © Gillian Rudd 2007

The right of Gillian Rudd to be identified as the editor of this work has been asserted by her in accordance with the Copyright, Designs and Patents Act 1988.

Published by Manchester University Press
Oxford Road, Manchester M13 9NR, UK
and Room 400, 175 Fifth Avenue, New York, NY 10010, USA
www.manchesteruniversitypress.co.uk

Distributed exclusively in the USA by
Palgrave, 175 Fifth Avenue, New York NY 10010, USA

Distributed exclusively in Canada by
UBC Press, University of British Columbia, 2029 West Mall, Vancouver, BC, Canada V6T 1Z2

British Library Cataloguing-in-Publication Data
A catalogue record for this book is available from the British Library

Library of Congress Cataloging-in-Publication Data
A catalog record for this book is available from the Library of Congress

ISBN: 0 7190 7249 2 paperback

ISBN 13: 978 0 7190 7249 9

First published 2007 by Manchester University Press

First digital, on-demand edition produced by Lightning Source 2010

Contents

	Acknowledgements	*page* vii
	Introduction: green reading	1
1	Earth	21
2	Trees	48
3	Wilds, wastes and wilderness	91
4	Sea and coast	133
5	Gardens and fields	165
	References	207
	Index	217

Acknowledgements

My thanks go to the Arts and Humanities Research Board for awarding me a Research Leave Grant, and to the School of English at Liverpool University, as well as the University itself, for granting me the semester's leave which allowed me to apply for the AHRB grant. More personally, I would also like to thank Alastair Minnis, Jocelyn Wogan-Browne and John Anderson for their unfailing help and support with this project, and Jonathon Bate, Ruth Evans, Terry Gifford, Lisa Kiser, John Parham, Ralph Pite and Felicity Riddy for their various helpful comments and reactions to the several conference papers and drafts which presaged the current volume. Paul Baines has read most of these chapters with remarkably little complaint, while, as ever, my family has been long-suffering over the course of their composition. I am also very grateful to The Landmark Trust for permission to use the picture of St Winifred's Well on the cover of this book. St Winifred's Well in Shropshire is owned and maintained by The Landmark Trust and is available for holiday bookings (see www.landmarktrust.org.uk).

In writing this book I have tried to bear in mind readers whose acquaintance with middle English literature may be comparatively slight. As a consequence I have tended to quote from editions that are readily available and offer a good deal of help in the way of glosses and commentary, rather than necessarily the most scholarly (the terms are not necessarily exclusive). For similar reasons, letter forms have been modernised, even when quotations are from editions that retain thorn etc. Naturally, much reference has been made to the scholarship and criticism surrounding the texts discussed here; I trust my debt there is evident in the notes and bibliography.

St Winifred's Well

Introduction: green reading

The picture at the front of this book is of a small cottage which was originally a shrine to St Winifred in the hamlet of Woolston, not far from Oswestry in Shropshire.¹ The shrine building dates from 1485, although the site itself has been regarded as holy since the twelfth century, when a well was reputed to have sprung from the spot where St Winifred's remains rested briefly en route from her burial site to Shrewsbury, where her relics were to be housed. St Winifred's Well, as it is now called, is not the famous well at Holywell, but it is dedicated to the same saint and the architecture of its humble cottage echoes that of the larger Holywell buildings. This lesser site has waxed and waned in popularity and the area immediately around it has changed concomitantly. Currently it is situated on a triangle of land, nestling quietly between working farms, with trees, hedges and a pool, fed by the spring which is still guided out from underneath the cottage through stone basins. A quiet public footpath runs through the plot, rather neatly separating the old cottage from the newly adapted pigsty which has been renovated to be a simple but nonetheless modern bathroom. Sitting in the doorway or on the edge of one of the basins it is possible to feel thoroughly surrounded, cocooned even, by the natural world. Tree-creepers, wrens, owls, goldcrests, toads, voles, shrews, harvest mice, kingfishers, swifts and bats all add to this feeling, and the careful restoration of the cottage itself to a quietly modified version of its fifteenth-century origins adds a sense of 'stepping back in time' which is frequently attested by the comments in the visitors' log book. Nature, apparently untouched and undisturbed by the holidaymaker's presence, is all around.

St Winifred's Well encapsulates many of the paradoxical elements that cluster together in environmentalist thinking and ecocriticism alike and epitomises my own interests in bringing current green literary criticism to bear on late medieval texts. The cottage occupies a geographical, environmental and commercial position made up of many of the contradictions inherent in our human relations with the non-human world. Its appeal lies in its apparent remoteness, but in fact it nestles on several different kinds of borders. Most immediately it is tucked between working farms, whose buildings are carefully screened from sight by trees and hedges cropped by their cattle. Regionally, it is situated in the borderlands of Wales and England and so partakes of both without being limited to either. It is a site where various reactions to and version of the natural world meet, blurring the division between spontaneous and man-made landscape. The spring itself is natural, occurring without human aid or intervention and is a constant source of fresh water, but now inaccessible to larger animals because of the buildings around it. The bathing basins and timber-framed cottage are not natural per se, but are constructed from natural materials, both originally and in its latest restoration by the Landmark Trust who now owns it (itself a reflection of modern interest in historical accuracy and environmental issues). Their existence reflects the natural human impulse to both sanctify and seek to contain natural sites like springs. Many of the trees have been deliberately planted, others encouraged, cut back or converted to hedges as human preference or need required. The pool in its current form is the result of human intervention, created by digging out the banks of the stream which ran from the well, but the wildlife that visits or lives in its environs has made its own way there – although it is now actively encouraged as enhancing the aesthetic and commercial appeal of the spot. Yet however much one detects artifice in even the most 'untouched' aspect of this place, here, as elsewhere, the influence of the non-human should also be acknowledged: the sycamore tree in the hawthorn hedge is likely to be fortuitous, even if 'allowed' to remain by the human custodians of the land. Human and non-human influences intertwine, and the non-human world is as ready to exploit us and the environs we create as we are it and them. Relations are fluid, depending on the species concerned and the time of year, but they are not entirely one-way. Many visitors bring animal companions, as I did, somewhat to the detriment of the rodent population, but arguably to the delight of the grasses whose seeds are carried further afield by the coats of enthusiastic pets charging in and out of hedges new to them. Finally, the effects of such visits are carried away by the visitors and for a while at least affect how they view their usual environs and the stories they tell.

This last function raises questions about the purpose of preserving such places. Its carefully maintained lawn and pond could be cited as proof of humankind's inability to let the non-human world exist unless it has some value in human terms (here that of recreation) while also of giving humans the sense of being benign controllers. At the same time the array of wildlife, plant as well as animal, could be taken to show that is it not just humans for whom such pockets of land act as a refuge. Taking that line further, it becomes possible to argue that insisting that such places serve only a human purpose denies the non-human world autonomy and denigrates other species's evident ability to turn our manipulation of habitats to their advantage. Of course, this is by no means always the case: humans have destroyed a good deal in pursuit of their own convenience or pleasure, but in this particular case it is not possible to argue straightforwardly that human intervention has been bad for other forms of life. St Winifred's Well is thus simultaneously an example of humans imposing their preferred version of what is desirable on the non-human world, an instance of the seemingly innate human impulse to venerate the non-human world, and a demonstration of the resilience of the actual, real world in the face of human control. Most importantly all these elements coexist, however much they may seem to be at odds in the abstract. The result is a sense of unease, which, once noticed, is hard to allay, but which itself is a rich response, albeit one that makes it impossible to arrive at a single, unambiguous and uncompromised reaction to places such as this.

All of this is pertinent to ecocritical literary study. The questions raised and the contradictions foregrounded by considering the existence and effects of such places as St Winifred's Well are the same as those found when analysing texts in the light of current green concerns. Not all the questions are asked of the texts; some will highlight the contradictions inherent in green reading, but that is right. Ecocriticism cannot be a school that seeks to create and maintain a single, uniform outlook. Central to ecological thinking in general is a recognition of the importance of diversity – of species, of environments and even of approach. Balance is achieved not through the eradication of one thing and the total dominance of another but by a constant movement of position that keeps everything in play, as now one thing takes precedence, now another, and each responds to the other elements, wittingly or not, in the constant shift of life and death, survival and extinction.

In this volume I explore some of the literary borderlands where human and non-human meet. The meeting grounds I have chosen are late medieval English texts, here presented as sites where modern 'green' concerns with how humans relate to, construct and inhabit the world coincide with how these things are articulated by medieval literary texts. Such 'green reading' is not, of course, to be confused with claims that any given text is itself 'green'. Rather the chapters that follow should be regarded as essays in the true sense: explorations of ideas here conducted with the premiss that the arguments need to be led by what is in the individual texts themselves, with the aim of revealing what ecocriticism can bring to the fore that is usually either relegated to the background or simply overlooked altogether. In order to make this process more accessible I have elected to concentrate on mainstream texts thus providing some degree of shared and familiar territory for most readers. At the same time, working with material such as Chaucer's poetry, the works of the *Pearl* poet and Langland will show that green concerns are not restricted to texts that deal exclusively and obviously with human/non-human nature relations. That is not to say that green analysis of less well-known material should not be done, merely that it is not done here.

Which brings us to the question: what is ecocriticism? Rebecca Douglass has provided a succinct definition in her article 'Ecocriticism and Middle English Literature' where she says: 'ecocriticism is reading with attention to treatments of nature, land, and place, informed by a desire to understand past and present connections between literature and human attitudes regarding the earth'(Douglass 1998: 138). This is certainly a place to start, but green reading goes beyond simply paying attention to how nature, land and place are treated in terms of representation. Close attention has already been paid to the role of landscape in literature in these terms, not least by Pearsall and Salter who begin *Landscapes and Seasons of the Medieval World* (1973) with an assertion which simultaneously highlights the frequency with which landscape occurs in medieval romance and dismisses a large number of such appearances: 'Where landscape has no symbolic purpose to fulfil, it hardly exists, except as a series of glimpses caught by the knight from the road, or the lady from the castle window' (Pearsall and Salter 1973: 52). The kind of attention advocated by Douglass means that we do not allow even 'glimpses' of landscape to pass without comment, instead we ask the question: why is that particular unsymbolic glimpse of landscape included there? And we are not satisfied with an answer that accounts for such passing sightings in terms of adding local colour or even a touch of realism. Rather, ecocriticism calls upon us to recognise the extent to which, as Glen Love puts it, the 'enveloping natural world is a part of the subject on the printed page before us [and] even when it is not, it remains as a given, a part of the interpretive context' (Love 2003: 16). That interpretative context will include such questions as: how far humans are regarded part of the world, how far set apart from it; whether nature (or Nature) is seen in hierarchical terms or as made up of a vast array of different things each equally worthy; whether humans are stewards of nature with a duty to protect as well as use it, a privileged species who by nature and divine decree may exploit the world around with impunity, or simply one of a vast number of life forms, no more nor less valuable, albeit more capable of making a distinctive mark; what the effects are of regarding the non-human natural world as a reflection of the divine mind and sometimes a tool for divine retribution. The list is long and by no means homogeneous, nor do the items listed here exhaust it, but this version serves to indicate the reach and variety of topics explored by green reading.

Although the elements focused upon inevitably alter according to which text is being read, some concerns persist throughout. Chief amongst these is the issue of anthropocentrism. Buried within Douglass's 'desire to understand past and present connections between literature and human attitudes regarding the earth' is the admission that humans are too readily self-referential in their attitudes. Ecocriticism strives to move away from the anthropocentrism which creates and operates a value-system in which the only things that are seen, let alone valued, are those that serve some kind of purpose in human terms. This in turn raises the difficulty of how we may speak for the Other (all that is not human) without either perpetuating the human/non-human divide or absorbing that Other into the human. Clearly to speak for it risks abrogating it into the human, the very thing ecological theory urges us to avoid, yet not to speak for it seems to relegate it to the realm of silence and thus render it invisible, again, a position greens seek to avoid. This debate is perhaps most clearly conducted in terms of anthropomorphism, and it has been tackled in these terms by both Jonathan Bate and Val Plumwood. Where Bate's main aim is to trace the rise of human awareness of the non-human as a valid Other, Plumwood explores the consequences of both adopting and rejecting anthropomorphism, finally arguing that such metaphorical habits may be the most effective ways humans have of attempting to apprehend and value the non-human world.[2]

Given that we are human it may be a fallacy to say we can ever move beyond the bounds of our own views of the world. Yet ecocriticism, like the green movement in general, believes that the attempt is worth the effort for the shift in attitudes and worldview it offers. Rachel Carson, whose *Silent Spring* has been credited with starting the environmentalist and ecological movements, asserted that 'the more clearly we can focus our attention on the wonders and realities of the universe about us, the less taste we shall have for destruction' (1954).[3] While for some that assertion may seem utopian, it has the virtue not only of advocating the kind of attention promoted by literary critics like Douglass but also of introducing the idea of wonder as a positive and valid response to the non-human world. For Carson, as for many others (green critics among them), wonders and realities are not opposites but two ways of describing the same thing. To acknowledge wonder is to acknowledge a sense of humility and also of integration of ourselves with the world as a whole. For the texts focused upon in this volume that world is also very clearly a created whole and, as the section on Hugh of St Victor and *Piers Plowman* illustrates, wonder is an appropriate and indeed necessary response; one that reveals proper attention to the Creation of which we are an integral part.

Understanding ourselves as constituent parts of a wider whole and further appreciating that this means that our actions have consequences for all other elements of the world is part of the notion of interconnectedness that is central to green thinking. That is that species and elements that seem distinct are in fact bound by a web of connections, each dependent on others to greater or less degrees. None is truly able to function without the other, or at least not for long. Such thinking is now frequently presented under the short hand term 'ecosystem' and we are becoming accustomed to references to very small ecosystems, such as can be created by the close proximity of plants in a house or garden, and the much larger ecosystem that defines our world. It is not possible to exist outside an ecosystem of some sort and all things necessarily partake of the largest one of the planet as a whole. Even on a local level, where it is possible to say that particular individuals (human or other) are not part of a given system, it is still the case that their being outside it helps to define it.

Bringing Carson and Love together it is possible to see an analogy between ecosystems and literary analysis. The effects and applications of green reading reach from detailed close readings of passages embedded in larger texts to wider, general conclusions about habits of thought, representation or attitude. As with current ecological and environmental debates, the two may conflict with each other, as what emerges from a close reading may be at odds with the evident general attitudes of the larger text, yet that does not mean that either the micro or macro interpretation is wrong. It merely shows that the two coexist. This recognition is particularly liberating for ecocriticism as it allows it to explore texts that are not overtly 'about' nature. Indeed, although ecocriticism can be said to have its roots in the study of American nature writing or the British Romantics, it is now reaching into every genre and period. As the title of Armbruster and Wallace's 2001 collection of essays indicates, ecocriticism is expanding *Beyond Nature Writing*.

As the range of texts subjected to green criticism is increased, a debate about ecocritical methodology comes to the fore.[4] In part this is due to an understandable desire to get away from being boxed into dealing only with descriptions of landscape in literature, but it also reflects the range of disciplines ecocriticism draws upon, each with its own established methods of investigation. Thus philosophy, literary criticism and scientific exposition jostle each other in arguments over what kind of methodology green readers should adopt.[5] Such diversity is welcome. Ecocriticism has its roots in the ethical and political concerns of ecology and environmentalism. Like feminism, therefore, it draws its energy from a clutch of attitudes and beliefs, not all of which will be regarded in exactly the same way by all practitioners, and not all of which will be to the fore in any given reading of a text or topic. There is a risk that too great a concern with methodology will rule out types of approach that not only yield interesting readings in themselves but also reflect ongoing extra-literary green concerns. There is a danger, too, that too much emphasis on method will detract attention from the literature itself. Karl Kroeber hailed ecocriticism as a welcome new development in literary and critical studies precisely because 'ecological criticism resists current academic overemphasis on the rationalistic at the expense of sensory, emotional, and imaginative aspects of art' (Kroeber 1994: 2) Yet while decrying rationalism, Kroeber and others of this party evince a strong desire to prove things empirically, thus laying themselves open to the charge of reintroducing rationalism via another route. Hence calls have gone out demanding greater focus on the 'materiality of nature', to borrow Onno Oerlemans's phrase,[6] which overtly privileges the crossover between science and the arts. The balancing act thus becomes one between a desire to give due consideration to the actual, material world and a recognition that 'nature' is to some extent a human construct, liable to change according to shifts in human society.[7] One effect of this balancing act may be a sense of unease, of things shifting as we look at them, and it is often such unease that provided the starting points for the readings offered in the following chapters.

As green literary debates continue in general certain concerns, topics and terms recur, apart from the self-evident concern with 'nature'. While the critical focus is on the non-human world, at least as much as the human (for some, more than) and while human/non-human relations continue to form a central part of ecocritical investigation, other concerns are beginning to be acknowledged as just as important. Increased emphasis is being placed on the myriad ways in which things are related, interdependent within ecosystems, in ways not fully acknowledged heretofore. Connections between animal, mineral and vegetable species are acknowledged to be more intricate than they at first appear, creating ecosystems in which each element is dependent on the functioning of all the others. Such ecosystems can be either very big, encompassing the whole planet and its atmosphere, or very small as when a group of pots in a yard or corner of a room create a micro-environment. Importantly, the systems are organic, that is, they change constantly and respond to external elements as well as the various forces created by the workings of the system itself. This makes them both highly adaptable and very fragile. Fluctuations are integral, but the removal or marked alteration of any given element results in change which may be fatal, or evolutionary, depending on your point of view. Each micro-system is also likely to have effects on the larger macro-system, although such effects may be hard to trace, which means that apparently individual and local actions may have unforeseen consequences. That in turn means that every species is implicated in the fates of others.

The most developed version of this notion of ecosystem is that propounded by James Lovelock in the 1960s and fully articulated in his book *Gaia* (1979). Here the planet Earth is presented not only as a complete ecosystem but as a self-sustaining unit, a complex organic system, that acts to correct imbalances, however caused. Lovelock's Gaia thus has life but does not have an identifiable consciousness or self-awareness, is not, in that sense, alive. None the less, his suggestion that it should be treated as if it was alive and his choice of name (that of an ancient Greek earth goddess) have encouraged others to regard Gaia as a single identity, rather than as a system resulting from the interplay of its constituent parts. In part this reflects the human inclination to venerate natural phenomena, an inclination to which literature bears witness in many ways, but it must also be said that the notion of Gaia as a conscious being can also encourage heedlessness. Humans can act as they like, secure in the knowledge that an older power will right all wrongs. Rather than creating respect for the system as a whole, the Gaia concept thus unintentionally creates a sense of licence for humans to act as we please. The concept is further complicated by Gaia being evidently female, with all the connotations of fertility, mothering and subservience that brings. Ecofeminists, most notably Val Plumwood and Carolyn Merchant, have pointed out how such associations have legitimated the human habit of exploiting the non-human world, while yet increasing a trust in it as somehow always working towards what is best for us – where 'us' comes to denotes a predominantly western male concept of the human.[8] Such attitudes overlook the fact that Lovelock's Gaia acts in her interests, not ours, and there is nothing to say she must consider the perpetuation of humans desirable. Given which, we do well to heed any warnings that the wider system might send us that things are changing in ways that we find disconcerting or even hostile.

The implications of Lovelock's choice of name for his hypothesis is thus at odds with his own account of its consequences. It is just such conflations and their consequences that green reading seeks to foreground, reminding us that, for good or ill, we are part of the world and tend to be bound by our conceptions of it. The phenomenal world self-evidently exists, but it is not static. Nor are our perceptions of and attitudes towards it: our ways of perceiving the 'natural world' necessarily superimpose, albeit crookedly, whichever concepts of nature dominate at a given moment. It is impossible to slough off such concepts entirely.

However, while 'the relation of image to world will doubtless remain very much alive within the literature and environment movement' (Buell 1999: 706), both the material and the mode of ecocritical debate continues to expand, bringing with them, it is to be hoped, a useful diversity of approach, allowing what Buell refers to as a 'map of interlocking but semi-autonomous projects' to develop.[9] It does no harm to bear in mind that one of the most fervent cries from environmentalists has been for the protection of biodiversity. Species and habitats flourish best where there is room for change and adaptation as well as for simple regeneration of what already exists. This seems to me to be an exciting and useful paradigm to follow in critical practice. It serves to unbalance any emerging hierarchy, allowing for new appraisals of the material before us and for refreshing reactions to and thoughts about both the texts and the ideas behind them. A case in point is that way recent calls to focus on the actual nature being represented in and by the literature give rise to some challenging questions regarding allegory which are particularly pertinent for medievalists.

Following D.W. Robertson's *Preface to Chaucer* of 1962, we have become accustomed to read medieval literature allegorically

Green reading

('iconographically' is Roberston's preferred term) and indeed, despite a period of unpopularity, belief in the importance of allegorical reading is once again enjoying some prestige.[10] This may seem a particular requirement for reading medieval literature, and certainly Robertson's call to more figurative reading was a welcome counter to reading every aspect of Chaucer's descriptions as either realistic or conventional, but we must be careful not to assume that each and every element in a description is allegorical. Robertson himself allows for non-figurative elements, albeit relegated to a secondary role: 'even more significant than the appearance of these formally iconographic descriptions, ... is Chaucer's tendency to mingle details of an iconographic nature with other details which produce an effect of considerable verisimilitude'.[11] For Roberston it is the presence of the iconographic that gives meaning to the 'other details'; his readings translate the allegory, but have little to say beyond the above comment about any non-figurative trees or horses, and nothing at all about the actual ones that are over-written by the allegory. One of the consequences of reading ecocritically is to focus on those 'other details' and give them credit for doing something more than merely adding to an effect of 'verisimilitude'. Green reading poses the question of exactly what such non-iconographic, descriptive elements are being true to: of whose 'real' is operating at any given time and what undercurrents may be at work in those apparently insignificant 'other details'. This is not to say that the figurative use of the non-human world should be set aside as irrelevant to green reading altogether. Human language is riddled with metaphor, simile and analogy, all of which combine to create an allegorical habit. The challenge must be to read with an awareness of allegory, while also focusing on the actual animals, plants, rocks or seas under debate. For literary critics it is not a case of either/or but of both-and.

In the following readings of medieval English texts I seek to maintain this awareness of both-and, of different but equal, in the hope of displaying further riches within the texts considered. Frequently this involves devoting attention to elements of the works which are usually regarded as marginal, and bringing to the fore aspects which have been previously overlooked. Focusing upon them, reading as it were through green lenses, will bring out new facets of the texts and allow us to refocus our views accordingly, but this is done with the aim of adding to our appreciation, not of replacing more established readings wholesale. For example, consider Chaucer's short poem 'The Former Age' which, with its use of an ideal rural past, is the very kind of literature we might expect to find subjected to green criticism. Like all texts that make use of the idea of a Golden Age, this lyric is evidently more preoccupied with the flaws of the present age than the ideals of the former one. That does not mean that it is not available for ecocriticism: the point is not to claim that texts are themselves 'green' in outlook but to reveal how pervasive the tensions between human and non-human are, even when being portrayed as being in harmony. Apparently unambiguous phrases can be shown to carry additional implications which betray a response to the non-human natural world of which the author was probably unaware. The job of an ecocritic is to show the range of attitudes in play, just as that of a feminist is to reveal the set of gender associations at work within any given text: neither necessarily seeks to claim that the text, far less the author, shares their own outlook.[12]

Structurally, 'The Former Age' revolves around the traditional contrast between the 'blisful' idealised Golden Age, that bygone time when humans were at one with their surroundings and not obliged to work, and the 'cursed' current, corrupt, state of affairs. It begins:

> A blisful lyf, a paisible and a swete,
> Ledden the peples in the former age.
> They helde hem payed of the fruites that they ete,
> Which that the feldes yave hem by usage;
> They ne were nat forpampred with outrage.
> Unknowen was the quern and ek the melle;
> They eten mast, hawes, and swich pounage,
> And dronken water of the colde welle.
>
> Yit nas the ground nat wounded with the plough,
> But corn up-sprong, unsowe of mannes hond,
> The which they gnodded and eete nat half ynough.
> No man yit knew the forwes of his lond,
> No man the fyr out of the flint yit fond,
> Unkorven and ungrobbed lay the vyne;
> No man yit in the morter spyces grond
> To clarre ne to sause of galantyne.
>
> ('Former Age' 1–16)[13]

Green reading

Chaucer's Former Age is like many another. All is simplicity and content: no delving, no spinning, and no sweaty business (that comes later, in line 28). In keeping with the tradition, Chaucer creates a notion of an idyllic past long gone while also relying on the common knowledge that such past never existed. Chaucer's picture of this former age is surely intended to be one of humanity and nature in harmony, a right relation which results in a balanced earth. Yet several of Chaucer's words here are smugglers; some carry undeclared commercial connotations that run contrary to the clear surface meaning of the lyric, while others hint that life in this ideal world was not so idyllic.

The term 'feldes' seems innocent enough, and is easily read as equivalent to our modern 'fields' that is a piece of land with defined boundaries, often cultivated or used for pasture. These meanings are indeed acting here and were in common use by Chaucer's time, as the *Middle English Dictionary* shows. However, consciously or otherwise, Chaucer's use in this poem may also retain the older, but still current connotations of 'felde' as an open space or plain. This concurs with the idyllic notion of a spontaneously generous nature, but it also carries with it the customary linking with woods, attested by the *MED* citations and reflected here in the movement across four lines from the 'feldes' apparently yielding 'fruites' to the 'mast, hawes and and swich pounage' which are also part of the contemporary diet and which are more usually found in hedgerows or woodland. Significantly, too, the mention of 'feldes' calls up a comparison with the latter-day life of grinding corn in mills, reminding an attentive reader that the natural fruit of plains is more likely to be grasses and their corn than the berries the word tends to summon up. Wide open plains are not in fact good places to find food that humans can simply pick and eat. Thus in Chaucer's 'feldes' the open flat plain jostles with the bounded, farmed area of land as the poem holds both definitions in play. If the Golden Age is truly one of pre-agrarian economy, then 'feldes' is simply open ground, but why then is it 'feldes' plural, rather than the more straightforward 'felde'? That final 's' concurs with the general trend of the poem towards fields as bounded areas, defined by humans and serving their needs. Even if we allow such Golden Age fields to be free from cultivation, this second concept of field is necessarily the result of some kind of human intervention. Boundaries are implied, and even if these are made up of such naturally occurring markers as rivers it is still an act of human projection to declare the space between a field. The fact that this is an anthropocentric world-view is soon made apparent as monetary concerns prevail with people regarding themselves 'payed' by the crops which the fields yield 'by usage'. To gloss the 'usage' as 'by custom', naturally (without cultivation)' as the Riverside editors do supplies the immediate meaning, but overlooks other associations of 'use', for example that those who produce the crops have the right only to work the land; they do not own it and are obliged to give some kind of payment either in produce or work to those who do. The terms thus imply that the humans own the fields and so receive due payment from those who have the use of them. The plants have become in effect the peasant workers, or possibly tenant farmers, of the lord's land. The implications reach further when the effects of 'yave' are taken into account, as Chaucer (following Boethius) selects the most indolent version of the golden age for his poem.[14] These fields habitually and spontaneously yield crops and the tone of the poem blithely assumes that such crops are intended for human consumption; are indeed presented as a gift ('yave'). The fields are not quite personified, but the humans are securely at the top of the hierarchy in this idealised world.

The second stanza devotes some effort to fending off precisely these connotations by reiterating the uncultivated state of the land. Inevitably one effect of the denials and of the prolonged anaphora on 'No', which begins in verse two and continues throughout verse three, is to bring to mind all that is so fervently rejected. This is common to invocations of the Golden Age because the sharp contrasts between the bygone era and the current state of affairs are created by steadily subtracting contemporary evils in order to reach back to a time before they existed. However the existence of the literary convention should not blind us to other undercurrents within those contrasts. In this case we should pause over line 11: 'The which they gnodded and eete nat half ynough.' Normally this is understood as showing that the land spontaneously supplied more than enough food for all, implying a picture of people leaving half of what is available, having eaten their fill. However this is not what the words actually say. The image here is in fact one of starvation, of not eating half enough; an image already suggested by the humble diet of 'mast, hawes, and swich pounage' mentioned in line 7. 'Pounage' in particular is significant as it is food given to pigs and is exactly what the starving people of Piers's half-acre are reduced to eating in the famine scene of *Piers Plowman*.[15] That is a step beyond the lack of overindulgence indicated in line 5 and is altogether more disturbing. It is additionally interesting from a green point of view as it fleetingly places humans and animals on the same level.

Once we see one such disconcerting undercurrent, we may begin to notice others. So, for instance the fleece which 'was of his former hewe' (18) is ostensibly part of a purer lifestyle not unlike that advocated by many today, wherein fabrics are left in their 'natural' state, not bleached or dyed. Arguably, though the natural place for a fleece is on the sheep's back, so here again Chaucer's language contains a covert allusion to farming, which even in this comparatively benign form could be described as the exploitation of one species by another. While it is just possible to argue that crops could spring up spontaneously, it is less convincing to envisage a sheep voluntarily casting its fleece for the benefit of humans. The idea of sheep arises again in line 50, where 'lambish peple' invokes an analogy between human populace and the meek flocks we associate with kept livestock. Doubtless the intended comparison is with peaceful, content, harmless creatures, with a possible allusion to the Christian flock of obedient believers and, more tenuously, to Jesus as Lamb of God. Certainly the contrast is between these 'lambish' people and the warmongers who have haunted the poem since line 23. Yet this very contrast allows for a further, latent connotation to arise in the form of 'lambs to the slaughter' as Chaucer's poem takes its darkest turn to end with 'manslawhtre, and mordre in sondry wyse' (63). The contemporary world he decries is clearly no place for those 'voyd of alle vyce'.

Notably, too, the 'swety bysinesse' (28) of the first sin and the cause of human downfall which ushers in the 'cursed tyme' is not the sexual intercourse we might expect from Christian tradition, but the literal digging mourned in the classical tradition for giving rise to covetousness, as precious metals and stones are first revealed and then desired.[16] What makes such stones desirable is, of course, the human value system of commerce which has quietly risen to the surface of the poem, having been latent in the 'payed' of line 3. Digging things up is thus not only a source of anxiety, but of strife, and indeed strife infiltrates the whole poem not only between people but also between humans and the soil. Ploughing is described as wounding (9) inverting the harmony of the mythic Golden Age in which 'corn up-sprong' (10) to create the state of affairs in which it is 'the cursednesse of coveytyse' that 'sprong up' (31–2). Green reading thus reveals that, whatever he may wish to imply, Chaucer is not in fact depicting an entirely untouched world. His Former Age is necessarily ephemeral and, in keeping with his literary predecessors, his imagination has not been able to sustain the vision of a natural landscape free of human intervention. We should not berate him for this; rather, it is interesting to note that, even when rhetoric demands a picture of a world in which humankind is a content and passive presence, our cultural imagination fails to deliver.

Such a reading of Chaucer's poem enhances rather than undermines the traditional view of it as a social satire, drawing on Boethius and Ovid, or the historically precise interpretation of it as a political satire directed at Richard II (Minnis 1995: 487–9). Indeed we need to have some appreciation of each work's literary and historical context if we are to understand how the elements brought to the fore by ecocriticism function within it. That is not to say that our current green readings must be circumscribed by our understanding of medieval attitudes towards the non-human world, but we should be aware when the conclusions we draw from a text or the elements we see at work are the results of anachronistic reading. In the readings that follow I have therefore assumed a general, basic knowledge of medieval English literature[17] and worked out from there. Throughout, I aim to maintain an attentiveness to and awareness of the non-human, while also being conscious of the paradoxes surrounding reading texts which are themselves self-evidently human constructs. Some of the results are rather wry, some pessimistic, some, contrariwise, joyfully celebratory. Such diversity of conclusion arises from the diversity of the texts considered and of their own treatment of the non-human world. Thus this book as a whole will be a conglomerate of some of the attitudes towards nature (to use a convenient short hand) that can be found in late medieval English literature, as well as the inevitable effect of my own ways of reading. It will not be an attempt to present a 'typical' medieval view of the non-human organic world, not least because, as David

Green reading

Salter so clearly puts it, 'the culture of the late Middle Ages was capable of speaking with more than one voice when it came to debating humanity's place within the wider world of nature' (Salter 2001: 147).

In order to reflect some of the voices thus speaking in the Middle Ages, this volume is divided into five sections each taking a concept important to green concerns as its particular theme (earth, water etc.). Most sections also concentrate on two main texts or authors to supply examples and work through ideas. In a bid to consider a reasonably broad range of texts, I have not usually returned to these texts in other sections, even though there would be clearly things to say about, for example, the use of water in *Pearl* or Malory, or the role of trees in *Piers Plowman*. In the end, too, I have decided not to include a separate section on animals, preferring to include consideration of animal nature as it arises within the other topics, rather than as a separate entity. The topic is a large one and much good work has already been done on it (Salter's *Holy and Noble Beasts* and Salisbury's *The Beast Within* spring to mind as two of the more recent examples). Indeed, overall I am aware that the readings offered in this volume constitute only a beginning of what is possible in the arena of ecocritical readings of medieval texts. While the conclusions offered here emerge from my adoption of a green point of view (as I understand it), that is not to say they would be the same if applied either to other texts or by other critics. If, as Leo Marx has asserted, it is the job of literature to educate desire, then it is surely criticism's role to discover the terms as well as the objects of that desire. In fulfilling that role ecocriticism may also demonstrate the fruitfulness of mixing green concerns and literary analysis.[18] The aim of this volume is to show some of what alters when we read ecocritically, refocusing our customary view in order to read as it were through green lenses. My hope is that *Greenery* provides some indication of the potential yield of green criticism, but also that it will somewhat disconcert readers. I take being disconcerted as a good thing, as it makes us aware of conflicts between first reactions and subsequent interpretations through drawing attention to details that don't quite fit. The readings offered in the chapters that follow seek to first identify such potentially disconcerting elements, and then offer explanations for why they are nevertheless effective, without striving for an homogenous overview which I believe would be both improbable and undesirable.

Notes

1. The well and cottage above it are described by Niklaus Pevsner 1989: (323). Appositely for this study, Pevsner's introduction contains the assertion 'Those who visit Shropshire and come back are enthusiastic as a rule about landscape – and landscape should always come before buildings' (p. 11).
2. Bate touches on the relatively slow emergence of green criticism in his preface to *Song of the Earth* while Plumwood tackles the issue of speaking and indeed conceiving of the non-human in her discussion of the role of reason in *Environmental Culture: The Ecological Crisis of Reason*. She is particularly engaged with the issues surrounding anthropomorphism, and cautions against dismissing it out of hand, suggesting it may offer our best way of thinking about the world of which we are a part. See Plumwood (2002), p. 38–61.
3. This quotation now serves as the epigraph for the Rachel Carson website; see www.rachelcarson.org.
4. There was much call for an ecocritical methodology at the ASLE-UK (Association for the Study of Literature and the Environment, UK branch) conference held at Bretton Hall in July 2002. Moves have already been made towards this, most usefully, for those interested in the application of ecocriticism to medieval literature, by Rebecca Douglass in the paper she gave at the American ASLE conference in 1997. An expanded version of this paper may be found in Douglass 1998: 136–63.
5. The two contrasting articles by Glen A. Love and Dana Phillips in the special number of *New Literary History* (1999, 30: 3) devoted to ecocriticism offer a good way of entering the debate over how and what ecocriticism should cover. Love advocates an increase in interdisciplinarity, particularly in terms of approach, while Phillips challenges any reliance on the truth of scientific methods as applied too casually to literature and supports a more theoretically informed approach.
6. Onno Oerlemans (2002). The introductory chapter of this book offers one of the many fair overviews of ecocriticism to date, although it necessarily concentrates on the areas most pertinent to literary discussions of Romantic literature.
7. One of the best articulations of the difficulties here is Hayles 1995.
8. Val Plumwood (1993 and 2002) presents a feminist ecological philosophy based on a critique of dominant forms of reason, which denigrate 'female' habits of thought and attitudes that include (rather than dismissing) emotional and imaginative forms of association between humans and other species. Carolyn Merchant focuses on the long-term and long-standing consequences of the close links made between women and nature, but also offers ways in which such links could become positive forces. See 1982, 1992 and 1995). Freya Matthews (1991) explores the links between human identity and environment, while Rosemary Radford Ruether (1992) discusses the

Green reading

various aspects of the theological consequences of Lovelock's hypothesis. Stephen Clark (1993) offers a consideration of most of the prevailing models for thinking about the world as a whole and evaluates them from an ecological standpoint. An overview of the way Lovelock's idea was taken up by others may be found in Laurence Joseph (1990).
9 See Buell's (1999) presentation of the development of green criticism.
10 This was evidenced by the decision to hold a panel session devoted to discussing the legacy of D.W. Robertson at the thirty-ninth International Medieval Congress at Kalamazoo 2004.
11 Robertson (1962), p. 242.
12 A useful analogy may be Arlyn Diamond (1997), which tackles the problem of seeming to claim that Chaucer was a proto-feminist and the difficulties that surround praising his presentation of women in his work.
13 All citations of Chaucer are taken from the Riverside edition.
14 Examples of the various classical versions of the Golden Age may be found in Lovejoy and Boas (1935; 1997) although, as the Riverside editors point out, Chaucer is following Boethius and drawing on Ovid.
15 See *Piers Plowman* B.VI.172–330. This scene and its allusion to annual starvation are discussed in Chapter 5.
16 Merchant (1982: 29–41) is again useful here in tracing the attitudes towards mining in the context of her consideration of the alignment of nature and woman. In the context of Chaucer's lyric and his own merchant links, it is interesting to note that in the Classical tradition is it trade, not mining, that is the downfall of the Golden Age.
17 Hence, as indicated in the Acknowledgements, my decision to refer to editions which provide a good deal of help to readers unaccustomed to Middle English.
18 At the conference of the UK branch of the Association for the Study of Literature and Environment (ASLE-UK) held in July 2002, Leo Marx issued the challenge of whether or not environmentalism, a political movement, had anything to do with literary study, and thus whether literary criticism had any business tangling with ecological concerns. I believe that challenge is answered not only by his other assertion that it is the job of literature to educate desire but also by the examples of feminist and postcolonial criticism in illuminating literary texts.

1
Earth

I ended the Introduction highlighting the sense of unease that I think is often the result of, as well as spur to, green reading. I begin this chapter by looking at a word and its attendant associations that denotes simultaneously one of the most familiar elements in our lives and one of the most complex. The word 'earth' can summon up homely ideas of the countryside, the soil, something accessible, available and to be relied up, even sensible (down-to-earth) or things rather too basic for comfort ('earthy language'). Alternatively it can indicate the earthly as opposed to spiritual, this world as opposed to the next, or this planet as a whole. The entries for this short word run to several pages in dictionaries of both modern and medieval English, indicating that not only are our relations to this word and all it signifies complicated now, but that they have been for some time and often for the same reasons. The range of meanings and associations available, both literal and metaphorical, means that it offers much opportunity for the kind of allusive and elusive poetry we find in lyrics. This chapter will thus be concerned for the most part with readings of medieval English lyrics, and I will start with one of the most famous and most elusive.

> Erthe toc of erthe erthe wyth woh,
> Erthe other erthe to the erthe droh,
> Erthe leyde erthe in erthene throh,
> Tho heuede erthe of erthe erthe ynoh.
>
> (Murray 1964: 1)

It is hard to imagine a poem more fully concerned with earth than this. To judge from the number of variations that survive in both English and Latin, this deceptively simple verse has always attracted attention, but it is this manifestation as a concise four-line lyric which remains the most powerful as well as probably its earliest recorded form.[1] Every noun except two ('woh' and 'throh') is 'erthe' and in the final line in particular it is possible to wonder if there is one 'erthe' too many. Earth as soil co-exists with earth as metonym for human, as almost every possible connotation of the word is employed within four lines and every reaction to the earth is thus potentially in play. The semantic range of 'earth' in the thirteenth and fourteenth centuries seems to have been very similar to that available today, and this continuity allows the connotations of soil, world, earth as opposed to heaven, and grave to resonate through the poem and thus also down the centuries. It is this that has led to this short poem attracting the degree of critical attention that it has, most notably from Hilda Murray, Rosemary Woolf, Edmund Reiss and, most recently, Bennett Huffman,[2] as well as figuring briefly in accounts of the Harley lyrics generally. The overwhelming tendency has been to puzzled over it, sometimes interpret it at length and inevitably regard it as a rather bleak and enigmatic reflection on human mortality. Above all, consideration of the poem offers many ways into the various attitudes towards earth itself available to writers and readers in the fourteenth century. Interestingly, the poem also speculates on what the earth's attitude towards humans might be. It is therefore an obvious starting point for any ecocritically minded investigation of late medieval English literature.

As is often the case with short poems written using simple words, it is easier to apprehend the meaning than it is to translate it into modern English. A crude rendition might run like this:

> Earth took earth from the earth with sadness.
> Earth drew the other earth to the earth.
> Earth laid the earth in an earthen tomb.
> Then had earth of earth earth enough.

However, it is immediately apparent that this is hardly a translation and indeed barely suffices as a transliteration. The difficulty, of course, is to arrive at a version which adequately reflects the extraordinarily compact nature of the poem. Paraphrase would be easier, but also more unsatisfactory as decisions would have to be made about exactly what each 'erthe' meant, and much of the power of the poem lies precisely in avoiding such finite decisions.

On the other hand, there is general consensus on the meaning of the poem. We understand at once that we are dealing with a mortality lyric, which warns us against valuing the things of this world too highly, and indeed this interpretation shaped the way the lyric was expanded and altered through the fifteenth century (see Murray 1964: xxix–xxxviii). Read thus the emphasis tends to fall on the 'woh' of seizing earthly goods while alive, reminding us that they will benefit us little once we are in the grave. 'Woh' thus becomes a mixture of sorrow and sin and the things of the earth are, by implication the artificial things of wealth, property and, possibly, high or debauched living. In this kind of interpretation the lyric gives voice to the desire to acquire earthly goods, which are then tacitly, but closely, aligned with excessive sexual gratification, both of which seem to be regarded as inevitable human traits. The rather rueful end presents the expected consequence of such actions and in doing so presents the whole story as the expected norm, offering no further comment. Such pithiness is in the nature of lyrics as well as riddles, and recognition of this ought to counter our impulse to 'solve' the poem by working out a comprehensible narrative and then consider we have understood all that it has to offer. Lyric-like, the general meaning and tone of the poem is immediately comprehensible, but, riddle-like, the poem makes sense only when we are prepared to hold several meanings of the word in our minds simultaneously.[3] The simple device of repeating 'erthe' so many times in such a short space forces a scrutiny of the concepts and associations of the word that we rarely give it, but are worth exploring.

Given that a Christian context surely operates for this poem, the image of earth being taken from the earth must bring to mind the story of Adam's creation and, consequently, lead to reading the subject of the lyric as generic man. Man, or humankind, could then be either 'erthe' or the 'erthe toc of erthe'; that is, either clay or the clay taken from the earth in the act of creation. The question of why the earth should regard such creation as sorrow ('woh') remains open, unless it is a suggestion of a postpartum sorrow which tacitly draws on the concept of mother earth. If so, this sorrow is soothed only by the final reunion of human and earth in the third and fourth lines of the lyric. Alternatively, retaining the primacy of the Christian reading, the first 'erthe' could be man who then takes earth out of earth as he works the land. 'Woh' here becomes synonymous with the toil that became man's lot after the Fall. Possibly it is very simply this arduous, physical toil that leads the gradual decline traced by the poem to the death and final rest of the last line. This reading recalls not only the Creation of Man by God, but also the precise gender roles assigned at the Expulsion, as Man is condemned to toil in the sweat of his brow, and Woman to the pains of childbirth. Finally, still within the Christian frame of reference, the poem could be read as specific, not generic, in which case 'erthe' could refer very precisely to Adam himself, recalling the possible derivation of 'Adam' from *adamah*, earth.[4] The aptness of this reading is illustrated by the entry from *The New Catholic Encyclopedia* on Adam, which could almost be a paraphrase of 'Erthe toc erthe':

> the author of Gn 2.46–3.24 makes skillful use of this derivation because man (adam) was formed from the ground (adama), he is destined to till the ground (Gn 2.5) in hard labor (3.17–23) and ultimately go back to it in death (3.17). (McDonald 1967)

This in turn opens the poem to being read as précis of the Fall, as Adam and Eve give in to earthly desires and are therefore expelled from Eden to the fallen world, with its curse of perpetual toil, 'erthene throh', ending only with death. Finally, moving on from the first Adam to the second, the lyric's second line could be taken as an allusion to the incarnation of Christ, with the third referring specifically to his death, as the act of redemption. In such a reading the final line speaks of restitution, of payment in full, rather than of having one's fill.

Other, secular, readings are also viable, as simple human lives and conditions are reflected in many of the available meanings of the words. There may be suggestions of toiling on the land in the words 'woh' (woe) which could mean general hardship, 'droh' (drew) possibly as in tilling ground and 'throh' (throe) which can mean any form of pain, although it usually signifies acute suffering (physical or emotional) rather than chronic ache. Alternatively connotations of sex and birth may be detected. 'Droh' has connotations of drawing down into sexual coupling, some of which also form part of the semantic range of 'leyde',[5] while 'throh' can mean specifically labour pains. It can also refer to death pangs, of course, and indeed also carries the meaning 'coffin'. While this naturally leads to reading the third line as a description of burial, it also carries an implicit undercurrent of the body as an imperfect housing for the soul, which is shed only when the one kind of earth, the corpse, is returned to another, the soil. Perhaps this adds to the tone of almost gentle acceptance in that final 'ynoh' (enough) as death is a release from the hardships of life. This last move makes clear how the religious and secular are interwoven, as each sphere of understanding informs the other, rather than ousting it from the lyric entirely.

So it is that we arrive at an accumulated understanding of this deceptively simple text. In reading it we must consider earth as the world, as the clay from which man was made, as the soil which is both tilled and which is our final resting-place and also as worldly goods. All this is done with relative ease: we readily appreciate the underlying theme of man, that is made of earth, returning to earth, and might easily accept interpretations of the poem that all but dismiss it as an extraordinarily compact working of this common theme. The tone of lament and resignation sounded by the rhyming 'woh', 'droh', 'throh', 'ynoh' accord with our expectations of mortality lyrics, while the abiding image of burial in line three allows us to overlook the final puzzle of who, or what, has had 'ynoh' of what (or who) in the final line. Traditionally, it is assumed that it is man, recently dead, who finally and perhaps regretfully, admits that he has had his fill, or even excess of 'erthe'. 'Erthe' as worldly affairs and worldly goods are left behind as 'erthe', soil, surrounds him.

Yet all these various readings persist in avoiding reading the word 'erthe' as simply that: earth. If we seek to reinstate this meaning a more disconcerting interpretation becomes possible, one which may seem perverse, but which is still within the available meanings of the terms, and certainly fits the overall tone of the poem. What, then, if it is Earth, the soil and even, by extension, this planet, that has had enough of mankind, that jumped up bit of clay, and finally, after years of endurance and suffering, simply reclaims him, re-absorbs and thus eradicates him? In this light 'woh' becomes a more dangerous word; man is actually inflicting harm on the earth and such wounding will not go unpunished. My use of the male pronoun is deliberate here, as the common trope of the Earth as female can also be detected in this poem, not only in that suggestion of embrace, as one 'erthe' draws in another, but also in the possible birth references of the first and third lines and, of course, in the implied notion of a return to 'mother earth' at the end.[6] With all this too come the contradictory responses towards earth as both mother and devourer.

The power of the lyric lies not in resolving such contradictory readings, but in encapsulating them and condensing them together by focusing as fully as possible on 'erthe'. As we read and react to the lyric we are forced to run through a wide range of our cultural and individual understandings of the significance of 'erthe'. Many of those reactions are doubtless appropriate primarily to a given reader and to a given moment of reading, but, although any one reader may decide to relegate some of those reactions to the realms of possible-but-not-currently-pertinent, they do not therefore deserve to be summarily dismissed. What emerges is a very direct sense of humankind's paradoxical but intimate relation to the earth and this sense of paradox and of immediacy is lost if our reaction to the world becomes solely one of allegorical translation. Time spent reflecting on the poem and teasing out some of the layers of meaning results in a recognition of the underlying anxiety that seems to inform much of our attitude towards earth. It is as if we are as a species profoundly uneasy about what our right relation to the rest of this world should be. We almost seem to expect retribution.

Yet at the same time there is an inclination to turn to the world as a healer of all our sins. Through looking at and appreciating it we hope to find some kind of guidance or, better still, assurance. If the earth is simply the foundation of our being and the source to which we return, then there is a sense of relief and homecoming bound up with our anxieties about death. Perhaps this latter view is a sop to our fears; more dangerously, it can become a reason to be uncaring about how we affect the planet, but if we are tempted in that direction, the very lyric that offers us solace also offers us warning in the wider resonance of 'ynoh'.

So, reading this lyric leads us to enact the double sensation of bafflement and admiration which frequently mark our appreciation of what we tend to term 'the natural world' – a term which, while seeking to make a distinction between it and us, implicitly renders us 'unnatural', thus creating further complications. Moreover, the poem's dexterity with the word 'erthe' foregrounds our marked unwillingness, even inability, to read it as simply 'earth'. Instead most efforts at interpretation succeed in overwriting the earth itself, replacing it with other things that are more humanly comprehensible and comfortable: artefacts or (the nearest to the primary meaning) the worked ground. Such habitual sliding away from a sustained focus on the thing itself, 'the physical world, its facticity and material presence', as Oerlemans would term it,[7] is what makes much nature writing so resilient to critical interpretation. Oerlemans makes his argument with regard to the writing of the Romantics (prose, shorter poems and sections within longer narrative texts) but the questions of focus and interpretation he raises are thrown into greater relief when, as with the medieval poems under discussion here, we are dealing with free-standing lyrics that are often anonymous, frequently without certain date and usually without a known precise reason for their composition. In this they are most like found objects: they do not need to refer their moment of composition, or invoke a context beyond that they create in themselves. Without the props of human narrative or philosophical debate to give us something else to focus upon, we are brought up against the fact of what is being observed and described.[8] Once we have judged whether or not the depiction is 'accurate', we have little more to say about the subject of the poem and tend to move to its aesthetic and formal qualities. However, the challenge is to resist such reactions by pondering exactly what the subject of the poem actually is and what we mean by accuracy of depiction. The resilience of many nature lyrics in the face of critical interpretation may in itself be an accurate rendition of the final unknowability of the phenomenal world. It is certainly there, but it is not obliged to offer itself as a source of meaning to the human mind. Paradoxically for the critic, the effectiveness and success of such texts lies in the very thing that makes them poor in interpretative terms and the reaction is often to seek meaning in iconographical or allegorical terms. Such readings may be convincing, but they overlook, or over-write, the material of the poems, much as I have tried to show that 'earth' is over-written in interpretations of 'erthe toc of erthe'. Some lyrics, though, do not yield much even to allegory: none the less they remain compelling. They are not naive, but they are resistant and their continuing effect raises questions about how we begin to interpret such writing.

A solution to the difficulty created by the lyrics' lack of overt context is often provided through the creation of context within anthologies by editors. Ways and means of doing this vary. At one stage the habit was to invent titles for each poem, and then group the poems in a collection either by date, or in terms of secular or religious, or by placing several similar poems together. R.T. Davies's widely used and much reprinted edition *Medieval English Lyrics* (Davies 1966) deploys all these strategies and has thus affected the reception of his chosen poems for several recent generations of readers. The choice of title necessarily reflected what the editor thought the poem was about, or, perhaps, what was deemed most significant about the chosen text. This habit has (rightly) fallen out of favour, and the common practice now is to use the first line as the title or to number the poems sequentially through the anthology (sometimes, as in the case of Duncan 1995, both) except for those few poems which have become so well-known by a title that it would seem perverse to alter it now – 'A wayle whit as whalles bon' being one such. Significantly, though, the desire to provide some kind of comprehensible context remains. Duncan opts for a division into familiar groupings: love lyrics, penitential and moral, devotional and miscellaneous. Such grouping is not without its problems: the line between penitential and devotional is fine, as is that between love and devotional, while the need to have the catch-all 'miscellaneous' betrays the difficulties attendant on creating categories at all. Intriguingly, after providing a clear explanation in their introduction of why titles and the division into religious and secular should be avoided, Luria and Hoffman elect to group their (numbered) selection into titled sections. The titles they choose are often based on phrases drawn from one or other of the poems and serve to create the kind of spurious, yet welcome, framework that tends to direct interpretation and even offer a kind of overall understanding of the collection. Thus 'Worldes bliss' is followed by 'All for love', 'I have a gentil cok' and then (a contrast) 'Swete Jhesu'. The final, tenth, section is ' When the turuf is thy tour', which in effect brings the collection full circle, since the theme of the transitoriness of worldly goods (highlighted in the first section) tends to be underlined by reminding us of our body's final resting place in the ground.

Reiss's book of short critical essays gets round the problem by simply presenting each poem and then launching into analysis.

Earth

This certainly avoids questions of title, but it is significant that he tackles the issue in his introduction, where he declares 'my concern has been with the particular poems and not with generic concepts or chronological developments' (Reiss 1972: xiii). He goes on to discuss the problems attendant on dividing lyrics into religious and secular, rightly pointing out that neither the poems nor, as far as we can tell, the original audiences, thought of the two concepts as being as firmly distinct as we tend to in our more anxiously secular societies. Nevertheless, when it comes to the discussions themselves, Reiss is willing to make use of comparison in order to illuminate his reading of a particular lyric. A case in point is his consideration of 'erthe toc of erthe' which contains a section on 'Pees maketh plente' (p. 55), included to demonstrate the artistry of the lyric. It is a useful comparison, but, because 'Pees maketh plente' deals in abstracts, or even personifications, this comparison aids and abets our desire to slide away from focusing on the material earth and the concrete noun, and look instead at the concepts and allusions surrounding it.

Similar slippage can be detected within some individual phrases, showing that the lyrics themselves almost encourage this kind of deflection. A good example is the phrase 'worldes bliss' and similar terms. The world here is emphatically not that of rocks, seas, plant and animal life, it is one of simple human projection and the joys associated with it are likewise solely human and frequently man-made, typically wealth, social standing and, implicitly, debauchery. It is these we are being warned against with the familiar assumption that too much time spent enjoying such physical delights detracts from the more important concerns of the immortal and spiritual. Although it is clearly the opposition between human body and human spirit that is meant to be operating here, it is none the less true that the use of 'worldes bliss' relies on the unspoken premiss that the human is separate from the natural world. Frequently this separation is integral to the meaning of the poem, as is the case in 'Fare well, this world!', where it is 'this worldes joye' that 'lasteth but a season' as the poetic persona faces death and God's judgement, or in 'Worldes blisse, have good day!' where the world of human affairs is being renounced in favour of devotion to Jesus crucified. Such separation is present, too, in another tellingly brief mortality lyric that also draws on the connotations of human as earth:

> Wrecche mon, why artou proud,
> That art of erth imaked?
> Hider ne broutestou no schroud,
> Bot pore thou come and naked.
>
> When thy soule is faren out,
> Thy body with erthe iraked,
> That body that was so ronk and loud
> Of alle men is ihated.⁹

Here the easy association of pride with wealth and social position is aided by the admonitory effect of 'schroud' which implies a contrast between the winding cloth (itself a human affectation) and the presumably showier clothes worn by the living addressee. That addressee is us, of course, for the poem is ostensibly general in its address, and hits its mark whether our own dress is costly or humble. However, tones of disgruntled social comment can also be heard, as it tends to be the wealthy who are most thought to be in need of reminding that they have once been 'pore and naked'. The powerful combination of rhythm, rhyme and final placing serves to make the last line particularly striking and suggests that the particular 'wrecched mon' at whom the poem is aimed is already widely 'ihated'. In such a light the second line can acquire a secondary meaning, i.e. that privilege is built on worldly things alone and, be it social respect or material wealth, it is a human product. This reading simply augments the more obvious one that the human body is organic matter, and it is this which becomes the dominant reading in the second stanza, where the corpse is both covered with and raked out with the ground. The poem's disgust at misplaced human pride infects the attitude towards the earth here, as the second stanza closes off any sense of death as homecoming that the first stanza left open. Ground and body are mixed together and they both seem to attract this lyric's hatred with 'ronk' calling to mind the closely sounding 'rank'. The poem's emphasis on the human, its anthropocentrism, makes any form of appreciation of the world impossible, except in so far as earth becomes the final leveller, allowing one 'wrecche' to rejoice in the downfall of another. The earth and the grave here are a form of comeuppance; there is none of the gentleness or relief after hard labour that may be heard in 'erthe toc of erthe'.

Despite its dour tone, the reaction elicited by 'Wrecche mon' is not entirely negative. As Rosemary Woolf put it of death lyrics in general: 'there is an undoubted pleasure in seeing how a short verse will suddenly compel the imagination to focus on what it would normally exclude and forget' (Woolf 1968: 68). Woolf is talking about how lyrics make us attend to death and, more particularly, the fear of death, but her words also ring true for their ability to make us focus on the natural world which we so often overlook, even as we seem to invoke it. I have indicated above how phrases like 'worldes bliss' and 'worldly joy' actually indicate human enjoyment and usually made goods, but there are poems which allow such phrases to mean the pleasure that can be seen to exist in the non-human world. It does not always follow that perceiving such joy elicits similarly joyful reaction; indeed for another of the Harley lyrics it serves only to heighten the sense of distance. The first stanza (of three) runs:

> Winter wakeneth all my care;
> Now this leves waxeth bare;
> Ofte I sike and mourne sare
>   When it cometh in my thoght
>   Of this worldes joye how it geth all to noght.

Here 'worldes joye' clearly includes the good things of the natural world. In fact it is not necessary to read into the phrase the meaning of human pleasures, it is the recognition that the joyful things of the non-human world are just as transient as the human ones that sounds the note of sadness here. Moreover, this poetic voice seems to be in harmony with the non-human world: it is winter, the season of death and sadness, that has elicited this train of thought. This notion of seasonal appropriateness is familiar to us; we find it used in more light-hearted tone by Henryson at the beginning of his *Testament of Cresseid* where we are told 'Ane doolie sessoun to ane cairfull dyte / Suld correspond and be equivalent'. However, Henryson's lines state a proposition, and the description of the harsh weather that follows creates the dreary season that matches the sorrowful tale. In other words having said that conditions and story should correspond, he then ensures they do. Moreover, his poetic persona quickly loses sight of the actual conditions. The cold blasts have penetrated into his study and made him retreat to the warmer place in which we find him. Here, having indulged in an increasingly rhetorical and ornamental use of the elements across the opening five stanzas of the poem, he is in enough comfort to select a tale to fit the weather. Although this is a more considered and cosy reaction to the relation of season to mood than that expressed by the lyric, *Testament* none the less acknowledges the same basic response, even as it over-writes it.

Henryson's opening with its references to the zodiac, the gods, human ageing and even the (rather forlorn) hope that Venus, goddess of spring as well as love, his 'faidit hart of lufe scho wald mak grene' (*Testament* 24) offers a good example of Rosemond Tuve's argument for the influence of the Classical tradition of the sequence of the seasons on medieval literature. Tuve illustrates how far this tradition was absorbed into the medieval literary consciousness; sometimes so fully absorbed that the text does not foreground, arguably is not conscious of, the associations that come with the depictions of seasons used.[10] Nevertheless, the associations persist. Here, in both 'Winter wakeneth' and *Testament*, while winter is readily connected to human old age, and the ageing of the world, it is also rightly understood as part of the greater cycle, in which all things must die as the world goes through a fallow season so that new growth may ensue. Thus a proper appreciation of winter includes the acknowledgement that it is not only an essential part of the natural order of things, but that it must give way to spring.

That appreciation lends a wry humour to Henryson's *Testament*, but goes no further. In the Harley lyric, however, there are odd tensions at work that make the tone all the more disconcerting. It seems odd to refer to leaves 'waxing' bare, when the usual associations of 'wax' is to grow larger, often with connotations of coming into fruit. The sense of things being awry reappears in the first two lines of the third and final stanza:

> All that grein me graveth grene;
> Now it faleweth all bidene;
> Jesu, help that it be sene,
>   And shild us from helle,
>   For I not whider I shall ne how longe her dwelle.

Some question hovers over the first of these lines. As printed here (following both Luria and Hoffman and Duncan) the less ambiguous 'grein' is preferred to the equally possible 'gren', thus making it securely 'grain', and 'graveth' is preferred to 'graueth', thus narrowing the meaning to 'bury' and losing the connotations of growing offered by the alternative. However the overall meaning of the two lines is clear: all the seed-grain, that was sown when it contained the vigour and potential to grow, is now withering. Even if we invoke John 12: 24–5, as Speirs and Reiss do (Spiers 1971: 58–9; Reiss 1972: 78), and recall that the fertile grain must die in order to sprout anew, there is something amiss. The order of events in that case should be that the green seed dies and then becomes green again, but here the fading follows the green, and is emphasised by the rhyming 'bidene', driving home the finality at the end of the line. If we maintain our focus on what is happening to the grain here, as ecocriticism encourages us to do, we are faced with crop failure and the prospect of famine. The cry to Jesus in the third line, 'Jesu, help that it be sene', can thus become a despairing plea that, in the face of the barrenness of the fields and the withering leaves, some growth may yet be seen. If we then remember that in the Middle Ages hell was a place of ice as well as fire, it becomes possible for the poem to remain closely tied to the actual land throughout its three stanzas. The hell against which shelter is sought is the actual approaching winter with its threat of hunger that wakes the care at the beginning of the poem. Similarly, the final uncertainty about where this desperate human may go, or how long stay in the one place, may become a reference to the fear of how long remaining in any given place will be sustainable, and to the subsequent wandering instigated by famine. Thus a possible and more optimistic set of associations based on the inevitable revolution of the seasons which lead to new life and even, through the connection of Christ with spring, to redemption, are chased out by other more immediate concerns, which are all the more moving when we realise that underlying the text are these contrary, more positive, possibilities.

Such green reading does not offer a less harrowing poem, but it does bring to the surface elements which are habitually overlooked and reminds us of what it is actually like to be human and what directly affects us in the world around us. Our emotions inevitably form part of that effect and, as Karen Jolly has pointed out, what the world is and our emotional and religious reactions to it were all regarded as part and parcel of what the world was understood to be up to the twelfth-century renaissance, when reliance on material proof comes to the fore (Jolly 1993: 221–6). It takes a long time for such things to change. It is not unreasonable to say that vestiges of this older appreciation of the world persisted into the fourteenth century and indeed have continued in various forms and with varying degrees of credence up to the present day. The division between rational proof and emotional knowing is once again being challenged in the early twenty-first century as debates continue which seem to focus on reinstating the place of pleasure as a response worthy of respect in literary analysis. In ecocritical terms this is connected to the wider challenge to value systems that asserts the notion of interconnectedness. Initially this claim was simply the ecological one that ecosystems are surprisingly finely balanced and depend upon even the smallest constituent part for their continuing function. Any disruption thus has unforeseen effects which often reach beyond a single arena into other, wider, ones that seem at first utterly distinct. Once the claim of such interconnectedness has been acknowledged, the concept becomes more readily available for use in other spheres, and this is what some ecocritics are now asserting. Douglass provides one such example. For her it is a case of:

> an understanding of the interconnectedness of the literary text to human and other organisms. 'Ecocriticism' combines ecology with literary criticism to form a discipline that examines (criticises) the relationship of texts to literal and figurative environments. (Douglass 1998: 136)

I would argue that some of that relationship is aesthetic, not only in Woolf's terms of 'undoubted pleasure' (Woolf 1968: 68) but also in terms of our initial response to the surrounding world. Alexander Nehamas (Nehamas 2000) explores this area in terms of the value of beauty, asserting that being struck by something as beautiful is accompanied by an impulse to share that perception (if not always the thing, the case apparently alters if the beautiful object is a lover). For him, finding a thing or person beautiful is a sign of wanting both to be a part of it and to partake of it – to have it or them become an integral part of one's life and, by extension, character. To extend his argument into the realm of literature, that very impulse to share denotes beauty, and, if we as readers find some kind of enjoyment or shared ground in the reaction a text elicits, then, necessarily, we have also sought to enter into a kind of communion of understanding. This is not far removed from ecocriticism's interest in connectedness, and also allows for the thing shared, the connection, to be uncomfortable, ugly even, without destroying the sense of beauty which is acknowledged by the initial effect. Part of the pleasure to be had from simple lyrics is that they create a kind of shock of recognition, which creates this sense of communication even where what is being communicated is the unknowability of the world around us. When pleasure in the literary artefact coincides with recalled or recreated response to the non-literal world, the effect is doubled, but we must not lose sight of the fact that at least part of that response to the physical world is mediated by our social and literary creation of it.

In some cases that process of mediation clearly forms part of the text itself. 'Mirie it is while sumer ilast' is a good example:

> Mirie it is while sumer ilast
> With fugheles song –
> Oc nu necheth windes blast
> And weder strong.
> Ey! ey! what this nicht is long,
> And ich wid wel michel wrong
> Soregh and murne and fast.

It begins well enough, but that 'while' warns us that summer merriment and birdsong cannot last. As with 'Winter wakeneth al my care', the contrast between the seasons serves only to highlight the misery attendant on winter, the 'now' of the poem. The tone here seems bleaker: although the rhymes link the lasting of summer with the equally inevitable winds of winter, which might offer a notional balance, the poem refuses to focus on that. Instead the linking power of the rhyme goes on to present the 'fast' as likewise inevitable. Like 'Winter wakeneth', it is possible to read this as a religious lyric, taking the 'long night' metaphorically as the life of this world, before the hoped for rebirth into the everlasting day of heaven. However, if we want them, we must import those notions of heaven or of penance duly done in terms of sorrow and mourning in the last line. The poem itself keeps us within this world; there is neither reference nor recourse to a world beyond. Here, unlike in 'Winter wakeneth', there is no overt appeal to a power beyond that of the natural world.

What we are offered is a justified sense of resentment at the state of affairs that brings suffering through the long winter nights. In this reading the 'wel michel wrong' of the penultimate line is great external injustice, rather than personal wrong doing and again one might be tempted to perceive a note of social comment underlying the text. For ecocriticism, though, what is significant is that, whichever reading one favours, the lyric enacts the human tendency to relate everything to ourselves and judge it according to how it affects our own comfort and convenience. The poem works precisely because we are so accustomed to seeing the world used figuratively in this way: our impulse is to interpret rather than just see. In a way this, too, is part of the interconnectedness advocated by some green critics, but its drawback is its obvious anthropocentrism. 'Mirie it is' may present an accurate picture of human literary relations to the world, but it is not necessarily a politically or ethically desirable one.

On the other hand the alternatives are hard to come by, partly because that habit of using the world figuratively, and thus implicitly asserting humanity's central position, is so pervasive. Nonetheless, it is possible to find places where the world around us is seen as being no less important than us, yet also resistant to being absorbed into our general outlook. The upshot is juxtaposition, which does not result in either conflict or collusion but simply remains the placing next to each other of two distinct things. When it comes to facing us with the effects of such placings the advantage of the lyric form is that it is free of any requirement to provide sustained narrative or, indeed, meaning. Its associations with music allow sound and effect to be at least as important as content and to present themselves as an object without necessary reference to anything beyond themselves. At the same time the associations with the human voice (regardless of whether or not a particular lyric is ever sung) give lyrics an intimate tone and allow them to be regarded as an individual expression of a given moment. Lyrics that make use of the natural world can add to that the largely observational quality of nature writing, again without any absolute requirement to explain or interpret what is seen. Altogether, then, the lyric is best placed to take advantage of the power of juxtaposition: it is allowed to simply record. Part of what it records is the difficulty humans have in the face of a world that does not need to have human significance. Our value-systems are thus challenged at their very root and we are brought up against a world that seems impenetrable, obdurate – and that juxtaposition is the very thing lyrics can present superbly.

> Westron wynde when wyll thow blow,
> The smalle rayne downe can rayne –
> Cryst, yf my love wer in my armys
> And I yn my bed agayne!

The first two lines of this sixteenth-century song do not need the second two; nor, strictly, do those second two rely on the first for any semantic clarity, although they do supply a reason for their expression.[11] Even so there is a slight disjunction: the wish of the first two lines need not give rise to that of the second. Except, of course, that these four lines more than adequately articulate the wry resentment that so often epitomises our reaction to the non-human world, especially the inanimate world. As literary analysis comes into play we might wish to note that, following Tuve, it is possible to see here the tradition of the seasons at work, with the gentler west Zephyr being invoked as spring is longed for in the face of (presumed) winter hardship. Or we might comment on the aesthetic power of the monosyllabic second line, with its repetition of 'rayne' reminding us that it is both noun and verb. This then raises the question of whether 'can' is working simply as an auxiliary, emphasising that it rained, or if it carries here the meaning 'is able to' even 'knows how to', indicating that even the finest of rain can give us a thorough soaking and hinting that it may be well aware of this. The first line's alliteration and suggestion of onomatopoeia as the many 'w's are sounded could also attract attention. The more direct tone of the third and fourth lines is thus highlighted and contributes to the comic effect as well as to the sense of the poem as a whole. It may even be tempting to weave whole scenarios around these four lines: is the lover being urged to become softer, just as the year is? Do we assume a male speaker here? It is worth noting the inclination, compulsion perhaps, to animate the wind and the rain, as 'thou' lends force to the rhetorical question. It is not 'when will the wind blow from the west?' but the anthropomorphising apostrophe 'Western wind, when will you blow?' Likewise 'smale' has a personifying effect, possibly heightened by 'can', if we take that to indicate know-how and doubtless further intensified for twenty-first-century readers by E.E. Cummings's 'nobody, not even the rain, has such small hands'.[12] However, for ecocritics, the point is precisely that this lyric's undeveloped juxtaposition of weather and human reaction reminds us that our response to the non-human world is often a desire to withdraw from it, either literally by returning to our beds or figuratively by endowing it with human attributes. Yet the power of the lyric is also that, while it tacitly acknowledges this response, it neither endorses nor repudiates it. We are left with the western wind presumably not blowing and ourselves not wrapped by the arms of a lover in bed. Interconnectedness does not necessarily lead to comfort.

Importantly, this is not a mortality lyric. There is no moral to be drawn, no allegory to be decoded. The literary tradition of the seasons may be part of its make-up, but need not be part of its meaning. Its initial impact, however, is part of its meaning, even where that impact includes bafflement, because that reaction is part and parcel of the piece. However the reader hears the lyric – as rueful, plaintive, pleading, miserable or even comic – the formal juxtaposition of a natural world doing what it does and a human wishing either that it were not or that at least they need not be part of it remains. Such juxtaposition is fairly common and is often accounted for as being part of a literary and philosophical trope, whereby humankind is seen to be in tune or out of kilter with the rhythms of the natural world. Thus this device can reiterate a sense of simultaneous connection and lack of connection with nature: in common with all living things, humans feel the approach of spring, yet they alone (or just the persona of the poem) are not able to be another unreflecting part of the world's expression of the season. That sounds more convoluted than it is; a couple of examples will demonstrate the point.

Like 'Westron wind', 'Foweles in the frith' relies on juxtaposition, declining to explore or explain the natural observations it uses, but unlike it, the two arenas are linked by 'and':

> Foweles in the frith,
> The fisses in the flod,
> And I mon waxe wod.
> Mulch sorw I walke with
> For beste of bon and blod.

The force of that 'and' should not be overlooked. It implies not just the notion of being out of kilter with the rightful process of nature ('the birds are in the forest, the fish in the sea, but I must go mad'), but also the suggestion that such madness is the expected mode for humans (just as birds belong to forests and fish to seas, so humans go mad). The middle English also allows, fleetingly, for the image of the man naturally heading for the woods, as 'frith' and 'flod' inevitably summon up the similar, but not identical word 'wod' meaning 'forest' rather than the 'wod' of 'madness' which must be the primary word here. There is, too, the possibility of 'mon' being a noun, reinforcing the notion that just as birds and fish are doing what comes naturally, so is man, although whether as species or gender is unclear. The two areas of human and non-human are teasingly united in the final line as 'beste' can be both 'best' and 'beast'. However, although both meanings are possible and indeed can even operate simultaneously, with the 'beste' being also recognised as a corporal being, the 'mon' is still separated from the rest of the world as a result.

Regardless of whether one reads this as a love-lyric, a religious lyric or a statement of the human lot, the emotional effect lies in the contrast between non-human and human world. It is that which gives the poem resonance and also presents the by now familiar puzzle of what, exactly, is our relation to the rest of the world. Does this poem imply that humankind is the highest species, the 'beste of bon and blod'? That reading offers not only the rueful comment that knowing the best of creation results in permanent discontent with all else but also that it is the animal, beast, side of humankind that incurs this sorrow. Is the text suggesting that sorrow is an integral part of humanity, or is this a particular set of circumstances, such as lost love or deep appreciation of the superiority of Christ? Whatever the answer or answers to lines three to five may be, the starting point is the simple statement that birds are in the forest and fish in the river – and these statements remain as incontrovertible as they are unelaborated. This lack of elaboration adds to the force of the lyric and enacts the way thought, however internal it may seem, frequently originates externally. Some observation or chance occurrence triggers a reflection that may lead us either into familiar territory or to new arenas, and often that line of thought leaves the instigating object or observation untouched. Perhaps this is the example par excellance, of Oerlemans's 'materiality of nature': the thing is there; it is included in the poem in recognition of the part it plays, but there is no more to say.

This lack of more to say is what I mean by the obduracy of nature in the face of human reflection. The end result is the same as that described by Silverstein who epitomises the lyric form as one of 'abstraction, saying less than the reader knows about the events involved, hence suggesting more than is said' (Silverstein 1971: 6). 'Suggestion' should not be taken to be nebulous. In the context of human/nature relations it is precisely because there are things that defy precise verbal description that suggestion is such a powerful tool. Being evocative is here more accurate than being definitive and such evocation is often most subtly created through simple devices like juxtaposition. It is here that these lyric poems come into their own: they are able to articulate, to evoke or recreate our human relations to nature precisely because they are not formally expected to narrate or explain – it is permissible for a lyric just to encapsulate. Indeed one form of lyric, the reverdie, has been identified as just that: an expression of nature without recourse to further conventional associations, in particular a celebration of the new life of spring. The best known instance must be the much anthologised 'Sumer is icomen in', which, according to Silverstein again, has no moral imperative other than that the cuckoo never stop singing (1971: 37). Much of this song's popularity must rest on its evident singability. The music is at least as bouncy as the words and the round's imitation of the repetitive cuckoo call gives a certain satisfaction, even if it can also infuriate after too many repetitions. There is a great temptation to regard the poem as a particularly successful recreation of a spontaneous outburst of joy arising from suddenly, absolutely, realising that spring has indeed sprung. And we must not deny that this is an important part of the song. It is necessarily part of such recognition that it is belated – summer can be seen to have come in only when it has well and truly arrived and it is only perhaps because the association with summer is overridingly positive that in this instance belatedness does not bring with it its customary sense of loss. This song encapsulates, apparently, simple and sheer joy in the burgeoning of nature, which is reflected in its metre and rhyme as much as in its images. Here, seemingly, is the natural world untainted by human interference, unimpeded by any sense of humanity being out of joint. For once humankind seems to have managed to step off the stage and appreciate what is going on all around.

Apparently, seemingly – because while it is perfectly true that such joy is at the heart of the song, this is not a world entirely untouched by humans. What is being rejoiced in is a season of prosperity in which it is more than likely that human toil has had a hand. The seed which now grows and the mead which flowers have both been sown, just as the wood is doubtless managed. Indeed the very term 'wod' or 'wude' denotes a place of trees and clearings which was full of life that could be put to good human use. Trees were coppiced, game both encouraged and hunted, berries and fruits gathered. Woods were fertile places and not at all left to themselves. Places not so tended and harvested would be regarded as 'waste', not as we now tend to think of waste as being barren, but as uncultivated land whose potential fertility and use (from a human point of view) was thus being wasted. Likewise, as Reiss points out, the animals mentioned all belong in the barnyard (Reiss 1972: 10) where the female animals have shown their value by producing young, which will also result in milk. It is possible, though admittedly not entirely necessary, that the reason the cow is calling for its calf is because the two have been separated to prevent the calf getting all the cow's milk. Such intervention means that the humans get diary products, as well as the sounds of an idyllic summer. Meanwhile the young male animals display their health through energetic cavorting which promises good breeding in subsequent years, and perhaps good meals for those privileged enough to eat meat.

Defying this agricultural, human-centred reading of both world and song is the repeated call of the cuckoo, which, literally, provides a counter point. Thankfully, the bird is no good for the table (although it had some medicinal use as a cure for fatigue,[13] but would not have been bred for such purposes) and thus reasserts the rights and pertinicity of the non-human world throughout. Not seen, but continually heard, it echoes through the text and the imagined scene, blithely unaware, we assume, of its associations with cuckolds[14] who are, arguably, also most in evidence in the good weather when all minds seem to turn to procreation. A moment's reflection on the nature of cuckoos might further undermine the apparent unmitigated joy of the season, since each cuckoo reared means some other bird's brood ruthlessly supplanted, but the triumph of this song is that we do not think of such things, even though we know them. It pulls off its trick of presenting itself as 'a pure spring song', a reverdie (Silverstein 1971: 37), and it is only when we challenge its effect and its surface that it is possible to see what underpins such 'purity'.

Other lyrics are, as we have seen, more eager to direct our attention to the underpinnings of seasonal joy, and what is surely the most famous celebration of incoming spring, Chaucer's opening to *The Canterbury Tales*, unashamedly converts the whole process of nature into an excuse for human holidaymaking 'Whanne that Aprille' provides suitable weather. Carolyn Dinshaw has shown how the Prologue sets up heterosexual norms for the world of the pilgrim tales that follows.[15] Her argument that the Prologue thus establishes 'one of the founding markers and guardians of the Christian West' (1999: 117) can be extended to include not only human sexual relations but also the expected relations between human and non-human life in general, as the Prologue consistently presents the non-human natural world in terms of human concerns. In doing so the opening of the Prologue shows the fate of reverdie when it is adopted by a narrative poem. There is no attempt here to hold our attention on the actual, physical landscape, partly, of course, because the whole thing is invented – this is description not of one given place but of an attitude. The landscape is very much one of the mind. Thus April is immediately personified and governs the piercing, bathing and engendering that take place in the opening four lines, when Zephyr takes over. It is a skilful use of the season convention, which, as is now well established, follows with a degree of accuracy the right progression of events: first the rains soaking down to the roots, then the rising of the sap through the veins of leaves to result in flowers. As Dinshaw points out, it is this episode that establishes the heterosexual norms that will control the world of the pilgrims' tales, but, as she also asserts, the fact that the Prologue endorses such norms does not constrain us to read the Tales in accordance to them. Green criticism allows us to go a step further and notice that this Prologue is not in the least interested in the world it apparently seeks to describe, and in that it offers its most accurate reflection of at least one human attitude

Earth

to the surrounding world. When Chaucer's pilgrims set forth they do so secure in the belief that the world is given meaning by their reaction to it. The fulfilment of the 'Whan' that opens the poem is the 'Thanne' that sets them on their way.

The first nineteen lines of Chaucer's *General Prologue* thus enact the very thing that ecocriticism challenges: the habitual abrogation of the non-human world into a human framework and value-system. Repeatedly ecocritics must come up against the question of how and how far it is possible for us to think in any other way; yet the attempt is worth the effort, if only because each fresh attempt disconcerts us, preventing us from becoming stuck in a rut of response. It is also important to realise that others have been here before us, that although twentieth-century ecological concerns have lent new urgency to our efforts to imagine the world differently, such efforts have been made previously, in other modes, but these too, were powered by consideration of humankind's right relation to the world. A challenge to Chaucer's masterful absorption of the natural world into human value-systems is to be found in the lyric 'When the turuf is thy tour'. This poem, like 'Erthe toc of erthe', focuses on the earth, but here it is human attitudes which are paramount. Significantly, the word 'erthe' is not used at all, although its ostensible topic is what happens after burial.

> When the turuf is thy tour,
> And thy put is thy bour,
> Thy wel and thy white throte
> Shulen wormes to note.
> What helpet thee thenne
> All the worilde wenne?

This is perhaps the most decorous and courtly of the lyrics considered here. Its play with terms of privileged lifestyle and physical beauty ('tour', 'bour', 'white throte', 'worilde wenne') is no less effective for being immediately obvious. The dexterity with which the contrasts are marked has been commented upon by Woolf, who concisely places it in the general context of the ironic trope of the grave as a house (Woolf 1968: 82–83). The context is valuable, but it keeps the lyric within the human realm, overlooking the central, perfect irony of the worms who also value the lovely skin and beautiful throat, but for rather different reasons.

Reiss goes to some effort to establish that the division of the poem into the expected when/then parts happens not, as he declares we would expect, purely after line four, but begins to happen at the end of line two (Reiss 1972: 84). The impetus for his rather careful argument is a latent unease at what the poem does. Reiss wants the worms to be part of the shocking contrast of grave with life, but this is not what the lyric offers. Syntactically the 'then' clause is made up of the final two lines only; the operation of the worms is simply part and parcel of the new quarters in which we will all find ourselves eventually. Reiss admits this, but is clearly uncomfortable with it, hence his attentive argument. Similarly, his ingenious suggestion that 'note' be read as 'uote', hence 'wote' – to guard – would serve to bring the worms more fully into the human sphere, making them ironic guards rather then straightforward consumers. Like Woolf, he is resisting the lyric's casual displacement of human preoccupations (and physical remains) from centre stage, which is so wittily accomplished by those worms.

The English poet is here being more subtle and more sardonic than the Latin counterpart whose lyric appears above this one in the manuscript. In the Latin the skin and throat are simply food for the worms ('cibus vermium'), in the English the worms are credited with some aesthetic appreciation as they 'note' these physical attributes. The effect is further compounded by the lyric's trick of making us into the worms, for we, like them, have been focusing our attention on the skin and white throat of the third line. The irony is then supplied by the reader, who is thus forced to reassess 'thy wel and thy white throte' in terms of their nutritional worth, rather than their conventional and assumed beauty. As we do this, we in effect acknowledge a shift in our own value systems, as we imagine that worms will not share our aesthetic. However, the lyric actually leaves open the possibility that they might, or that they might have one of their own, which is not just a question of food source: 'note' involves assessment and implies deliberation. The suggestion, if indeed it is there, is slight and playful, but nevertheless contributes to the sophistication with which this established trope is deployed.

In the context of green reading, there is a further shift through the poem that demands consideration, that of turf to world. The precise sod, which covers the tomb and is thus implicitly compared to the building material of the tower with which it alliterates, becomes first the soil of the pit, then the smaller, more intimate private chamber of the grave, and finally, through contrast, the world, or its treasures ('winne'). In a scenario in which the human creations of fortress and chamber have become grass and soil it is we our bodily selves who have become the gains of the world, but this world is that of the worms. Like 'erthe toc of erthe' and 'wrecche mon whi artou proud', this lyric foregrounds the organic nature of our bodies, but here the personal pronouns add a certain bite, which lends a potentially vindictive tone, beyond the ironic detachment preferred by most commentators. It becomes a puzzle to locate the voice of this poem. We could easily imagine one person directing it with more than conventional force at another, a tack which would lead us into the realms of courtly writing and rather embittered thwarted love-lyrics. Yet if we maintain the effort to resist pulling this text into the human social arena, we are left with the possibility of hearing a similar voice to that posited for 'Erthe toc of erthe': that of the earth itself. If so, then this is a voice of retribution or at very least of sarcasm. What help indeed to apparently conquer the world when in the end it will inevitably encompass us?

Perhaps this is not the definitive voice of the poem, but that uneasy, disconcerted relation to the world does seem to me to be acting here, just as it forms at least part of the tone of 'Erthe toc of erthe'. Yet, like that lyric too, it is possible to detect a less fraught response to this voice – the worms that devour are accepted easily and simply as part of the process by which the human goods of the world are brought into proper proportion. This tension between half-expected retribution and half-desired inclusion seems to me to be a mark of humanity's anxious relation to the wider world. We are not sure whether we are separate from the rest or an integral part of it, and most of us waver between the two positions, maintaining a kind of third way. While treading this way we rarely attempt to relate to the world as a totality. More often we deal with sections of it, changing our relation according to our circumstances. Somewhat in the spirit of that habit the following sections of this volume concentrate on particular aspects of the world – trees, fields, water – but the kind of general apprehensions I have outlined in this initial chapter will be seen to recur in various forms throughout this study.

Notes

1. The version cited here is that found in Harley 2253, a manuscript compiled probably in the later 1300s held in the British Library, which contains a variety of lyrics, political poems and longer prose works in English, Latin and French. Full description of this manuscript and a copy of its contents may be found in the facsimile edition published by the Early English Text Society in 1965 with an introduction by N.R. Ker. The four-line version of 'erthe toc of erthe' cited here is called the A version by its editor, Hilda Murray, whose 1911 edition of the poem for EETS (1964) provides an exhaustive account of the poem and its variants.
2. See Murray 1964, Woolf 1968: 84–5, Reiss 1972: 50–7 and Huffman 1997: 22–38. Murray's scholarly investigation of the 'erthe upon erthe' tradition remains unsurpassed. Woolf treats the poem very briefly at the end of chapter three, 'On Death', half of which may also be found in Luria and Hoffman 1974: 290–309. Reiss offers a fuller consideration of the lyric, concluding that it is both 'bothersome' and 'compelling'. Douglas Gray touches on the poem in the context of the mortality lyric tradition (Gray 1972: 196–200). Huffman treats it from an ahistorical, aesthetic angle, which also takes some account of ecological criticism. I am indebted to Bennett Huffman for directing my attention to this lyric, especially in the context of ecocriticism. Many of the interpretations of the lyric I offer here have their origin in his consideration of it, which may be found in his MA thesis *The Aesthetics of Mortality in the Middle English Lyric*, University of Liverpool, 1997.
3. Rosemary Woolf shortcuts discussion of this lyric by referring simply to the medieval sense of pun as synthesis, which she distinguishes from the modern use of pun as signalling confusion. I disagree with the latter conclusion, but certainly the notion of synthesis is valuable when considering this and other compacted lyrics. However, the aptness of the term runs the risk of encouraging us to skip over identifying the various parts that are being synthesised, and also to ignore the effect of the poem as a whole.
4. See Ruether 1992: 19–22 for a brief discussion of this putative derivation.
5. In this 'leyed' acts much as our colloquial 'lay' does today; see definitions under 'leien' in the *Middle English Dictionary*.
6. The lament of the aged man in Chaucer's Pardoner's Tale, 'leeve moder, leet me in' (PT 731), likewise draws on this tradition. A useful précis of mother earth in literary terms may be found in Merchant 1982: 6–29.
7. See Oerlemans 2002: 4 for this precise articulation, but it forms the theme of his book and is broadly explained in his Introduction.
8. This is not to say that all lyrics are without narrative. Some enact encounters, typically between a lover and a beloved, or voice political or social discontent, or take part in philosophical debates. However the genre offers even such dramatic lyrics the option of being free-standing: the voices do not have to be named, the context does not have to be precise.
9. Except where indicated otherwise, all quotations from lyrics are cited in the form found in Luria and Hoffman (1974). I have chosen this edition as being the most readily accessible at the time of writing, but readers will find much interesting and useful information in the introduction and notes to Duncan's Penguin edition (Duncan 1995).

Earth

10 See Tuve (1933, 1974) 3–5, 13–14 and 23–4. At this point in her study Tuve is concentrating on the representations of spring, but part of that is the emphasis on the due order of procession exemplified by the change of seasons.
11 I have cited the text of this lyric as it is found in Gray 1985. Other editors punctuate the text differently, notably Davies (1966) who decides to show the first two lines as a single question, thus closing off the possibility that the second line at least could be heard as an exasperated assertion.
12 See E.E. Cummings, 'somewhere i have never travelled, gladly beyond' (Firmage 1994: 367). Cummings's line is perhaps more widely known through Woody Allen's use of the poem in his film *Hannah and Her Sisters*.
13 See Reiss (1972: 10–11) who refers to Hildegard of Bingen's *Physica* as a source for this 'common' tradition.
14 'Cukewold', as cuckold derives from the bird's name because the female was thought to be unfaithful to her mate. Although the two words seem to have been distinguished through separate spelling, the derivation would have been fairly well known and anyway the simple sound of the word makes the connection. Interestingly, the cuckoo was also proverbial for knowing nothing beyond itself, evidenced by the fact that its song is a constant, unrelieved, repetition of its name. As such, it fits in well with the spirit of a reverdie, to be simply an unreflective record of a given moment.
15 Dinshaw's discussion of this part of the Prologue forms part of her explanation of why the Pardoner seems 'illegible' but is a thoroughgoing examination of the seasons passage of the Prologue as an articulation of normative heterosexuality. See Dinshaw 1999: 116–21.

2
Trees

This chapter discusses trees as individual specimens and as groups, be those groups woods, groves or forests. Orchards are not included, as the medieval orchard is closer in concept to a garden than to any form of woodland. There is also a distinction to be drawn between woodland and forests, since, although the terms were to some extent interchangeable (as they are still), the conceptual difference between 'trees', 'woods' or 'woodland' on the one hand and 'forests' on the other, is marked. Broadly speaking, 'forests' are closer in imaginative terms to wildernesses (spaces that seem to be untouched by human intervention) than woodlands (areas open to, if not actually created and maintained by humans). Wild places are discussed in Chapter 3, but, given the overlap in terms of reference between 'forest' and 'wood', it is worth pausing to consider forests briefly before passing on to the consideration of specific trees that forms the focus of this chapter.

Much work has been done on forests in the Middle Ages, both on actual forests and on the concepts and associations which attach to 'forest'.[1] It would be needless to repeat such work here, but it is important to remember that although today we assume that a forest cannot be a forest without trees, in the Middle Ages the defining element seems to have been deer.[2] This was particularly true of areas designated Forests (and receiving the capital 'F'), which were in effect game preserves, the animals in which were the property of the king or lord who had the rights over that area of land. Usually these rights extended to cover all that lived there, animal and vegetable, human and non-human, although in some cases other people (not necessarily those living locally) could be granted or gain the right to harvest wood, fruits or pasture pigs or other animals. One result of these extensive rights and the official designation 'forest' was that traditional foraging of any scrub and woodland by the local population for firewood or harvesting of berries was criminalised. Another was that the land so designated was then maintained with the interests of game in mind, which typically resulted in maintained clearings amidst well-spaced trees which were usually free of lower branches (the result of grazing as much as pruning) with unwanted saplings being weeded out. Where hunting took place there would be careful clearing of the ground to help avoid falls and generally assist the passage of the hunt. Clearings in forests might also be 'assarts': places deliberately cultivated to provide wood for fuel or building, with named people having the right of assart over a designated area, quite possibly within another person's property. The plant life within a forest might be a mixture of spontaneous growth and planted vegetation of various kinds and might look more like bush or scrubland than wood. However, while it is clearly true that the word Forest could be used of actual, geographical areas only sparsely populated with trees, it also seems true that literary and imagined forests were dense with trees, unkempt growth and wild animals. In fact, although strictly speaking medieval terminology did not require trees to define a forest, it seems that the association was wide spread.[3] None the less, it is perhaps more accurate to speak of woodland than of forests where the area referred to is covered largely by trees. Such woodland could be made up of obviously cultivated plantations, harvested for timber, with trees being coppiced or pollarded as required, or could be relatively unmanaged areas, used for pasture and forage. Pasturing is one aspect of woodland we have largely lost and refers mainly to pigs, who prefer wooded areas, than to sheep or cattle with their preference for grassland or scrub. The fact that the Domesday Book assesses size of a forest by the number of pigs it could sustain is a mark of how far woodland could be envisaged, let alone recorded, only in terms of human use.[4]

A further use to which forests in particular were put, both in actuality and in the imagination, was as places of exile or refuge. This association seems to have been an effect of the laws preventing the killing of any animal within a designated Forest, except by those who held the hunting rights, but it also blended with notions of wilderness and escape from human civilisation, which are the elements that most interest Le Goff and Saunders. It is noticeable that, despite the precision of terms available, literary authors rarely maintain the rigid, legal use of the terms 'forest'. Instead, the conceptual use dominates, whereby a forest is an area of woodland that is apparently unmanaged, wild and thus potentially dangerous for humans. In short, the kinds of suspicion that Harrison traces in his book *Forests: The Shadow of Civilization* seem to dominate at first. The challenged posed by such reaction to the idea of woodland is to see where, if at all, actual trees are allowed space within a text. The temptation is to be caught up in a series of increasingly allegorical readings, all of which have something to offer, but all of which contribute to making the trees themselves increasingly difficult to see. A matter, perhaps, of not seeing the trees for the wood.[5]

The roles assigned to woods and trees in Chaucer's Knight's Tale, and their eventual fates, offer one of the most vivid expressions of the anxiety which forms so great a part of humanity's relation to the non-human world. In marked contrast to the unornamented style of the lyrics discussed in the last chapter and their direct engagement with the natural world, this Tale is both the longest and the most straightforwardly courtly of *The Canterbury Tales*. As such it partakes of an overtly formal and anthropocentric world in which literary conventions thrive; there is no interest here in expressing a direct relation to the natural world, nor in seeking any kind of unmediated apprehension of it. Far from it: the landscape's primary purpose is as a backdrop to human affairs, the woods and trees are cultivated and dispensable and the foremost role for animals is as metaphors. The Knight himself sets the tone in his opening lines:

> I have, God woot, a large feeld to ere,
> And wayke been the oxen in my plough.
>
> (KT 886–7)[6]

It is a neat use of a device which simultaneously shows his rhetorical skills and, latently, highlights his distance from the actual business of ploughing. Indeed, there is an implicit joke that we would be as bored listening to all the details of Theseus's conquest of the Amazons as we would by hearing a description of ploughing. We are supposed to appreciate the clever use of the analogy, but not really visualise the image. Two lines suffice; then the Knight moves on to the more courtly business of Theseus's encounter with the grieving women of Thebes, which sets the ball rolling for the story of Palamoun and Arcite. This is the kind of rhetorical use of the natural to which we are accustomed and the very fact that we are so accustomed to it means we are apt to overlook other moments when there is something more disconcerting going on in, or perhaps under, the text. These more disconcerting elements come into view when we shift our attention from the dexterity of the rhetoric on to the physical world being linguistically, and in some places actually, exploited.

Not surprisingly for a tale concerned with knightly affairs, there is no actual ploughing in the Knight's Tale. There is, however, a good deal of literal digging, as first the grove in which the two protagonists are discovered fighting is grubbed up at Theseus's command to make room for imposing lists (KT 1862), and then yet more trees are felled in order to provide Arcite with a fit pyre (2860–67). It is easy to read both these events as simply part of the ostentation which marks much of the tale, but a green reading of this passage focuses attention on what happens to the trees and shrubs and so reveals a deadly strife between human society and woodland, which has dire consequences for both. The destruction of the grove, described at the beginning of part three of the tale, starts a chain of events that ends in disaster, not only for humans, especially Arcite, but also for increasing areas of woodland, as response becomes revenge and annihilation. Indeed, trees come off particularly badly in this tale; even when they appear as elements of rhetorical colour only, they are deployed in an unsympathetic manner. The first example of this comes in lines 1299–302, in the description of Palamon after hearing news of Arcite's release:

> Therwith the fyr of jalousie up sterte
> Withinne his brest, and hente him by the herte
> So woodly that he lyk was to biholde
> The boxtree or the asshen dede and colde.

'Asshen' here seems to be at first a simple word, simply used, denoting the ashes of a fire as per the meaning offered by the *MED* n (2) and thus deftly making the metaphorical fire of jealousy into a real one that consumes Palamon to ashes within the space of these four lines. Yet there is another level of meaning here, which is called into the text by the proximity of 'boxtree' followed by that 'or' which leads us to expect the name of another tree: and of course 'asshen' is also the ash tree (*MED* n (1)) and taking it as the tree makes perfectly good sense. The bark of the tree is a greyish colour, making the comparison of Palamon's appearance to ash easy enough to understand, though hardly complimentary. The submerged pun on ash as tree and ash as the remains of a fire thus neatly ties together the metaphorical fire and the trees of the simile, while the decision to use trees for the simile at all might be the result of the lexical suggestion of both 'fyr' and 'woodly' (although it is important to remember that 'wod' (mad) and 'wod' (wood) are two different words). However, that still leaves the question of why box is the other tree mentioned. As an evergreen, one would expect it have associations with life and vigour, not, as here, with death. The puzzle is solved, however, if we think not of the living tree, but of the timber: box is pale, almost yellow (indeed Trevisa tells us box is white when it is well planed)[7] and ash is so light as to be nearly white. Despite that assertive 'boxtree', then, Chaucer is in fact thinking of the cut wood here, as he is also when he calls Thisbe 'pale as box' in *The Legend of Good Women* (line 866). In other words, the only place these trees have in Chaucer's imagination here is as lumber to be grown and harvested for human purposes – lexical and physical.

Chaucer's attitude here is an example of assimilation, or incorporation, as Val Plumwood describes it in *Environmental Culture*. Plumwood defines the concept in terms of colonisation of one people by another, whereby 'the speech, voice, projects and religion of the colonised are acknowledged and recognised as valuable only to the extent that they are assimilated to that of the coloniser' (Plumwood 2002: 105). This process can be seen to be going on in relation to the human colonisation of the non-human world also. In the case of the Knight's Tale, the box and ash appear in the text, and thus are available to the imagination, only in terms of the use to which they will be put eventually by humans, not as autonomous species in their own right. Such incorporation occurs at various different levels of language but the net effect is always to make the incorporated disappear, either because the way it is described denies some vital elements of its being, or, more brutally and directly, because the end product is the death of the being incorporated. Traditional and even postmodern literary criticism might object that this emphasis on the trees is mistaken: the box and ash are similes, not real or even representations of real trees. An attentive critic might argue that rhetoric is cleverly mimicking life here as this is simply what happens to trees; they exist in order to be incorporated into the human economy, so the text's metaphorical use of them simply mirrors their eventual fate as having no value, no meaning and no life without reference to humans. Green criticism's response is that such objections and Chaucer's use of the similes spring from the same anthropocentric attitude, which denies trees any intrinsic value. Ecocriticism thus highlights and reassesses our reading, drawing attention to the fact that we are not expected to notice, let alone be shocked by, the detail that the box and ash must have been felled in order for the comparison to work. For green critics such details matter and the incorporation here revealed is at least questionable if not indeed reprehensible.

An example of such incorporation can be found in the fate of the grove which provides the setting for much of the action in the Knight's Tale, but itself is eradicated. We first encounter it when Palamon decides to hide out during the day, having ignobly escaped from prison. By choosing to take refuge 'in a bussh, that no man myghte hym se' (1517) he renders literal the old saying 'feeld hath eyen and the wode hath eres' (1522). This witty use of the device raises a smile because it makes us realise the anthropomorphism that always lies behind this proverb and leaves us comfortably in possession of not only eyes and ears but also fields and woods.[8] Palamon himself is in no position to appreciate the joke, of course. For him, concealment is a matter of deadly earnest, as he lurks in the bushes 'with dredeful foot' contemplating ways and means of winning Emeleye. His awareness of being in mortal danger places him on a level with the shrubs amongst which he hides, an irony of which neither he nor the Tale's narrator is aware. When happy accident brings Arcite, Palamon's erstwhile sworn brother, now sworn rival, to the very same place, the appropriateness of that word 'dredeful' becomes apparent. Not only has Palamon himself been full of fear as he hid, but now he and Arcite become a source of danger to the grove. Initially that danger is specific, arising entirely from the swordplay between the two men and imperilling only a representative, non-existent oak tree:

> The brighte sweredes wenten to and fro
> So hidously that with the leeste strook
> It semed as it wolde felle an ook.
>
> (1700–2)

Strictly speaking, the danger here is only apparent, made doubly safe by being not only speculative but also held within the bounds of the comparative clause ('it semed as') however the putative danger posed to the imagined oak swiftly becomes the actual fate of the whole grove. When Theseus, bowing to the pleas of the ladies, commutes his initial sentence of death to trial by tournament, he also decrees that the list be built 'in this place' (1862), the very grove which provided shelter to Palamon and enough space for the one-to-one fighting Theseus finds so despicable. This decision to destroy the grove reflects more than a nice sense of place on Theseus's part: it also betrays a deep unease at the effect this inappropriate setting has had on the two young nobles. It rendered them literally unrecognisable, to the extent that when he came upon them fighting 'breme as it were bores two' (1699) 'what they were, no thyng he ne woot' (1703) – he knows what they are like (boars) but not what they are. The simile of 1699 makes us suddenly aware of the extent of uncertainty available in the common use of 'what' for 'who' in line 1703. It is possible to read Theseus as having real doubts about the identities of these skirmishing creatures as the Tale fleetingly suggests that they have thrown off their courtly veneer to such an extent that they have become mere wildmen, scarcely human at all. Such uncertainty is so unbearable as to be unacknowledgeable and is quickly transmuted into the more familiar demand to identify themselves in social terms, as Theseus commands these two unknowns to tell him what kind of people they are: 'telleth me what myster men ye been' (1710). Couched in these terms, his request tacitly asserts that the two figures must be human, thus enabling Theseus to suppress his initial, more radical, uncertainty over their species which line 1703 briefly admitted.

Theseus's confusion is reflected in the animal imagery used to describe the two combatants:

> They foynen ech at oother wonder longe.
> Thou myghtest wene that this Palamon
> In his fightyng were a wood leon,

> And as a crueel tigre was Arcite;
> As wilde bores gonne they to smyte,
> That frothen whit as foom for ire wood.
>
> (1654–9)

As with the Knight's allusion to oxen, the animals' function here is intended to be purely metonymic. Palamon and Arcite's social status is acknowledged through comparison to the lion, tiger and boar: noble beasts whose typical adjectives, 'wood' (mad), 'crueel' and 'wilde', indicate the attributes humans like to apply in their quarry, and also invoke in warriors in the thick of combat. None the less, there is an implication of ignoble loss of the human state in that picture of the maddened anger of the frothing boars. This is metamorphosis in the wrong direction. Instead of the elevating effect of simile we might expect, we find ourselves moved increasingly on to the animal side of the comparison, a move commonly assumed to be debasing. This is a contrast to the effect achieved later in the descriptions of Lygurge and Emetreus, the noble supporters of Palamon and Arcite, whose glances are described respectively as like those of a gryphon (2133) and a lion (2171) and who are surrounded by various animals renowned for their hunting prowess and in various degrees of domesticity. Significantly, we meet Lygugre and Emetreus as they enter Athens to take part in the tournament; at this earlier point in the narrative there is something wrong and that something is the setting, which has transformed the men from the noble beasts of simile into actual wild animals. The solution is to change the setting, and that is done by altering the landscape, not by relocating the combat.

To Theseus's mind the rivals's surroundings, like their battle, needs to be rightly controlled if the two heroes are to regain their standing as worthy suitors of the fair, if oblivious, Emeleye. Without such control, the scrubland setting of their encounter brings out not their heraldic nobility but a base animal nature, which the text, in the person of the patriarchal Theseus, regards as inferior to and unworthy of humans. Following this reading, Theseus represents the civilising forces of culture and humanity, which seek to put distance between human and non-human, and is in no doubt about the superiority of the human. He thus restores the 'right' order by first condemning their behaviour and then shifting the basis of the rivalry from direct one-to-one fight to full-scale courtly spectacle complete with specially constructed lists and a hundred men on each side. By now a green reader will be feeling distinctly uncomfortable with the way the plot is developing. Ecocriticism makes us all too aware of the value judgements being made that unhesitatingly relegate the animal and non-human world to an inferior place, designated unruly, ungoverned, dangerous and so in need of relegation and control. For ecocriticism, then, accepting the common reading of this incident as a straightforward instance of social order being imposed on untamed and unlicensed brutality means noting that as such it is also an instance of the conglomeration of attitudes humans hold concerning the non-human world which makes us likely to destroy it rather than leave it be. There are a few additional details which are part of that conglomeration, consideration of which should serve to further disconcert our easy acceptance of Theseus's judgement.

Each of the animals mentioned in the descriptions of the fighting rivals elicits that combination of fear and respect from humans which has so often resulted in a desire on the human's part to kill them. Yet while lions and tigers were exotic cats, boars were a common hunting quarry, and as such bound into a specific form of relations with humans. That relation reflects the influence of their surroundings, as the clearing in the woodland is in fact a grove in a forest created primarily to facilitate noblemen's enjoyment of the hunt. In the light of this, the fact that the two pugnacious protagonists are described as 'hunters in the regne of Trace' (1637), not as warriors, takes on an added significance: each tries to establish himself as human hunter bound to vanquish the other as animal quarry. Or at least so we would assume, but in fact a further step occurs, as the text moves into the imagined thoughts of one of these Thracian hunters:

> 'Heere cometh my mortal enemy!
> Withoute faille, he moot be deed, or I,
> For outher I moot sleen hym at the gappe,
> Or he moot sleen me, if that me myshappe.'
>
> (1643–6)

By the time we reach the end of this vignette we have forgotten that one of the mortal enemies is animal. The imagined lion or bear of line 1640 is pulled into an entirely human world-view through the interpolative force of 'or he moot sleen me', which attributes to the animal the same thought processes as the man. By using exactly the same phrase the lines seamlessly transfer to the animal the conscious desire to kill offensively (possibly in both senses) that is present in the human hunter. This overwrites the fact that the lion or bear invoked by this passage (1640) is prey, deliberately sought out by his human 'mortal enemy'. If the animal slays, it will thus be in self-defence, not as part of some arbitrary proof of prowess. Thus, while at first sight this instance of anthropomorphism may seem beneficial to the animal, in that both hunter and hunted are given matching thought processes and so presented as equally worthy combatants, there is a fatal catch: the conflict is entirely of the human's making.

The hunting terminology contains a further element that serves to remove the animal and natural into the realm of allegory altogether, for Theseus happens upon these two while himself on a hunting trip of a very specific kind. This is a May hunt, pursued as part of a courtly routine, in which the members of the court ride into these particular woods because 'ther was an hert, as men tolde' (1689). The prevalent use of the hunt as a metaphor for courtship is at work here, complete with the hart/heart pun which makes the motif so elegant.[9] Not only does the terminology thus make explicit the dualism which divides human from non-human (which Palamoun and Arcite both seek to evoke in order to establish themselves as human, the other as less than human) but it also provides a way in which the animal can be denied recognition as a separate entity altogether, becoming merely an allegory for a pattern of human emotions. There is a further textual twist. The allegory of the love hunt could be seen to offer a way to collapse the dualism of human and animal through the operation of the hart/heart pun (underpinned by further puns such as deer/dear) which presents the love object as the animal and also an object of honour and worship rather than of denigration. In a similar way the fact that 'hart' is a male deer, but in the allegory usually taken to be the lady, undermines too easy a hierarchy in the male/female divide. The quarry may be feminised by being hunted, thus allowing the stag to become a hart and eventually the human, female, heart, but at the same time it is supposedly the lady who commands and to whom the courtier/hunter is subservient. Thus it makes sense to reflect her in the allegory as occupying the dominant, 'male' position; hence the use of the male deer. The hunting motif implies that both animal and lady are also subject to the simple power of the human male, yet simultaneously the human male hunter is subject to the rules of the hunt, which are supposedly presided over by the female principle deified in Venus. These puns thus reveal that the apparently clear-cut hierarchical opposition of human/animal is as artificial a construct as the courtship convention of the love-hunt allegory. With a final flourish, that very allegory is here brought up against a literal hunting and fighting for love, which itself is denigrated, not applauded, and rendered powerless by the forceful imposition of the patriarchal law of Theseus's sword and subsequent decree that the battle be done 'in a lystes roially' (1713).

Accordingly, the fate of being struck down, which initially threatened only the oak tree and even then only notionally, now becomes the actual fate of the whole wood. Significantly, no words are wasted on the description of destruction, not even the briefest of *occupatio*,[10] instead Part Three of the Tale opens with the list already built and it is the decoration of the temples that command attention. This reinforces our inclination to read the clearing in the woods as a natural, wild setting for an uncultivated, uncivilised bout, which is rightly replaced by an altogether more elaborate affair. Taken this way, it becomes inevitable that Theseus will tame the potentially disruptive natural world of the original grove through imposing the construction of the ornate tournament ground, with its wall, temples and gates on the spot which has been both refuge and arena for such improper and unrefereed behaviour. Such behaviour is a tacit admission that it was the power of the place itself that elicited the fracas Theseus come across. Yet while it is tempting to interpret this as an example of the human imposing due order on the natural work, such an interpretation is not quite satisfactory for two, not entirely reconcilable, reasons.

The first is that this clearing is several times referred to as a 'grove', which carries implications of forest management.[11] This is no wild, untamed and dangerous wilderness, but a clearing in the royal woods deliberately cared for in such a way as to allow for harvesting wood and providing cover for the game that is to be hunted there. The second, which runs counter, is that, even if we persist in reading the surrounds as wild and untouched by human hand, this does not, in fact, endorse the dualism of man/nature according to which entering the natural world signals a loss of humanity. On the contrary, the aspiring knights of medieval romance head into wildernesses to prove their valour in the mastery of the non-human. In Malory such wild places are frequently explicitly called forests and tend to be the providers of adventure (where 'adventure' indicates the unpredictable and quite possibly non-human) which makes them fit backdrops for bouts between individual men eager to prove their worth.[12] True to Carolyn Merchant's description of nature itself as a social construct,[13] we have different conceptions of nature and different uses of the available attitudes towards the natural world acting within the same text. Each of these uses may change depending on the immediate context within a given passage, but what remains consistent is the assumption that human is superior to and dominant over non-human nature. This assumption is the predicate of the binary opposition human/nature, but as we see the discourses of appropriation struggling to contain the actual landscape within the text we are free to ponder the validity of both the opposition and its founding assumption.

In Chaucer's Tale, however, the opposition stands unchallenged and what we see is a tussle of language which shifts from a subtle struggle between various methods of appropriation (rhetorical turn, heraldic symbol, proverb, hunting trope) to out-and-out attempts by the narrative to subsume and contain the natural world within it. On a simple textual level there seems to be a recognition that one cannot just destroy nature – it must go somewhere and so we find that when the lists are royally built, making use of every available machine, science and stone, some aspect of the destroyed grove appears with nice, but probably unintended, literary irony, painted on the walls of the temples set at each gate. Venus has her garden and flowers, Mars a forest and Diane, of course, a hunt set in woods, as well as a picture of Daphne being turned into a tree. Such pictorial and literary appropriation of nature is so familiar as to make it habitually unremarkable.[14] Here in the Knight's Tale the effect is to cast the destruction of the actual landscape into the background, converting it from physical place to literal painted backdrop to human affairs. However, the fact that this is a familiar use of the natural world should not deter us from scrutinising exactly what is going on within it: closer analysis of the descriptions of the temples of

Diane and Mars in particular reveals some unexpectedly disturbing elements.

It is no surprise to find forests depicted in Diane's temple; as a huntress she must have habitats that support deer. Here again it is worth remembering that such game would have been found most easily in woods that were patrolled, even husbanded, to use a deliberately loaded word for the environs of a virgin goddess. However, the temptation to read her as the goddess of pre-agrarian society must not lead us into too Romantic a view of her habitat. Diane exists to be chaste/chased in both senses and the tacit acknowledgement that the right fate for all women is to be caught underlies the representation of her as both huntress and virgin goddess, patron of childbirth and queen of the underworld. In a conglomeration of attitudes readily familiar to all feminist thought, and particularly eco-feminism, this goddess exists to be mastered (to evoke Val Plumwood's phrase)[15] just as her environment, the forest, does. In terms of plot, too, her position as weakest of the three gods is reflected in her inability to grant Emelye's desire to remain unmarried. In this light the picture of Daphne takes on a new dimension: not only does she figure on the walls of the least powerful deity but furthermore it becomes increasingly apparent that in the particular context of the Knight's Tale transformation into a tree offers no security. Even in the original legend one has to admit it is dubious sanctuary, especially since the upshot is to have her young branches appropriated for Apollo's laureate wreath. Here, though, the omens are even worse because all the trees that appear in the poem end up being felled to make way for some (male) human purpose or other.

It is perhaps more surprising to find a forest included in the paintings of Mars's temple[16]. Here it is listed as one of the terrifying areas in the world 'in which ther dwelleth man ne best' (1976). The unnatural state of this forest briefly aligns the animal world with the human, implying that a world which supports beasts, even those dangerous to humans, is more conducive to human life than an expanse of trees without so much as a rodent. Significantly the trees in this forest are 'knotty, knarry' and, most tellingly, 'bareyne' (1977). They are also 'olde' and, while there is no explicit statement that such ancient trees are the only ones there, the absence of any young growth is implied through silence. Of course this is not supposed to be a realist painting, far from it, the aim is to terrify, and the use of this image of old twisted barren trees in a wood devoid of birds and beasts contributes towards that aim tellingly. Chaucer is tapping humanity's atavistic fear of deep forest in this depiction of Mars.[17] All the god's guises of dangers fatal to humankind are listed, so it is surely significant that the most serious of these dangers seems to be posed by the forces of the natural world, rather than by human agents. The light of human reason has no place in this dark temple in which imagination belongs to Felony (1996) and Madness laughs in his rage (2011). As is the case with each temple, the description presents the unfettered action of its deity. If, then, human equals rational, the absence of reason results in a slide into the in-, un- or non-human – and it is alarming. Here, it is the unexplained rumble of wind in the knotted branches that terrifies, not the appearance of Juvenal's stabbing smiler. Even more disconcertingly, this dark forest is the setting for Mars's temple as well as being painted on its walls (1982), a detail which produces the curious and disconcerting effect of feeling one is walking in an Escher landscape. From this position it is a positive relief to enter into the more familiar territory of Felony, cloak and dagger thieves and death by misadventure. In this wide-ranging and unglamorous depiction of the remit of the God of War, armed combat itself is given no explicit representation. Instead, the division between human and animal, which seemed to have been abandoned in favour of a simpler dualism between animal (including human) and non-animal as a recourse against the threat of the forest at the beginning of the passage, is re-asserted as 'this god of armes' stands on a cart with the stars Puella and Rubeus overhead and a wolf eating a man at his feet (2040–48).

Certainly the powers of human government and their notion of the proper role of landscape is forcibly reasserted by their main representative in this tale, Theseus. Watching him, we are forced to admit that in the Knight's Tale Diane and the realm of the natural environment as represented by the forest are doomed to be buried beneath the built environment of humankind. Arcite's death inspires Theseus to even greater acts of deforestation as the woodland is once more made to bear the brunt of human activity. This time the grove is associated not with Palamon, in comic anthropomorphic safety, but with Arcite, whose fires of love (so described by Theseus) are made into the literal flames of his pyre:

> That in that selve grove, swoote and grene,
> Ther as he hadde his amorouse desires,
> His compleynte, and for love his hoote fires,
> He wolde make a fyr in which the office
> Funeral he myghte al accomplice.
> And leet comande anon to hakke and hewe
> The okes olde
>
> (2860–6)

Suddenly those words 'hakke and hewe' take on a darker tone as the violence latent in them becomes explicit and the victim of the strokes is not the generalised grove but individual trees:

> But how the fyr was maked upon highte,
> Ne eek the names that the trees them highte,
> As ook, firre, birch, aspe, alder, holm, popler,
> Wylugh, elm, plane, assh, box, chasteyn, lynde, laurer,
> Mapul, thorn, bech, hasel, ew, whippeltree –
> How they weren feld shal nat be told for me
>
> (2919–4)

Here again a familiar literary device adds an extra dimension as the *occupatio* necessarily makes the felling more emotive. The narrator is naming the trees, where naming is beginning to take on a personal, direct connotation, rather than being a simple, unemotive, list. Moreover, as old oaks are felled 'anoon' (2865) to make Arcite's byre and an astounding array of other trees are hewn down in order to create a good blaze for his pyre, specific mention is made of the creatures that lived among these trees who are being harshly deprived of their habitat. The continuation of the device which casts the description in terms of what the Knight is not telling us (perhaps recalling the weary oxen with which he began his tale) merely adds to the effect of reckless destruction:

> Ne hou the beestes and the briddes alle
> Fledden for fere, whan the wode was falle;
> Ne how the ground agast was of the light,
> That was nat wont to seen the sonne bright;
> Ne how the fyr was couched first with stree,
> And thanne with drye stikkes cloven a thre,
> And thanne with grene wode and spicerye
>
> (2929–35)

It is difficult to know exactly what effect is intended here; perhaps no single effect is the aim. Certainly, it is hard to read this passage without some sense of flagrant waste, not so much of a young man's life, though doubtless that is how many will wish to interpret it, but of an entire habitat as trees, shrubs, flowers and all are pressed into service. The Riverside Chaucer notes point us towards the *Teseida* 11.22–4 'where the forest, unspoilt at the time of Arcite's funeral, functions as a symbol of peace, security and permanence through natural change' (Riverside 840, note on lines 2919–24). The note goes no further, but the implication is that the consequence of a young nobleman's death in a tournament is the destruction of that symbol. That alone should raise eyebrows (is it *really* so significant? Has the principle of natural change *really* been overthrown, or is this just human aggrandisement?). More worrying is the fact that it is not just the symbol but the actual fact of the forest that is destroyed.

Perhaps it is this function of the forest as symbol that accounts for the bizarre inclusion of four lines dealing with dryads, hamadryads, nymphs and fawns:

> the goddes ronnen up and doun,
> Disherited of hire habitacioun,
> In which they woneden in reste and pees,
> Nymphes, fawnes and amadrides
>
> (2925–8).

Here we have the final stage of the play with language we first encountered when Palamoun hid in the bushes in line 1522. Now, however, the trees really do have ears and are therefore actually sentient beings, even if the only way we dare approach such an extension of our concept of a sentient being is through the distancing devices of mythology. This sudden reach into classical inheritance may be taken as simply raising the rhetorical level a further notch, thus increasing the sense of grandeur and pathos, but it also removes this very real destruction into the safer realms of epic. Conceivably, this carries with it the expectation that the description of the fleeing birds and beasts that follows is likewise removed into a space of unreality and rendered comfortable, even comic, by that distance. If so, I feel that last step is unsuccessful. That word 'agast' carries too much resonance for this passage to be easily dismissed as mere literary device.

Arcite's funeral should, I think, make us uneasy. It could also make us reassess the manner of his death. Saturn's fiend was his solution to the impasse between Mars and Venus, but it is significant that it does not attack Arcite himself. Instead, Arcite's horse is pressed into service, as, rearing in terror at a fiend sent, significantly, 'Oute of the ground' (2684), it gives Arcite his fatal throw. The implication that the gods, like humans, press the natural world into service for their own ends perhaps elicits some of the latent sensations to which 'Erthe toc of erthe' gives space, especially when we recall Saturn's gleeful self-portrayal, which could almost serve as a description of current ecological warnings. The upheaval in which he delights is not only of personal human fortunes but also of storms at sea and sudden epidemics:

> My cours, that hath so wyde for to turne,
> Hath moore power than woot any man.
> Myn is the drenchyng in the see so wan;
> . . .
> Myn is the ruyne of the hye halles,
> The fallynge of the toures and of the walles
> Upon the mynour or the carpenter.
> . . .
> My lookyng is the fader of pestilence.
>
> (2454–69)

As well as stirring up rebellion in man, Saturn causes drowning, plague, and, interestingly, the collapse of man-made structures. It seems that at some level we humans cling to the idea that if we go too far, we will be brought up short. We seem to want a concept of nature that includes its ability to survive wanton abuse and then, later, riposte with revenge upon the excesses of humankind.[18] In this description of Saturn's defining powers we can read the revenge of a natural world carelessly trampled upon by humans intent only on building, fighting and courtship. In this light it makes sense that it is specifically the miner and the carpenter who are the victims of his ostensibly random actions: the miner cuts open the earth while the carpenter relies upon the cutting down of trees.

At this juncture it is useful to recall Robert Harrison's point that Virgil's *Aeneid* (8: 415–429) tells us that the deep forest became a refuge for Saturn when he was escaping the usurping, controlling Jove[19]. Crucially the new order evicts the old, but does not destroy it. Instead the pre-civilised power is pushed into the margins, whence it is always possible it may issue forth. As Harrison puts it: 'the law of civilisation define[s] itself from the outset over against the forests' (1992: 2). However, in so defining itself it makes the forests into a place of refuge, creating a paradox whereby one may be safer in the dangerous forest than in the ordered city. Certainly this is the instinct upon which Palamoun acts when he decides to lie low in the bushes rather than hide or disguise himself in the streets. The correlation between man and tree which began as a passing witticism in line 1522 thus becomes an acknowledgement of kinship between the human and the plant which is reaffirmed through the use of dryads and hamadryads. It is hard to say whether the metamorphosis is from human to tree or tree to human and in the event it hardly matters. The two forms of life meet in the space of proverb and deity, but that meeting is possible only because each element is under threat from the forces of civilisation and building. Although this would appear to be the perfect opportunity for the forest to come forward as a place of refuge or asylum (an association which was clearly available, see Saunders 1993: 158) Chaucer gives this no room to flourish. The trees are cut down and we are forced to remember that it is only Theseus who has the right to order such felling, for this woodland is more correctly regarded as royal forest, that is, a region defined as set aside for the provision of the royal hunt. Everything within the designated area, trees, wildlife, open spaces, is under the protection of the King, but also subject to his whim. Having seen the setting reduce two nobly born knights to the level of animals, Theseus elects to redefine this area by eradicating the trees, thus re-enacting the story of Jove putting Saturn to flight by imposing a new order on the old and declaring the old to be chaotic, ungoverned, ungovernable and so due to be destroyed. However, this time Saturn is already in the forest and is primed to take revenge. He is now the deification of vengeful nature, a Nature far removed from the caring and endlessly forgiving Mother Earth which is often the preferred version of Gaia. This avenging nature creates the 'furie infernal' (2684) sent up by Pluto at Saturn's behest, which makes Arcite's horse shy, causing his fatal fall. This 'furie' is clearly a figure of a demon, a force summoned up from those nether regions which have much earlier in the poem been denominated the specific realm of Diane, who, as we have seen, is treated rather shoddily by the plot of this particular narrative. The use of Arcite's horse as the agent of his destruction recalls Diane's use of Acteon's hounds whose ripping apart of the deer which is both their master and their quarry is a particularly black inversion of the love-hunt in which the hart is indeed human, and also male. In each case the animals are incited by a divine power to kill the very people they have been trained to obey. The implication is obvious – such training merely superimposes a code of behaviour on instinct, it does not erase it. Moreover, it actually provides a means through which the apparently triumphant, controlling human can be destroyed, just as the miners and carpenters are killed by earthquakes that force the collapse of mine and building. It would seem that, for all the felling of trees and building of lists, the power of the forest cannot be annihilated.

However it is important to remember that this is not where Chaucer's poem leaves us. Saturn's fiend may well be regarded as an embodiment of an avenging principle of nature and Saturn himself as a deification of chaos, but the human viewpoint is still securely privileged. Saturn is seen from an intensely and essentially anthropocentric viewpoint in which chaos is inimical and destructive and targets its actions against humankind in terms that are both immediately understood and directly personal. The devastating act of deforestation which evicts the animals and minor deities is the response to Saturn's action, not the cause of it. Theseus has withdrawn his protection from the land and this time there is no painting in which to enshrine the landscape thus destroyed. Instead the trees quite literally go up in smoke. The final appearance of a tree in the poem is the oak whose main function in Theseus's final speech is to die:

> 'Loo the ook, that hath so long a norisshynge
> From tyme that it first bigynneth to sprynge,
> And hath so long a life, as we may see,
> Yet at the laste wasted is the tree.'
> (3017–20)

As ever, nothing is quite what it seems. Theseus purports to be recommending the joys of human love to the pair before him, when in fact their marriage is a matter of politics and, according to the example he gives here, a life not pressed into the service of human institutions is one 'wasted'. One almost hears the aside regretting the loss of good timber when a tree dies simply of age, rather than being felled in its prime and turned to use. It is perhaps a small consolation that this particular oak has served its purpose through metaphor and helped build an argument, if not a ship.[20]

Tracing the fate of the grove through the Knight's Tale using this green perspective has uncovered a different narrative from the courtly tale of rivalry in love with which it is more usually associated. Here we have a story of humanity's fraught and often antagonistic relationship with the vegetative natural world. The huge and deliberate conflagration which seals the fate of the grove ironically attracts the following explanatory note in the Riverside Chaucer, with a 'merely' that by now must sound deeply sardonic:

> The tone of the passage seems lightly comic, rather than . . . burlesque. Crampton (Condition of Creatures, 90) suggests that Chaucer aims here at a sense of detachment from the generally hyperbolic depiction of the funeral by reminding us that the natural world and its guardians are merely inconvenienced by the death which elsewhere seems so important. (Riverside 841, note to lines 2925–7)

Regarded ecocritically, this passage is rather less detached or humorous. It remains true that Arcite's death is rendered less important by description of his funeral rites, but this is because a different passing comes to the fore. Arcite's pyre is also the death fire of the woodland which has been central to the narrative and spurred much of the action of the text. The death or eviction of nature thus signals the end of the tale, as the diversity of actual flora and fauna is replaced by the paradigmatic oak (surely the same one endangered by the protagonists' swordplay in line 1703) which is evoked only to die in metaphor.

We are arriving at the point where it is possible to say that for Chaucer trees are primarily a resource, whether literally as timber or in literary terms, as the raw material for rhetorical display. A single stanza from *The Parliament of Fowls* demonstrates the point:

> The byldere ok, and ek the hardy asshe;
> The piler elm, the cofre unto carayne;
> The boxtre pipere, holm to whippes lashe;

> The saylynge fyr; the cipresse, deth to playne;
> The shetere ew; the asp for shaftes pleyne;
> The olyve of pes, and eke the dronke vyne;
> The victor palm, the laurer to devyne.
>
> (*PF* 176–82)

The enumeration of trees and their associated uses indicates a cultivated mixed crop, in which trees are grown for specific purposes, not a spontaneous, unmanaged wood, which would not naturally include such a range of species. It would in fact be very difficult to get this exact combination of trees to thrive all in the same place, as each prefers its own precise conditions. Conceivably, there is a latent compliment to skilled forest management here, but it is more likely that, as several commentators have pointed out,[21] we are in no way dealing with an actual wood here. This collection of trees is firmly in the tradition of a 'mixed forest' (see Curtius 1953: 195) in which the list of species furnishes an excuse for an act of poetic display rather than being a depiction of any credible woodland.

It has often been remarked that the trees in this particular forest are identified according to the uses made of their wood rather than according to botanical species or external appearance. Such remarks are frequently made in admiration and themselves betray an essentially anthropocentric appreciation of the physical world as well as of the poetry. J.A.W. Bennett's 1957 study of the poem includes the following comment:

> These trees, for instance, that at first glance seemed to show Chaucer as a nurseryman, and at a second glance to be variations on a theme of Statius, at a third view are seen to belong to and be reminders of the world of actuality, the world of peace and war, . . . So in the midst of the forest, when our sense of its paradisal air is keenest, we do not entirely lose awareness of the human world . . . (Bennett 1957: 79)

Bennett's comments are absolutely justified – for Chaucer, as well as for his poem's narrator, the 'world of actuality' is indeed a thoroughly human world, primarily defined by human pursuits. The consequence of this is that the trees are denied actuality even as their physical presence is invoked: it simply does not occur to Chaucer to celebrate the trees as splendid living entities in themselves. In this way Chaucer's artistry renders specious

Boccaccio's equally human-centred view of woods as places where Nature is in her untouched, pure state. As Lisa Kiser has shown (1991: 47–8) and as *The Parliament of Fowls* openly declares, 'Nature' herself is a thoroughly human construct, deeply embroiled in human perceptions and concerns. It should be no surprise then, to note that the landscape in which she is to be found is carefully managed. The woodland of this poem is carefully created and maintained by humans who encircle it with protecting walls and gates, much as they circumscribe their concept of both natural woodland and Paradise by inventing the notion of such a mix of tree species arising spontaneously and thriving in sempivernal splendour.

This containment of the non-human natural world within human concerns is evident even within the immediate poetic context of this passage. Without doubt, this verse of trees is a stanza of celebration and its glade is clearly intended to carry joyful associations. The dreamer/narrator has passed through the gates (albeit with some rather direct encouragement from his dream guide, Affricanus) and is relieved to find he is in a verdant and well-kept park:

> But, Lord, so I was glad and wel begoon!
> For overal where that I myne eyen caste
> Were treës clad with leves that ay shal laste,
> Ech in his kynde, of colour fresh and greene
> As emeraude, that joye was to seene.
>
> (*PF* 171–5)

The fact that the trees are thriving indicates to the dreamer/narrator that his sojourn within this walled park will be under the benign auspices of fortunate love. He has found himself in 'that blysful place' (127) of eternal May, rather than in the more forbidding alternative where 'nevere tre shal fruyt ne leves bere' (137). He seizes on the excellent health of the trees as proof not only of the kind of place that he has entered, but also of the kind of fortune he will find there. We as readers may suspect that the two contradictory legends carved over the gates are inextricably linked, rather than mutually exclusive, but this notion does not seem to occur to the dreamer. Once again, the value of the trees lies in their associations, not in themselves and it is the association of thriving greenery and fortune in love that gives rise to the 'joye' of line 175, rather than a delight in the woodland per se. Nor is there any pause in which to reflect that if these are real trees their leaves will not last for ever – the season of bare branches must follow that of fresh green. So it is that the stanza enumerating species according to the use made of their wood is preceded by one that relies heavily on the use of the literary associations of trees in spring and summer. In either event the trees as living plants are hardly acknowledged at all.

However, there is one tree that is singled out for particular mention: the oak under which Delight and Gentilesse stand a few stanzas later.

> And by hymself, under an ok, I gesse,
> Saw I Delyt, that stod with Gentilesse.
>
> (*PF* 223-4)

It is possible that the oak is singled out for attention because Chaucer associated it with nobility, as Nicholas Havely suggests.[22] Certainly there seems to be some kind of connection between these gentlemanly personifications and the oak tree. Although it is not entirely clear whether it is the tree or Delyt whose identity is being guessed, the shape of the line indicates that the supposition 'I gesse' concerns the type of tree. Following Havely's suggestion, this means the thread of association is that the tree can be presumed to be an oak because of the nobility of the two standing under it: they would not stoop to stand under anything less. It is a tempting association (particularly given our latter-day, anachronistic concept of 'the Royal Oak[23]') which can also be seen to be present in *The Book of the Duchess* where the narrator

> was war of a man in blak,
> That sat and had yturned his bak
> To an ook, an huge tree.
>
> (*BD* 445-7)

The use of the presumed association would be particularly neat here because, arguably, the man in black has turned his back not only to the tree (presumably in order to sit more comfortably) but also on the restrained, correct, noble behaviour it represents. Such reading is entirely in keeping with the kind of use of the oak that Theseus makes in his platitudinous speech towards the end of the Knight's Tale (quoted above) that is, one in which our attention is directed from the actual tree towards its meaning within a literary trope. However, it would be unjust to say this is the only role fulfilled by the oak in *The Book of the Duchess*. In our minds' eye it must be an actual, physical tree, as well as one with added connotations, otherwise we lose the picture of the man leaning against its trunk, which is, after all, the primary image here.

The Book of the Duchess has more than this solitary oak in common with the Knight's Tale; it, too, draws on the courtly convention of the May hunt in a forest and the allegorical associations this convention offers.[24] However, this earlier wood is noticeably different from the one which suffers so much from the consequences of being drawn into the Knight's human drama and is different, too, from the catalogue of trees found in *Parliament*. Here the narrative's entry into the forest is altogether more benign. Rather than being thrust through gates by an impatient dream-guide, the *Book of the Duchess*'s narrator is called into his dream landscape by birdsong. Likewise, although the depiction of the Troy story in the windows and the Romance of the Rose on the walls proclaims that he has entered the same area of literary tradition as that inhabited by Palamoun and Arcite, this part of the realm seems more at ease with trees than that invoked by the Knight. The illusion that an actual forest is being described is endorsed by the assertion that, unlike the wood of *Parliament* whose leaves would be for ever green, this wood has known the harshness of winter, which makes its new growth is all the more welcome:

> Hyt had forgete the povertee
> That wynter, thorgh hys colde morwes,
> Had mad hyt suffre, and his sorwes;
> All was forgeten, and that was sene,
> For al the woode was waxen grene;
> Swetnesse of dew had mad hyt waxe.
>
> (*BD* 410–15)

The trace of personification, detectable in the pronouns 'hyt' and 'his', develops into fuller human projection as the narrator eagerly forgets the sorrows of winter through the influence of the lush greenness he sees around him and seems inclined to share that reaction with the trees. Line 415, with its oddly clumsy repetition of 'wax', checks this impulse towards fully fledged anthropomorphism by reminding us that this greening of the woods is simply a reaction to the dew. The wood, it seems, cannot be allowed the degree of sentient autonomy the first, intransitive, use of wax implies. Instead we are reminded to regard such natural processes in a more impersonal light, aided by the use of the phrase 'swetnesse of dew' which in effect provides a subject for 'wax' and thus makes the wood the passive object of this dangerously animating verb. The attempt is not entirely successful, as, despite the apparent reluctance of this text to admit any such thing, the suggestion remains that the trees find the dew sweet. Although such human projection is part and parcel of the literary convention of the *locus amoenus* and although the shape of the line makes it clear that it is the human narrator who considers the dew sweet, the text is still on the edge of conceding a degree of sentience to the trees. It is only when the next line begins a new verse paragraph that we are returned to thoroughly human–human exchange with the rhetorical 'Hyt ys no nede eke for to axe' and the lines that follow display the trees from a purely human perspective.

> Hyt ys no nede eke for to axe
> Wher there were many grene greves,
> Or thikke of trees, so ful of leves;
> And every tree stood by hymselve
> Fro other wel ten foot or twelve –
> So grete trees, so huge of strengthe,
> Of fourty or fifty fadme lengthe,
> Clene withoute bowghe or stikke,
> With croppes brode, and eke as thikke –
> They were nat an ynche asonder –
> That hit was shadewe overal under.
>
> (*BD* 416–26)

Our attention is directed towards the trees in admiration as the dreamer wanders through magnificent specimens whose thriving state indicates not only well-established trees but also remarkably healthy ones. There is a sense of permanence here as well as vigour; a sense increased by the fact that the trees are massive (421–2) and well-spaced (419–20). The whole verges towards the ideal, as the trunks are clean of any odd twigs or branches that would ruin the aesthetic of their huge trunks, rising to the impressive canopy. That word 'croppes' gives us a hint that this wood may well provide crops as well as canopy and the harvest is not only of timber or firewood: the forest is teaming with wildlife, mostly hunting quarry.

> And many an hert and many an hynde
> Was both before me and behynde.
> Of founes, sowres, bukkes, does
> Was ful the woode, and many roes,
> And many sqwirelles that sete
> Ful high upon the trees and ete,
> And in hir maner made festes.
>
> (427–33)

This is indeed a forest is the sense of an area maintained to support good hunting and it is this function that not only leads to the trees being given such good growing conditions (well-spaced trees are easier for the hunt to pass through), but also allows them to be seen as living plants rather than future timber. It is also this that makes it such an ideal resort for animals, who, it is worth noting, are clearly unperturbed by the dreamer's presence. It is as if the walk through the trees, which elicited such admiration from the dreamer, has brought him closer to the rest of the animal world, to the point where he is among the quarry as one of them, not as a potential hunter or even gamekeeper/forester. Indeed, both these roles have been ruled out for him, he has lost the hunt and now loses his way wandering through the trees: clearly no woodsman he.

It is this figure, apparently so in tune with the other animals and trees, who encounters the melancholic man in black, sitting under a solitary oak, the epitome of the mournful lover and hinting at the man sent mad who takes refuge in the forest.[25] With this encounter the poem enters a fully courtly, highly allegorical mode and the fleeting (albeit idealised) image of 'man' as one of the beasts, at ease with trees, is displaced. The poem as a whole invites metaphorical readings and usually receives them. However much we may wish to maintain a distance between Blanche, the much-mourned first wife of John of Gaunt and White, and indeed between the man in black who sits under the oak and Gaunt himself, the text demands that some degree of connection is made. Likewise, its extensive use of explicit allegories, such as the game of chess, opens the way for us to read other elements through allegory too. The forest thus easily becomes an external referent for the emotional tangle through which both dreamer and man in black find their way via courtly conversational exchange. This fits the tone of the poem perfectly, but it means the forest is no longer a forest. The trees, once so directly acknowledged, fade first into metaphor and finally disappear from the poem altogether.

It is easy to say that the woodland we find in *The Book of the Duchess* is primarily an idealised hunting forest in which the actualities of game preserve meets the ideals of courtly fiction,[26] but it is intriguing that it is in this artificial and consciously literary forest that we find the nearest approach in Chaucer to presenting trees within a text just as trees. Yet the moment is not sustained; as narrative and allegory take over, the landscape becomes a backdrop, adding to the anthropocentrically reflective atmosphere of the poem, but no longer a matter for attention in its own right. Perhaps such blending into the background is the best thing for groups of trees, as at least it keeps them safe from felling. This might be true even for those woods or trees whose presence Chaucer requires for comic effect. Thus the pear tree in the orchard of the Merchant's Tale is not only a simple plot device but also a place of disorderly human conduct, while the woods of the Wife of Bath's Tale offer cover to corrupt 'lymatours' as well as dancing fairies and knowledgeable hags. However, all such uses arguably ensure that trees, and particularly forests, are held within the notion of the fearful and chaotic precisely because they are visible only when their function is as a crop, or as dangerously untamed areas which have a detrimental effect on human behaviour and so must be severely controlled. The more benign associations of woods as places of refuge from a hostile human world, or as repositories of ancient wisdom, are largely ignored by the urban and predominantly successful Chaucer. Such associations are to be found in Malory, however, and it is tempting to speculate that they are there because Malory's human world was on the whole a place less reliable and easy to negotiate than Chaucer's. One can easily imagine the appeal that an image of unconstrained open forest would have for one writing from prison.

Tempting as such speculation is, it is doubtless spurious: a good deal of the associations carried by the forest in Malory's *Morte* come with the landscape, as it were. In choosing to rework the Arthurian romances, Malory took on a body of work which contained the forest as one of its primary settings. It seems purely imaginative: knights ride into the forest seeking adventures; hermits abound; madmen take refuge; courts and castles are happened upon, but cannot be trusted. All this indicates a conceptual forest which is unsurprisingly difficult to map, but which offers rich yields to the critics: Saunders is particularly attentive to the metaphorical and symbolic roles played by the forest in the *Morte* (Saunders 1993: 163–85). However, coexisting with such powerfully figurative elements as being sites for illicit but condoned love (as it is for a while for Tristram and Isolde) are details which summon up factual knowledge of woodcraft or horticulture. Such moments are in keeping with the assertion made by C.S. Lewis in 1963 and endorsed by Eugène Vinaver, that 'Malory almost everywhere [is] labouring to eliminate the marvellous and introduce the humdrum'.[27] It is significant that the 'humdrum' here is synonymous with 'practical realism' and even more telling that Vinaver's response is set in a context of grafting, as he begins his discussion of Lewis by quoting lines 92–7 of Polixenes' speech in *The Winter's Tale* Act 4:

> You see, sweet maid, we marry
> A gentle scion of the wildest stock,
> And make conceive a bark of baser kind
> By bud of nobler race. This is an art
> Which does mend Nature, change it rather, but
> The art itself is Nature.[28]

Vinaver goes on to use the notion of art as nature, a notion which perhaps has rather different resonances in this age of genetic modification and the organic movement. However it is the decision to cite this description of grafting which is most striking to an ecocritical reader and invites a brief consideration of the Shakespearean passage.

The speech in which these lines fall forms part of the exchange between Polixenes and Perdita on the pros and cons of cross-pollination and the value and associations with the results. Polixenes extends Perdita's argument from the realm of natural, chance, hybridisation to the results of human intervention through breeding and, in these lines, grafting. At this point Polixenes is defending such horticultural engineering, but this is of course ironic as we know he will soon take great exception to the idea that his high-born son should marry a shepherdess. For critics of Malory, the point of interest is why Vinaver chose to preface his response to Lewis with this quotation at all. His argument with Lewis concerns Malory's use of the real and the imagined, but the fact that it is begun in horticultural terms is perhaps a testament to the power of the landscape in Malory's writing. The idea of trees pervades this text, even though there are few individual trees mentioned and little space devoted to the description of woodland. There is, however, one passage in the Grail Quest which not only focuses on trees but makes implicit use of grafting. This is the story of the spindles that Percival's sister tells to Galahad and Percival in the Book of Sir Galahad.

The spindles have been made from wood of descendants of the tree planted by Eve after the Expulsion. That tree was initially white but later became green. The passage of interest runs:

> Thus was the tre longe of grene coloure. And so [hit] befelle many dayes aftir, undir the same tre, Cayme slew Abell, whereof befelle grete mervayle, for a[s] Abell had ressayved dethe undir the grene tre, he loste the grene colour and becam rede; and that was in tokenyng of blood. And anone all the plantis dyed thereoff, but the tre grewe and waxed mervaylusly fayre, and hit was the moste fayryst tre and the most delectable that ony man mygth beholde and se; and so ded the plantes that grewe oute of hit tofore that Abell was slayne undir hit. (584)²⁹

This highly symbolic tree clearly responds to events in a suitably symbolic manner, changing from white to green to red as it reflects Eve's virginity, the (divinely commanded) sexual relation between Adam and Eve and finally Cain's fratricide. The way Malory presents it, this is a literal family tree. Yet it is also a real tree which has been harvested not only for fruit (the 'most delectable') but also for cuttings, which in turn have flourished. Or at least did until Able's murder. Thereafter, all cuttings taken die off.

I refer to the 'plantis' as the result of cuttings because it is clear that these trees are very directly connected to the parent tree as it was at a given point. Such connection is more correctly maintained through cuttings and grafts than by planting seeds which will revert to the original form of the parent tree (and thus may not look anything like the parent plant). At this particular point in Malory's text we seem to be dealing with just one tree, although later in the passage (when the wood is being taken for the spindles) we appear to have three separate trees. Grafting of one plant on to the stock of another will allow for several different plants to grow from the one main trunk, making literal the phrase 'the plantis that grew oute of hit', but although this means that the rather bizarre image of a single tree being simultaneously white, green and red is possible, it is also unlikely. This intricate horticultural feat is more probably the result of a simple slip on Malory's part, and that we are in fact dealing with three separate stocks, two of which (green and red) descend from the original and still flourishing third (white). None the less, the image of grafting is still important in order for the idea of the white and green trees giving rise to replica trees to work properly.

The gardening aspect of the metaphor continues throughout the story and works alongside the theological import. Cain's action is a heinous crime and a sin that blots all who follow and thus radically alters the original tree itself. Although that tree continues to flourish, it no longer produces good scions and so is paradoxically both fruitful and barren. Significantly, according to this paragraph, it is only when the tree is in its green state that it can produce good cuttings.[30] Horticulturally, this makes sense. It is not always advisable to take cuttings from saplings that are too young, in their white state, as it were. Once they are established and fruiting (the 'green' state of this passage) scions have a good chance of taking, while the original tree is strong enough to bear having such cuttings taken without it causing problems. However, once age or disease strikes, the matter can alter. Cuttings may no longer flourish as they will tend to carry whatever disease is afflicting the parent tree, whereas those taken before the disease developed will stand as good a chance as any of flourishing. The parent tree may, however, be strong enough to continue to grow pretty well, even fruiting, because it is well enough established to be able to carry a degree of disease. This may seem to be labouring a point, but the fact that such a reading (albeit a little tendentious) of this passing detail is possible at all reveals the real tree beneath the allegory and adds a sense of life to the passage as a whole. Suddenly these coloured trees are not only figurative but also plausible plants in an orchard or cultivated wood, owned, it transpires, by Solomon. The tending and nurture which has gone into maintaining this particular stock, and the knowledge about the specimen lineage it demands, is fleetingly apparent in the figure of the carpenter, whose implied respect for the trees as sentient beings makes him markedly reluctant to carve wood straight out of the living tree trunks (*Morte* 585).

Symbolism and reality become symbiotic here as our understanding of this paragraph works in two directions simultaneously. The ramifications of Cain's crime mean that it makes sense that the tree that reacts to Abel's blood should be barren, for not only has Abel been killed but the notion of a perpetually renewing family that flourishes healthily and with ease has been radically undone. The fact that such murder can be imagined infects all who follow and so we more readily comprehend the importance of the comment that while the original tree continues to thrive, any offshoots die. At the same time an appreciation of how disease can suddenly afflict a mature tree, making it useless for cuttings, yet allowing it to carry on well enough because it is strong enough to withstand some element of affliction, also broadens our understanding of the story of Cain and Abel, for the fratricide does not mark the end of the human race – it merely introduces a new and potentially fatal element, which itself is the result of other inherent aspects of human character, such as envy, greed and frustration. Disease and murder are not desirable, but they have become facts of life which must be dealt with accordingly.

The trees of this inset story, then, are both realistic and highly symbolic, thereby bearing out Vinaver's opinion that Malory's habit of blending the real and the metaphorical intensifies 'the feeling of the marvellous' in his text (Vinvaver 1963: 32). There are other individual trees in Malory's text, but none is treated with the same degree of precision as the ones which feature in the story of the spindles. Typically, these other trees are convenient places to tether horses and prop spears when resting or when dismounting to continue knightly engagement on foot, as Sir Marhalt does in the Book of Gawain, Ywain and Marhalt (*Morte* 96) and as Launcelot does in a more dismissive courtly gesture when he reclaims his own mount from the thieving unnamed knight who stole it some time earlier (554). Alternatively, these single trees serve as displaying posts for either one's own shield (indicating one's desire to be challenged) or the shields of those overcome in combat, the latter being how Sir Tarquin uses the tree by the ford to which Sir Ector is directed (*Morte* 150). Some individual trees seem to act as markers for paths or boundaries, which in itself is a credible enough use of trees, although it mitigates the notion that Malory's knights spend much of their time dense woodland. Individual trees do not stand out as clear markers amidst other trees, but serve the purpose perfectly well in the mixture of glades and woods which actually make up Malory's landscape.

Some trees are identified by species: there are a couple of oaks acting as markers for directions or as tethering posts for horses, the use Sir Lamerok is making of one when happened upon by Tristram (*Morte* 294), and there are the two apple trees (or perhaps just the one, encountered twice) under which Launcelot falls asleep, each time to his detriment. There is an understandable temptation to read these apple trees in particular as being symbolic: not only might they function as gateways to another, faery, world,[31] but they could carry connotations of the Fall. Malory does not seem interested in such connotations, however, and indeed provides an altogether more pragmatic reason for why Launcelot chooses to rest under an apple tree.

> So the wedir was hote aboute noone, and sir Launcelot had grete luste to slepe. Than sir Lyonell aspyed a grete appyll-tre that stoode by an hedge, and seyde, 'Sir, yondir is a fayre shadow, there may we reste us and oure horsys.' (*Morte* 149)

The spread of an established apple tree is not only good for shade but also easily recognisable, and so imaginable, by anyone who has ever seen the species. Here, it also serves to remind us that woods contained a variety of trees, some of which would be valued for their fruit crop, others for their timber and others still to provide shade and food for game. It is an open question whether apple trees would be deliberately planted in woods, or whether advantage would be taken of those that sprang up without human intervention. In other words, it is not clear here whether Launcelot and Lyonell are resting within the bounds of someone's cultivated woodland, or in land that is wooded, harvested, but not closely tended. We do know that they have just come into a plain, having travelled through 'depe forest', but that could mean they have reached the edge of someone's domain. Malory is clearly unconcerned about such detail; for the purposes of his narrative it does not matter whether this apple tree grows on the edge of Sir Tarquin's land or forms part of the estate of the castle to which Launcelot is taken by Morgan le Fay. However, by naming the type of tree, Malory has bought us into familiar, domesticated, territory and it is here that his knights encounter human adversaries: we are no longer in unidentified 'depe forest'.

In Malory's *Morte* then, individual trees, whether identified by species or not, seem to signal that we are in some kind of human world. Such trees are take for granted as part of the imaginary landscape, much as their real counterparts are in the actual world. Unlike Chaucer, Malory has no interest in the details of how humans use trees, either as timber or as providing fruit, nuts or firewood, not even as providing habitat for game. Nor does he trouble overmuch with descriptions of the woods through which his knights ride. In fact, given the predominance of forests in our mental image of Malory's literary world, it is remarkable how little he has to say about them. By far the most prevalent reference to a forest is a passing phrase as a given knight rides in, out or through it. However, that is not to say that Malory ignores the possible roles played by woods or forests in human affairs, actual as well as imagined. It is usually the imagined that has commanded most attention from critics and readers as the forests are easily (and not incorrectly) associated with the adventures the various knights seek. This connection is admitted by the knights themselves, most explicitly by Tristram who leaves his company on the verges of the Foreyste Perelous with the explanation 'for in thys foreyste ar many strange adventures, as I have harde sey, and som of hem I caste to preve or that I departe' (*Morte* 294). Tristram's words hint that he will be proving the truth of the rumours that the forest contains adventures as much as proving himself by undergoing them. Malory's text endorses those rumours, speedily providing Tristram with an unidentified knight to challenge and a string of consequent combats. The forest continues to carry this adventurous connection throughout the text, thus making it immediately significant that Gawain is unable to find an adventure when engaged in the Grail Quest, although it is also implied that he is rather choosy where adventures are concerned. 'For sir Gawayne rode frome Whytsontyde tylle Mychaellmasse, and founde never adventure that pleased hym' (*Morte* 558). The point is that, like everyone else, Gawain knows where the adventures are to be found – in the forest; they are simply eluding him. At the end of this section of Grail Quest Gawain is told explicitly why he has failed to make any progress and is even offered the chance to rectify the problem, but is too keen to follow Sir Ector (and avoid prolonged conversation with the hermit, Nacien) to learn. Interestingly, Nacien describes Gawain as

> so olde a tre that in the ys neythir leeff, nor grasse, nor fruyte. Wherefore bethynke the that thou yelde to oure Lorde the bare rynde, sith the fende hath the levis and the fruyte. (*Morte* 563)

The second sentence makes clear the symbolism of the simile, but the choice of comparison seems to imply that knights are as much a part of the forest landscape as trees.

With such references to the wooded forest pervading the text, it is no surprise that it has been the symbolic and imaginative aspects that have dominated discussion of forests and woods in Malory's writing in spite of the lack of descriptive passages. Saunders does not entirely ignore the real forest, but for her even that real forest is essentially emblematic. Her study argues convincingly that 'over the course of the *Morte*, Malory's presentation of the forest moves from historical to legendary and back again, reflecting the rise and fall of Logres itself' (Saunders 1993: 163). Having thus established that in the early books the forest 'acts as an image of an earlier, less civilized kingdom' (164), she goes on to say

> Yet, as the narrative unfolds, this literal and historical reading of the forest is interwoven with a more symbolic one, in which the forest appears as the dense and enigmatic landscape of romance, identified not by ambush, armies and proximity to familiar cities, but by glades, mysterious castles, and enchantments. (164)

In other words, the power of our associations with the forest as a place of myth and mystery overshadows the traces of real, non-symbolic, woodland within the text.

Such traces are clear to see, if we make a conscious effort to look, and Saunders is right to say that many of them occur in the earlier books. Focusing on the moments when actual woodland is present reveals the main functions served by woods in Malory's text, which themselves indicate a predominantly urban view of the woods in which (in marked contrast to Chaucer) trees are always growing plants, not future lumber. One important function of wooded landscapes early in the text is as terrain offering foot soldiers good chances of escape from pursuing horsemen. Thus Lot's advice to the other of the eleven kings ranged against Arthur is to let the infantry go: 'For thys noble kynge Arthure woll nat tarry on the footemen, for they may save hemselff: the woode ys nerehonde (*Morte* 23)'. This shows a straightforward appreciation of both the difficulty of riding at speed through mixed woodland with its uncertain floor and undergrowth and the concomitant difficulty of keeping quarry in sight. The very fact that it is difficult to ride through Malory's forests at speed betrays his use of the concept of forests as untamed, even ancient, places. His densely wooded ground is very different from the forest game preserves in which undergrowth would be cleared to ensure the hunt could pass without undue danger to itself and low branches be either removed or nibbled by deer. This rough and unruly terrain is also good for concealing surprisingly large groups of people, a fact Merlin makes use of when he hides the reinforcements he has brought for Arthur in the forest of Bedgrayne (*Morte* 16). Arthur in turn recognises that woodland has this advantage when he first rests in the forest by the Humber, where he is attacked by the Five Kings, and later returns there with Gawain, Gryfflet and Kay 'for they supposed to here of them that were ascapid, and ther founde the moste party of his peple' (79). It is not only companies that find forests good places to avoid people: Gareth turns into the forest in order to shake off the pursuing Gawain. 'That aspyed sir Gareth and rode wyghtly into the [foreste]. For all that sir Gawayne coude do, he wyste nat were he was becom' (218). The very qualities that makes woods good for escape makes them good for ambush, and this, too, is acknowledged, as, for instance, when Arthur leaves Sir Lyonel and Sir Bedwere in 'a boyshemente', taking the rest of the force to find the Emperor's pavilion, which, necessarily, is in a clearing (123). Forests as places of ambush and abduction continue as a motif throughout the text and, although the method of attack or abduction may be more or less magical or mysterious, the forest still provides the appropriate setting. Thus Morgan's abduction of Launcelot in the first third of the text is aided by magic (151), while Sir Melyas's overthrow by two knights representing his besetting sins in the Grail Quest, takes place in 'an olde foreyste' (529). The setting makes it credible that these two should materialise so suddenly and when they attack Sir Galahad shortly afterwards, we are told explicitly that they come out of 'the levys' (530).

Sometimes, however, the attack in the forest is straightforwardly human, such as the almost unmotivated plot enacted against Brangwayne.

> by the assente of two ladyes that wer with the quene they ordayned for hate and envye for to distroy dame Brangwayne that was mayden and lady unto La Beale Isode. And she was sente into the foreste for to fecche herbys, and there she was [mette] and bounde honde and foote to a tre (263)

As well as offering unknown attackers the opportunity to capture a woman, the forest here appears, unremarked, as a place into which women might well go on their own in order to gather herbs. Again, this tacitly acknowledges one of the major uses of actual woodland, as a place of harvest taken advantage of by all who lived close enough to pick herbs, fruit or nuts at the appropriate times of year. Such adventitious harvesting is entirely in keeping with how woods were used, and still are to some extent. This then unites with the phrase describing how Isode 'walked into the foreste to put away hir thoughtes' (263) to offer a far more benign set of associations than those of apprehension and mystery which arise from, and perhaps also give rise to, ambush and abduction.

In the episode of the kidnap of Brangwayne the two attitudes exist side-by-side, which may make woods more disconcerting, but also brings them into the realm of the everyday. By thus juxtaposing mundane details of how people live with and within woods with the fear of the unknown that Harrison has shown to be such a resilient part of how we think of forests, Malory quietly endorses the belief that woods are unreliable and yet also attractive places. He is able to do this, or perhaps does so inevitably, because of the prevailing associations with woodlands that are part and parcel of how we think not only of forests but also of the landscape we associate with medieval romance. In our minds knights ride through forests encountering adversaries, or each other, in sudden clearings; or they travel through dense woodland and so come upon a castle. In such scenarios the forest serves to indicate not only the distance between one court and another but also their remoteness from each other: communication is assumed to be partial and difficult, information unreliable and slow to get through.

Given all of which it is not surprising to find that it is not only possible but likely that one will get lost in a forest. Launcelot demonstrates this likelihood admirably when he escapes from imprisonment in a castle and sets out for the Cistercian abbey, where he is to meet King Bagdemagus's daughter, a mere ten miles away and seemingly well known to all in the area. As we would expect of someone eager to avoid detection, Launcelot heads for the trees, and immediately gets lost: 'And so he rode into a grete foreste all that day, and never coude fynde no hygheway' (*Morte* 153). Instead of finding an abbey he happens upon a pavilion, which he promptly enters (as is appropriate for a knight errant) thus setting off a train of events which results in a good knight, Belleus, being severely wounded and his lady being understandably annoyed about it all. Launcelot has very much lost his way: instead of making a quick and easy escape he has become embroiled in another knight's use of the forest (apparently for more romantic purposes). Although it is easy to put this down to inevitable knightly behaviour, it is worth noting that such behaviour is inevitable only in the forest and only for a very specific group of people: the questing knight or knight-errant.

If we look more closely at this episode it emerges that finding the abbey ought to have been a straightforward matter. Bagdemagus's daughter clearly assumed it would be easy enough to find as she does not give Launcelot directions, and evidently Belleus and his lady know where it is, as it is presumably they who tell Launcelot the way. It is therefore not true to say that all who enter the forest will inevitably lose their way. The conclusion must be that it is specifically the knight-errant who is thus strangely at a loss in the very forests which feature so heavily in his adventures. Of course, in order for the woods to remain places of intrigue and challenge, they must to some extent remain unknown to questing knights and this perhaps explains why Launcelot, chief among the secular knights, is such an inept woodsman. He seems almost incapable of entering a forest without getting lost, although admittedly in the Grail Quest the fact that he 'helde no hygheway' (555) may be more an indication of his spiritual state than a simple statement that he has no idea where he is. Further reflection shows that this lack of forest knowledge may be regarded as a defining characteristic of a questing knight. We have seen that knights know perfectly well how to negotiate forests when engaged in actual combat early in the text, and the later books are populated by hermits who were once knights, but have now retired and live knowledgably and in harmony with the woods. Admittedly, their hermitages are exceptionally well-appointed, as Malory rather charmingly acknowledges, but the point is that once they shed the identity of knight-errant they become men who know their way around a wood. Indeed they are often the ones who put their questing brethren on the right path, actually as well as spiritually.

These ex-knights and the other hermits are not the only inhabitants of the forests. Despite Saunders's assertion that we see little of the real people whose lives are lived within or on the verges of forests, Malory's text does in fact include several allusions to them. It is more a case of us colluding with the text and overlooking them, than of them being absent altogether. Thus, when Tristram goes mad and, significantly, sheds his knightly identity, he is taken in by herdsmen who adopt him as their fool.[32] In doing this they are not only taking care of his bodily needs but also, paradoxically, maintaining the idea that he comes from a different social sphere. It is possible to see this as an example of the inversion trope which is readily associated with life in the forests, according to which the lost noble becomes a beggar and the rustic takes on the role of lord. To an extent this reading works: lunatics were kept as fools, as a form of entertainment, but the role is more readily associated with courts than with herdsmen. Thus the act of adopting a fool could be seen as the point at which the herdsmen take on the role of a carnivalesque exiled court. However in doing so these ordinary people cease to be reflections of the real world and become participants in the imaginative realm of the narrative. A slightly different picture emerges if we retain the idea that these figures are elements of actual woodland life within the text. In that case we are struck by an incongruent juxtaposition of narrative elements. Real herdsmen and shepherds carve out a livelihood in actual forests: madmen are associated with forests only through literary convention. In this light the adoption of Tristram as a kind of court fool becomes a more nuanced strategy. By maintaining a distance between themselves and the mad Tristram the herdsmen are preserving the separate identities of both the actual and the conceptual forest. This in turn leaves the way open for Tristram to regain his original identity as a knight who may hunt in a forest, but does not naturally live there.

The case of Launcelot's madness is slightly different. Significantly, he begins his bout by jumping into a garden through a window and presumably into the thorn bush that scratches him so badly (487). After this all that we are told is that he 'ranne furthe he knew nat whothir, and was a wylde [woode] as ever was man' (487). He remains in this state for two years, but when he is taken in, in a move that is closer to capture than succour, his hosts are not woodsmen but knights, Sir Blyaunte and Sir Selyvaunte, whose only method of care is to keep him manacled in their castle. They give him food enough, but are unable to restore his sanity (497). In Launcelot's case, running into the forest, which he does explicitly only after his time in castle Blanke, is actually a sign that his recovery has begun. He does not remain within the forest, but seems to run through it to Corbyn in one day, thus beginning the retracing of his steps that eventually leads to him being placed in the presence of the Grail and having his sanity restored. The association of woods with places of refuge for those banished (as Launcelot has been by Guinevere) is doubtless an element here, but more powerful is the notion that ultimately knights belong in castles and their only business in forests is to pass through them, not remain within them.

The human life that goes on in a wood – that of forester, herdsman or hermit – is lived without much recourse to the knights and ladies who pass through, engaged in their various quests. The knights themselves are dimly aware that there are people who live such lives, but refer to them only when in need of a place to stay (usually when wounded) or, more rarely, when asking directions. In general, the knights and their adventures are a kind of superstructure to Malory's text, and while unarguably it is the superstructure that commands our attention, it is worth noting that Malory has included elements to remind us of the actual woodland on which it is all built. The final effect is to create in our minds an image of a heavily wooded country, which in turn is one of the principal means by which Malory sets his tales in a distant and golden past. In the late Middle Ages, just as now, the imagined landscape of the past was differentiated from the present most of all by the prevalence of woods and trees. Only in such a landscape can we be sure that we are in not only a historical past, but a literary and conceptual one as well. It is perhaps to fend off such romanticising nostalgia that Chaucer's use of trees is so deliberately contemporary. The careful regularity of his trees reminds us of the industries that create the actual woods through which his dreamer wanders in *The Book of the Duchess*. Such actual woods provide the pattern for our ideas of forests, but they are very different from the woods of our imaginations. In the main, Chaucer's trees are visible only because of his skill in incorporation – we are always aware of the human agenda and value systems behind their appearances in his texts. It is partly because he assimilates the trees into the human world so completely that they appear so real. Yet that very assimilation causes problems for a green reader and makes us unexpectedly uncomfortable with Chaucer's trees. We are not challenged to consider their otherness and indeed are scarcely allowed to acknowledge it. Malory, in contrast, calls up images of wild woods, more tangled, less mapable and more immediately associated with the idea of ancient forests. His combination of the mythic and the mundane offers both the security of the tree as tethering post and the challenge of the forest as the realm of the past. Trees in his text thus exist in the two time frames simultaneously and are key in bridging the two. Plumwood suggests that we honour trees 'as great time-travellers and teachers' (2002: 150) and it is this association of trees with time spans beyond human attainment which allows Malory to set his noble tales of Arthur in a past which is remote yet imaginatively near. So, although Chaucer and Malory draw on very different aspects of our human relations to and uses of trees in their writing, we may detect in each actual trees and real woods, if we look carefully.

Notes

1 Particularly useful in this context are Rackham's *The History of the Countryside* (Rackham 1986), Harrison's exploration of the concept of the forest, *Forests: The Shadow of Civilisation* (Harrison 1992) and Saunders's detailed literary study *The Forests of Medieval Romance* (Saunders 1993). Jacques le Goff's discussion of the imaginative world in *The Medieval Imagination*

(1998) is also highly pertinent, especially pp. 51–9 where he deals with ideas of the forest in close relation to those of the wilderness.
2. Rackham 1986: 64–5 where this point is made.
3. Browsing the *MED* it becomes apparent that the idea of trees is present, even if the plants themselves were not.
4. See Rackham 1986: 12–13 and also 24 for a useful caution about how existing records should be regarded.
5. Saunders 1993 is a case in point. While acknowledging the importance of 'the interplay of the real and the symbolic' (1993: xi) she ends up focusing primarily on the symbolic, but her work contains many useful facts about actual forests and their management.
6. All quotations of Chaucer's work are taken from The Riverside Chaucer ed. Larry Benson et al. (Boston: Houghton Mifflin, 1987 and Oxford: Oxford University Press, 1988). Citations are by text and line number.
7. See Trevisa ed. Seymour (1975) p. 918. This entry is also cited by the *MED* under box n (1) a.
8. Anthropomorphism is a complicated concept, especially for ecocritics, who are divided about whether it is to be criticised because it make everything human, or employed because it admits that non-human species are also capable of thoughts, feelings and ideas: anything thus accorded subjectivity stands a better chance of commanding human respect. Plumwood has a good deal to say on anthropomorphism and its relation to anthropocentricity (2002: 56–61).
9. Rooney 1993 is probably the best study of medieval hunting generally. Orme (1992) offers useful comments on the difference between actual and literary hunts, while Berry (2001) provides details on later hunting practices and also on the use of forests as game preserves.
10. *Occupatio* is a device much favoured by Chaucer, by which a description is provided while the narrator protests that they are refusing to give it: 'I shall not tell you about . . .'
11. Neither Chaucer nor his Knight bothers to identify the exact status of land that provides the setting for the Tale's action. However, it is helpful to bear in mind the difference between unadopted woodland, which all were free to forage for the fruit, quarry and timber to be found there, and afforested land, declared the property of the King, in which everything was protected and could be hunted, gathered or felled only with the King's say-so. Both Harrison (1992) and Berry (2001) offer useful insights into the differences between general woods and legally denominated forests. Chaucer would come to have some direct knowledge of the legalities surrounding forests and woodlands when he was appointed Deputy Forester for North Petherton some time in the 1390s, by which time he is believed to have begun on *The Canterbury Tales*.
12. *Sir Gawain and the Green Knight*, on the other hand, offers a variation in which the wilds themselves challenge the would-be hero as Gawain encounters monsters, wild men and Wodwos but finds the weather his hardest adversary. See Anderson ed. 1996: ll. 713–35.
13. Merchant (1992: 103) discusses the effects of the way this social construct changes over time. C. Harrison and J. Burgess make a more general point:

Trees

that followers of particular concepts ('myths' in their terms) inevitably learn different things about any given environment, depending on the myth operating at the time (Harrison and Burgess 1994: 298). David Pepper (1996) offers a different and useful overview of concepts of the environment, much of which is closely allied to attitudes towards nature, while Neil Evernden (1992) explores the topic at some length.

14 A case in point is the lack of consideration given to this episode by Derek Pearsall and Elizabeth Salter (1973). Their otherwise detailed survey of the development of various aspects of landscape motifs in medieval literature gives only a passng mention of Mars's temple on page 4.

15 As used for the title of her book *Feminism and the Mastery of Nature* (1993).

16 Although this description of 'the Thracian wilderness around the temple of Mars . . . is at the end of a line of development running through Virgil, Statius and Boccaccio' (Pearsall and Salter 1973: 4), forests are not among the first associations with Mars: battlefields spring more readily to mind.

17 Harrison 1992 remains the best survey of human reactions to and associations with the forest.

18 The notion of a resilient and fundamentally indestructible earth underpins Lovelock's 'Gaia' philosophy (expounded in Lovelock 1979), which carries with it the suggestion that the Earth will always right whatever imbalances humans introduce. Lovelock does not say, but it could be inferred, that such righting may not be carried out in ways comfortable for the human species. This last implication does not seem to have figured greatly in discussions of Gaia, but I believe the latent wish for a disciplining force can be seen in passages such as this one in the Knight's Tale.

19 See Harrison (1992: 1–2 and 49–52), where he deals with the founding of Rome as a city surrounded by and encroaching upon the Italian forest, and also 69–70 where he discusses the possible derivation of 'forest' from 'foris' meaning 'outside'.

20 'Wasted' is a tricky word here. The context of Theseus's speech seems to demand the interpretation 'spent, lost', but the word also caries connotations of being deliberately cut down, as in 'laid waste'. There is thus an ambiguity here: is the oak actually felled or does it die a natural death? If the former (rather then the more usual latter reading) Theseus's metaphor has overpowered the moral he is surely intending to convey, that of death as the end to even the longest life, and reveals instead the flagrant and habitual wasting of arboreal life that is part of the timber industry. In that case the tree might be said to achieve a victory over the tone of the line, albeit a Pyrrhic one – whatever the moral implication, the end for the tree is the same.

21 See, for example, Bennett 1957: 79; Leicester 1974: 22; Kiser 1991: 47–8. The notes of both the Riverside and Phillips and Havely editions rightly point out that this list shows Chaucer's indebtedness to an established literary tradition of such lists and his use of extant epithets for several of the trees.

22 Haveley makes this suggestion in his note to lines 218–24 of *The Parliament of Fowls* (Phillips and Havely eds 1997: 244) where he points out that the oak also figures in *The Book of the Duchess*. Havely also refers to Chaucer's lyric *Gentilesse*, presumably reading the 'first stok' as an oak, but on what grounds is not made clear.

23 The Royal Oak, familiar from so many pub signs, commemorates the oak tree in which Charles II hid after the battle of Worcester in 1651. Sprigs of oak used to be worn on 29 May to commemorate his restoration to the throne in 1660. The oak has long associations with Englishness, perhaps owing to its being one of the largest and longest lived of England's indigenous species but also in part because of its extensive use in shipbuilding. It is, of course, a false analogy to say 'English' is completely equivalent to 'noble'. Chaucer himself would have reason in later life to reject any such direct association, except in the most ironic terms, since he was robbed on 3 September 1390 (the first of three robberies in as many days) at 'le fowle ok'.

24 Phillips points out that hunts were associated with separation and death as well as with love (Phillips and Havely 1997: 37).

25 The figure of the madman taking refuge in the forest is closely aligned to the one fleeing to the wilderness and is dealt with in more detail in the discussion of Orfeo in the next chapter.

26 See, for instance, Saunders 1993: 155–7 and Rooney 2001.

27 Lewis makes the assertion in his essay 'The English Prose *Morte*' in Bennett ed. 1963: 7. Vinaver picks up the comment and elaborates upon it in his response to Lewis in the same volume, pp. 31–2. Vinaver's essay has been republished in *On Art and Nature* (2000).

28 I present the lines as quoted by Vinaver in Bennett, ed.1963: 30, where the play is also referred to as *A* (not *The*) *Winter's Tale*. Vinaver's essay has been reprinted in *Art and Nature* (2000).

29 All reference to Malory's text are to Vinaver's 1971 second edition of his single-volume Oxford text and refer to page numbers. The whole text is referred to as the *Morte* as that is its commonly used name, despite Vinaver's preferred title *Works*.

30 As the story of the spindles progresses it become clear there ought to be three types of tree, one white, one green, one red, from each of which is taken wood for the spindles. In order for the story to make sense, we must assume there were offshoots from the white tree, which remained white, but Malory's text does not actually say this.

31 The use of a single tree, often a grafted tree and most often an apple tree, as a gateway to another world was pointed out by A.J. Bliss in his introduction to *Sir Orfeo* in 1954 where he refers to examples in other Breton lays.

32 Tristram's relation to the forest is complex. His episode as a madman is balanced by his identity as an arch hunter and his time spent with Isode in apparent forest idyll. Saunders suggests that the figure of Tristram bridges the gap between forest and human society through this role of hunter. While this is a persuasive reading, it is significant that Tristram cannot remain in the forest permanently and that it is in the end his sojourn there with Isode which leads to his downfall. The inference might be that the real life of humans in the forest is as herdsman, not as hunter. A hunter, after all, is by this stage essentially a noble who needs to have a court to which to return.

3
Wilds, wastes and wilderness

The idea of wilderness is perhaps even more evocative than that of the forest. It conjures up images of vast expanses of untamed and untameable land which is either barren or supports a tangle of plant life which in turn provides a habitat for unknown numbers and species of animals. Above all, it is a place where humans are not and where it is felt they are not supposed to be, certainly not on any permanent basis. Permanence and wilderness are mutually exclusive in human terms: people, like the Bedouin, who live in wildernesses or deserts are itinerant and the Old Testament references to years spent in the wilderness signal that this is an interim state, regardless of how long the tribes spend there until they find a place to settle. Once settled, of course, the land is no longer a wilderness, even if the terrain is remarkably similar to that through which the wanderers have travelled. It is here that the concept of a waste or wilderness is different from that of a forest. As the previous chapter has shown, the idea of the forest seems to demand that anyone entering it will happen upon another person, or a castle or at the very least a pavilion or a hunt. Forests may be trackless, difficult to negotiate and contain beasts, but they are to some degree known quantities. A wilderness is not: its very unknowability defines it and, significantly, the wilderness resists the entry of humans to such a degree that those who enter it tend to be dehumanised in one way or another. Here, I suggest, the wilderness of the later Middle Ages combines the aspects of wilderness and wildness that Neil Evernden so carefully distinguishes in his discussion of latter-day wild spaces. Usefully he characterizes the two areas as follows:

> wilderness can be regarded as a thing, and as such, susceptible to identification and management. Wildness, however, lies beyond the

objects in question, a quality which directly confronts and confounds our designs. (Evernden 1992: 121)

The grounds of his distinction are close to those I am using to differentiate between the medieval forest and wilderness. Wilderness as a geographical space can be delineated, usually by defining the boundaries of owned and managed land, but, as with Evernden's wildness, the idea of wilderness is neither easily defined nor easily contained. As will become evident through the following discussions of *Sir Orfeo* and *Sir Gawain and the Green Knight*, this is because the idea of the unknown is integral to the concept of wilderness; to use Evernden's phrase 'wildness, otherness, *is* mystery incarnate' (1992: 121). Accordingly, the wilderness in these medieval texts becomes the place in which the mysterious can act as a palpable force, often being embodied in a being who is not necessarily bound by human rules. Here the parallels drawn by Sweeting and Crochunis between wilderness space and theatrical space are pertinent. They point out that, having been 'carved and framed though legislative or executive action ... space-based notions of wilderness ... create the wild within specific geographical confines' (Sweeting and Crochunis 2001: 325). Such geographical wildernesses are akin to realist stages, each being defined areas designed to be visited and viewed. Visiting and viewing are likewise key concepts in literary wildernesses, as Sarah Stanbury's excellent study of the *Gawain* poet demonstrates (1991). Thus, when exploring the wilderness of late medieval texts, it will be useful to think of it as a place that both is regarded as wild, in that it is uncultivated land, and also contains wildness, in the form of the untamed and unknown. These two together combine to make it a geographical and conceptual area that is utterly different from human space, utterly fascinating and often deeply disconcerting.

Part of that fascination may be the result of feeling our distance from this radically other landscape. Medieval wilderness in particular seems to exclude humans, or, more precisely, refuses to recognise those aspects by which we customarily seek to differentiate ourselves from rest of the world. Codes of conduct mean nothing and our habitual attitude of superiority is undermined by how difficult we find it to survive in such terrain as well as by the way other species take no account of us. It is thus that the wilderness 'confronts and confounds our designs', forcing us to confront and reappraise them likewise. Rather than being able to regard ourselves as the naturally dominant and successful species, we must alter our ways of being in order to enter the wilderness at all, for this conceptual wilderness has forms of life of its own, which themselves challenge the divisions between humanity and other species. It is here that we find the wildmen, Wodwos and faeries, and also the Green Man.[1] The net result is a clutch of terms indicating terrain which is hostile to civilised human life, but which is accessible to those humans who themselves wish to escape human society for one reason or another. The risk to the human is that of losing themselves, not merely geographically but also in terms of their identity, and it is this which makes wilderness a site of trial and transformation.[2]

Significantly, entry into the wilderness tends to be voluntary. The Orfeo of the middle English Breton lay offers a case in point:

> Into wildernes ichil te
> And live ther evermore
> With wilde bestes in holtes hore
>
> $(212-14)^3$

At first it may seem that Orfeo is simply reacting as a lover confronted with the loss of their beloved. His declaration that he will resort to the wilderness could call to mind the times Tristram and Launcelot both spend in the forest, each almost unrecognisable because they have been driven mad by the belief that his lady is unfaithful.[4] Yet, however much it may seem that Orfeo is acting according to the same convention by consciously seeking out the landscape associated with those who are at the end of their emotional tethers, in fact his case is very different. He sets his affairs in order, appoints a steward and leaves instructions as to how to proceed when (not if) his people receive certain news of his death. This is no impassioned, headlong rush, but a clearly stated intention to cast off his current identity and take on a different one in order to enter new and deliberately chosen surroundings. There is no apparent purpose beyond that change, for, as Gros Louis has pointed out, this is not the beginning of a quest: this Orfeo does not attempt to find Heurodis, nor is he seeking a way into the fairy kingdom.[5] Rather his action is purely and simply a radical removal into an entirely different way of living. Moreover, his chosen destination is specifically the wilderness, not the woods or forests. At first this may seem to be a difference without a distinction, but in fact the difference is important. As the narrative is careful to point out, entering the wilderness involves crossing the liminal ground of woods and heathland, which serve to separate the cultivated human world from the otherness of the wild: 'Thurth wode and over heth / Into the wildernes he geth' (237–8). Orfeo is electing to enter an area that by definition is untouched by human society and so defies accurate description, but it is only its contents that are thus inscrutable; it whereabouts are known, as is, evidently, the way to its boundaries.

However, although we may define its borders, we do not know for certain what lies within. More precisely, we know some recognisable creatures live there, wild boar, bears and lions for instance, but we are aware that much more remains beyond our ken, and so it is that the wilderness comes to epitomise a known area of ignorance. It is a mark of this inscrutability that the *Sir Orfeo* narrative cannot follow Orfeo into the wilderness proper. Instead we are provided with an extended description of the process of entering the wilderness which is performed through comparison of what Orfeo leaves behind. Here, again, Sweeting and Crochunis's suggestion that theatre space and wilderness share some characteristics is relevant, for Orfeo's leave-taking is nothing if not theatrical. He calls all his court into an audience to witness his formal investiture of his steward and hear his speech which is tantamount to a declaration that, having lost his queen, he has lost his own identity as king and so will seek out the wilderness:

> He cleped togider his barouns,
> Erls, lordes of renouns,
> And when thai al y-comen were,
> 'Lordinges,' he said, 'bifor you here
> Ich ordainy min heighe steward
> To wite mi kingdom afterward;
> In mi stede ben he schal
> To kepe mi londes overal.
> For now ichave mi quen y-lore,
> The fairest levedi that ever was bore,
> Never eft y nil no woman se.
> Into the wilderness ichil te. . .'

(201–12)

In the light of our focus on the wilderness, it is significant that the steward is given control over all Orfeo's lands (208) in terms which also imply guarding and preserving them: 'kepe' not just 'rule'. This further implies that the area Orfeo himself is about to enter does not come under such jurisdiction and indeed may be part of what the 'londes' must be guarded against. It is also significant that entering the wilderness is concomitant with never seeing another woman. This raises the question of whether the wilderness is a place without people of any kind, or just without women. Whichever it is, it is evidently a place that can be relied upon to release Orfeo from human social expectations, including those of marriage: he is no longer obliged to attempt to protect his wife, nor does he seek out a replacement for her. The consciously dramatic manner of Orfeo's announcement marks his recognition of the wilderness's effect as his highly theatrical speech is accompanied by equally theatrical actions. He casts off his kingly robes and, dressed simply in a wanderer's, or pilgrim's 'sclavin', goes barefoot from court, carrying only his harp. It is a masterly performance which bears some comparison to the careful arming of Gawain as he sets out on his journey in *Sir Gawain and the Green Knight*.

The narrative continues this performative process, providing an extended description of the various stages of exchange through which Orfeo embarks on his new life. His clothing of furs is replaced with coverings of leaves and grasses and his bed with purple linen becomes the hard heath:

> He that hadde y-werd the fowe and griis,
> And on bed the purper biis,
> Now on hard hethe he lith
> With leves and gresse he him writh.
>
> (241–4).

The pattern continues over the next twelve lines as castle and fertile lands reminiscent of summer are replaced with snow-covered, frozen, mossy ground; knights and ladies become snakes,[6] and the best food and drink, easily to hand, are replaced by roots, berries and fruit for which he must forage. An appreciation of the lay's deployment of this familiar rhetorical device (akin to the 'ubi sunt' trope) may lead us to overlook exactly what is happening in terms of text, which is that the extended list of comparisons serves to highlight the failure of language to encompass wilderness. We are given the illusion that Orfeo's life in the wilds is being described in detail, but in fact we are getting more about the luxuries he has left behind than the life he is embarking upon. In short, the poem can take us up to the point at which Orfeo enters the wilds, but thereafter is thrown back on its own devices to construct the environment in which he spends ten years. Those devices turn out to be those of initial invocation of what is lost, and subsequent description of the effects of wilderness living on the gradually wasting body of Orfeo: 'Al his bodi was oway dwine / For missays, and al to-chine' (261–2). The focus is thus kept on the knowable, human subject, although the transformation presented is extreme.

Such extremity is not unexpected, both Orfeo and the narrative concur in their projection of what the physical consequences of life in the wilderness will be. Orfeo puts it succinctly in his declaration that he will live 'with wilde bestes in holtes hore', but the narrative draws out the implications of such living in a 46-line (lines 234–80) description of physical privation and alteration at the end of which Orfeo is not only living with the beasts but has more or less become one of them. He spends all his time in an effort to find enough to eat: 'Now may he al day digge and wrote / Er he finde his fille of rote' (255–6). Summer offers the slightly better living of fruit and berries (although even these provide a meagre meal) but winter reduces him to roots, grass and bark:

> In somer he liveth bi wild frut,
> And berien bot gode lite;
> In winter may he nothing finde
> Bot rote, grases, and the rinde
>
> (257–60)

He becomes not only thin (261–2, quoted above) but also unkempt, with hair and beard reaching to his waist: 'His here of his berd, blac and rowe, / To his girdel-stede was growe' (265–6). The choice of 'girdel-stede' rather than 'wayste' reminds us quietly of the fine clothes he no longer wears – 'stede' allowing us to read 'instead' as well as 'place'. By the time we reach the end of this passage the transformation is complete, but is it worth noting that this picture, which is close to the expected image of a wild man, differs in some significant respects[7]. The clothing is particularly interesting. As noted above, the narrative specifically mentions Orfeo's relinquishing of his furs, but at the end of the passage he is covered in leaves and grasses, not, as we might expect, in animal skins. Furthermore, his meagre diet is exclusively vegetarian, consisting of fruit, berries, roots and grasses. Here, then, the use of pelts as clothing and animal flesh as food is exclusive to the wholly human life of the court. Orfeo's choice of words has proved to be very correct – he is living with wild beasts, not off them.

In *Sir Orfeo*, the lay, such extreme changes are worthy of remark, but not of censure: writing roughly a century later,[8] Henryson's attitude is rather different and betrays how often living in the wilderness is associated with becoming less than human. The second stanza of his poem *Orpheus and Eurydice* is very clear on how Orpheus's transformation is not just a change in circumstances but a degradation.

> It is contrair the lawis of nature
> A gentill man to be degenerate,
> Noucht folowing of his progenitoure
> The worthy reule and the lordly estate;
> A ryall renk for to be rusticate
> Is bot a monster in comparison,
> Had in despyte of foule derision.
>
> (8–14)[9]

Henryson is assuming that his readers know the tale of Orpheus well enough to know of his sojourn in the wilderness, either before finding Eurydice (as the lay has it) or after losing her for the second time (the classical version). However, Henryson omits any such episode of wandering from his version of the legend, replacing it with a journey through the heavens, planet by planet (184–239) during which Orpheus encounters the music of the spheres, but finds no clue as to Eurydice's whereabouts. Such a journey is nothing if not elevated and retains Orpheus's nobility even in grief. Ironically, further proof of his good breeding is to be found in the beautifully crafted formal lament he sings to mark the loss of Eurydice before he sets off on his cosmic travels. It is here, in the lyric not in the actuality of the poem, that we find the figure of the distraught and bedraggled Orpheus wandering in the wilderness that the legend's tradition leads us to expect. The conventions of song allow him to invoke the image of a man in despair verging on madness without suffering the indignity of adopting it. Despite his words, this Orpheus actually goes nowhere near the wilderness.

> 'Fair weill, my place; fair weile, plesance and play;
> And welcome, woddis wyld and wilsome way,
> My wikit werd in wildernes to wair!
> My rob ryall and all my riche array
> Changit sall be in rude russat of gray;
> My diademe in till ane hate of hair;
> My bed sall be with bever, broke, and bair,
> In buskis bene, with mony bustuos bes,
> Withoutin sang, sayng with siching sair,
> "Quhar art thow gane, my luf Erudices?"'
>
> (154–63)

Setting these stanzas from the two poems next to each other makes the contrast clear. According to Henryson, a noble lord may invoke the convention of the grief-stricken lover heading into the wilderness, but he refrains from actually enacting it, preferring his song to do that for him. In the Breton lay, on the other hand, the power of poetry is evident not in replacing but in displaying the changes Orfeo undergoes. It might be said, then, that the earlier text is more at home with the existence of wilderness as an integral, albeit mysterious, part of the world. In the lay the wilderness is a credible geographical place, but by the time we reach Henryson it has become primarily a literary concept, readily replaced by the cosmos as a place which is self-evidently there, but is essentially unknown.

Henryson's wilderness is so utterly bereft of redeeming qualities that he even denies it the presence of song. In his text the harmonising enchantment of music is to be found in the heavens alone as the beginning of line 162 fleetingly implies that it is the wilds that are 'withoutin sang', before the rest makes it clear that it is only Orpheus who will be songless. Even so, this is a strange assertion, given that the traditionally lasting image of Orpheus is that of the harpist surrounded by wild animals, gathered together oblivious of normal enmities by the sound of his playing. In the lay one of the ways we know Orfeo is not mad, even if he is unkempt and in the wilderness, is that he takes care of his harp, storing it in a tree to preserve it from bad weather or other misadventure, ready to play on brighter days. Indeed, it is only this harp-playing that assures us that Orfeo is still human and has not become one of the beasts or other more mysterious creatures who dwell in the wilds. Thus the lay is careful to say that although the wild animals will cluster around him when he plays, the moment he stops they cannot bear his presence, shunning him as a foreign presence in their domain:

> alle the wilde bestes that ther beth
> For joie abouten him thai teth,
> And alle the foules that ther were
> Come and sete on ich a brere
> To here his harping a-fine –
> So miche melody was therin;
> And when he his harping lete wold,
> No best bi him abide nold.
>
> (273–80)

Throughout the tale and in every version of the legend it is this harp-playing that distinguishes Orfeo from the beasts of the wilderness. Its magical quality is important: [10] it provides Orfeo with a passport into the fairy kingdom, with the means to regain Eurydice, with solace in the wilderness and above all with his own identity, being crucial in restoring his renounced kingdom to him in the middle English lay. However for green criticism the salient feature of this music must be that it is produced using a manufactured instrument. It is surely significant that Orfeo's music is not song: it is not a sound produced using the performer's body alone, but instead relies on an artefact. It is perhaps this which marks the distinction between human and other animals here. The picture offered by the poem is that of Orfeo, the wild man, at one with the beasts, playing to a crowd of various indigenous animals. Yet much as this image may seem to blur the boundaries between human and non-human, closer scrutiny reveals that it in fact marks them, for Orfeo is very much an instrumentalist performing to his audience.[11] The word 'abide' thus indicates that although Orfeo may be living in the wilderness, he is not part of the habitat.

In many ways, then, the picture drawn by Henryson in Orpheus's lament and that used more extensively in the lay have much in common. In each case the royal clothing is replaced with the coarse garment of russet cloth worn by a pilgrim (or possibly monk or friar) and in each the displaced king envisages himself sleeping with wild animals. In each text, too, the general 'beasts' indicates the point at which precise information runs out and the imagination tries to take over. Henryson's Orpheus envisages a land containing beavers, badgers and bears, just as the lay knows that Orfeo will be surrounded by snakes rather than lords, but beyond that both texts signal the essentially unknowable nature of the wilderness by resorting to generic terms – 'bes' in Henryson, 'bestes' in the lay. While in one way this asserts that the wilderness is a natural place, inhabited, like the rest of the world, by living creatures, it simultaneously indicates that 'wilderness' is a kind of blank canvas for the human imagination. We may not know exactly what the wilderness contains, but we can imagine it – and imagine we do.

What we imagine, though, has precious little to do with actual geographical wilderness and it is here that the associations of wilderness and wild places with the supernatural become most clear. The *MED* comments that by the fourteenth century the word 'waste' had taken on connotations of the ephemeral and this process can be seen to affect the concepts of wilderness and wilds as well. It is all too easy to attribute to the wilderness an element of mystery and such attribution happens in the minds of critics and readers just as much as it does in the texts themselves – Gros Louis, for example, writes of Orfeo's decision to 'move into the mysterious wilderness, by living out his life in strange and lonely lands' (1967: 249). Both 'mysterious' and 'lonely' are imported notions, each revealing our typically anthropocentric view of the world around us. The wilderness is mysterious only because we are outside it and the lands are lonely only if 'company' must mean 'human' – we have seen that the companionship of animals is available to Orfeo through his music. Yet this is not to say such imports are without textual support: the narrative of the poem assumes that the wilderness is indeed the appropriate place for encounters with the supernatural and its general attitude reflects our anthropocentric inclinations. Rather than attempting to describe the wilderness per se, the poem describes what Orfeo finds there and, significantly, what he finds, or more accurately, what he finds that the poem is able to portray, is the fairy court at play.

Wilds, wastes and wilderness

In effect the lay puts this supernatural fairy world on a par with the animals. Having described the birds and beasts clustering around and then shunning Orfeo (273–80) the next lines read:

> He might se him bisides,
> Oft in hot undertides,
> The king o fairy with his rout
> Com to hunt him al about
> With dim cri and bloweing,
> And houndes also with him berking
>
> (281–6)

At one level 'bisides' carries the meaning 'as well', as if the fairies, like the wild animals, have been summoned by Orfeo's harping. Fleetingly, too, there is the possibility that Orfeo himself is the quarry for this hunt, as line 284 offers the reading 'come to hunt him' as well as the 'come to hunt all around him' which finally prevails. These passing ambiguities dangle the notion that Orfeo has become so much a part of the wilderness landscape that he could be regarded by these other visitors to the wilderness as one of its regular inhabitants, thus making him, like the other animals, plausible game. However, we should be aware that these visions appear 'in hot undertides', a time of day particularly associated with visions, the appearance of demons and general supernatural activity.[12] Orfeo's position as spectator, distinct from what is being seen, is thus reiterated by the text and the net effect is to present both the actual creatures of the wilderness and the supernatural ones as equally credible and, therefore, equally strange. Orfeo is surrounded by marvels, be they the attentive birds and animals or the passing fairy court and while these things are indeed to be wondered at, their presence is not. The lay's prologue[13] has seeded the expectation that Orfeo's story will be a 'ferli thing' (4) of 'marvailles' (18) while the final lines assert its standing as a 'mervaile' (598) and it is here, in the wilderness section, that this marvellous element is most clearly in play. Yet, from the audience's point of view, Orfeo himself is as much a marvel as the rest because although we are being told what Orfeo sees, we are also aware of seeing him in this landscape: he is both observer and observed. So a more shifting pattern emerges, somewhat on the lines of a kaleidoscope, as different equivalents come into view depending on the perspective taken to the text. The constant factor is that of strangeness which maintains the distance between us as human audience and the action of the tale, which momentarily allows human, animal and fairy to exist on an equal plane.

The ability of the wilderness to maintain such shifting equivalences underlines our perception of it as an almost mythical arena. This sense is further endorsed by the way the narrative passes swiftly from Orfeo playing to the beasts, to three different fairy appearances: hunt, tournament and dancing. Each of these occurs at unspecific times: 'oft' for the hunt (282) and 'otherwhile' for the fairies in battle-dress and the dancers (289; 297). Such apparent precision but actual vagueness promotes the impression of being in another world, whereas in fact at this point we are still firmly in the actual, natural world: Orfeo does not enter the fairy kingdom until line 351. As well as being in keeping with the pace of the lay in general, such restlessness reflects both Orfeo's unease in the wilderness (the 'malaise' (240) and 'missays' (262) he has brought with him) and our own lack of secure knowledge about what the wilderness encompasses. More to the point, it reiterates our desire to fix the wilderness as a place of the unknown.

If the wilderness is the unknown, the fairy kingdom is not. However much we may wish to see in these supernatural people an embodiment of the wilderness, the poem itself will not support such readings. Explicit parallels are made between the fairy court and Orfeo's kingdom, not least through the use of the phrase 'castels and tours, / Rivers, forestes, frith with flours' which first describes the fairy kingdom as displayed to Heurodis during her ride with the fairy king (159–60) and is then repeated to evoke what Orfeo renounces when he enters the wilderness (245–6). Likewise, the fairy court itself mirrors the human one, albeit in more splendid and artificial terms while the presence of the dead and taken, frozen in the attitudes in which they left the human world, only goes to reinforce this suggestion that the fairy world works in parallel with our own. It is consciousness of this parallelism that ensures Orfeo's success as he invokes the codes of conduct expected of the most cultured, and thus arguably most artificial, human courts. It is thus by establishing a common link with the fairy based on their shared un-naturalness, that Orfeo wins the day.[14] Moreover, the point at which Orfeo starts seeking to enter the fairy world is the moment he reasserts his difference from the natural world of the wilderness. Significantly, this point is marked by speech:

> Parfay! quath he, ther is fair game;
> Thider ichil, bi Godes name;
> Ich was y-won swiche werk to se!
>
> (315–17)

Humanity sets great store by speech, frequently confusing the ability to speak with the ability to use any form of language and indeed with the ability to reason.[15] Lack of speech thus becomes aligned with lack of reason, even lack of thought, and both are associated with the non-human with an ease that borders on the facile.[16] One corollary of this is the power of silencing as a tool of oppression and this in turn has been highlighted by ecocritics, particularly ecofeminists, as one of the main ways the non-human world has been subjugated in human eyes and to human purposes.[17] On the other hand, there is also a long tradition of humans seeking to give up habitual speech as a sign of holiness. Here voluntary silence denotes removal from the common human world in a desire to achieve a higher spiritual plane. It is obvious how the wilderness unites both these aspects: it is both unspoken and without speech; it is irrational and also beyond the reach of reason and thus is both a place of madness and of religious retreat. More to the point here, it is a place without the need for speech because here the human does not reign supreme. We easily overlook this aspect, just as we easily overlook Orfeo's silence in the wilds. He plays his harp, but he does not sing. Indeed we do not hear his voice from the moment he gives up his kingdom in line 236 until he exclaims at the hawking party in line 315. In retrospect we can see how closely the lay has aligned Orfeo with the wilderness through this silence; like the rest of the non-human world, Orfeo has been spoken for and had views and significance attributed to him, but he has not been allowed to speak himself.

It is no coincidence that this moment of recognition is occasioned by seeing the falcons of the fairy hawking party catch their prey. The previous sightings of the fairy host have been as ephemeral as the wilds themselves – the hunts have run down no quarry and the massed men in arms have fought no fights. The dancers have danced, but their music, like the dim calls of the hunting horns, has been muted. All has been in the strictest sense surreal; that is, passing over the surface of the real landscape without impinging either on it or on Orfeo's life there. This last hunt is different. The party is made up entirely of ladies, it is a hunt with birds and the prey is caught, all of which seems to trigger some kind of response in Orfeo, resulting in first his laugh of recognition and then his spoken reassertion of his old identity, which also reasserts his position as observer only: 'Ich was y-won swiche werk to se!' (317). The commonplace turn of phrase 'to se' takes on a specific meaning here as Orfeo, as a man, could not have taken part in this ladies' hunt: 'Nought o man amonges hem ther nis' (307). Suddenly his relation to these ghostly figures and their various activities is clear: it is all entertainment, human sport governed by human rules. The supernatural fairy host is thus explicitly aligned with the human against the non-human natural world and the shifting of the kaleidoscope stops. Seeing this version of the human relation to the non-human world – that of genteel, social hunting which makes use of the innate skills of one species of bird to kill another – recalls Orfeo to his identity as hunter and king and it is this identity and this relation of human to non-human world that the lay seems keen to promote. Marvels are all very well, but they clearly have their place and are best contained within a larger, safer, human structure. In a moment the enchanted union of creatures in the wilderness evaporates and it is only now that Orfeo sees Heurodis again and, this time, resolves to follow her.

It is important to realise that Orfeo reclaims his old identity before seeing Heurodis because this sequence of events, the one clearly presented by the poem, undermines readings of the story that seek to see the restoration of Heurodis as a reward to Orfeo. The myth of Orpheus may lend itself to such interpretation, and indeed Henryson's version, which appends a lengthy, moral, reading of the tale, is simply one within this established and still flourishing tradition, but the middle English lay takes another view. For any moral or religious reading of the poem to convince thoroughly Heurodis must clearly reappear to Orfeo as a consequence of his actions, however she is no more 'brought to him' (Gros Louis 1967: 250) than he originally set out to find her. It is true that Orfeo voluntarily enters the wilderness and that the poem even describes this as 'exile' (493), it is undeniable that the image of a pilgrim is suggested in his decision to dress in a simple mantle and go out barefoot, but there is no indication that Orfeo is consciously embarking on a time of penance, nor that he believes such exile may earn him the return of his wife. If anything his abdication is explicitly a rejection of the human world and it is a further sign of how fully he enters into the non-human realm that he is reputed to have gone beyond man's ken: 'no man nist in wiche thede' (494).

It is this unknown, uncanny quality that marks the wilderness. Each appearance of the fairy host before the one of the ladies hawking has ended with a similar assertion of this uncanny aspect, as neither the lay, nor, we are told, Orfeo, knows whence these fairies come or whither they go. The hunt with hounds disappears 'No never he nist whider they bicome' (288) and the ten hundred armed knights evaporate mid description, with swords held high 'Ac never he nist whider thai wold' (296). Even the dancers seem to simply dance by 'softly' (300) with no indication of how they came or where they go.[18] All the time that Orfeo is himself a part of the wilderness he seems content to let such things pass him by without trying to discover their origin or questioning their existence. It is thus all the more significant that, when he decides he will approach the hawking party, it proves perfectly possible to reach them, which is how he happens upon Heurodis. Moreover, when he vows to follow them there is no suggestion of it being impossible. Even riding through a rock into the fairy kingdom offers no difficulty:

> In at a roche the levedis rideth,
> And he after, and nought abideth.
>
> (347–8)

Here again there is an unlooked-for significance in a familiar filler phrase. The term 'nought abideth' ought to mean simply that Orfeo does not hesitate, but it also suggests that once Orfeo has left the landscape the only thing left is nothing. And this of course makes sense, for we have no way of describing that which lies beyond our imaginative reach. The wilderness was accessible to the narrative, and hence to us, only as long as Orfeo remained there as a channel for observation and as a comprehensible object to focus upon.[19] Once he has gone the atavistic concept of wilderness reasserts itself and the unknowable once again becomes the unknown and unseen – a blank space on which we project our desire to escape humanity and our apprehension about what that might actually mean. In this context one of Gros Louis's comments takes on added significance. According to him, Orfeo 'realizes, as other Orphic figures do not, the vast difference between the natural and the supernatural, and acts accordingly' (1967: 250). In Gros Louis's reading that 'vast difference' exists between the human and the fairy worlds, but a green reading of the text shows that the greater distance lies between the natural, wild world and the societies imposed on it, whether human or fairy. 'Supernatural' thus takes on the meaning of being overlaid on the natural rather than being beyond or above it and Orfeo's actions are those of a human finally casting their lot in with the carefully constructed superstructure, human or fairy, which offers him a recognisable role rather than remaining in the wilds where he has eked out an existence rather more in the wilderness than of it.

Orfeo himself conspires to maintain the unspoken quality of the wilderness. The lay offers no room for him to tell the tale of his ten years in the wilds and the only time he refers to it is when he is inventing the story of his own death in order to account for how an apparent beggar has Orfeo's harp and to test the loyalty of the steward. True to the expected story version of the wilderness, Orfeo presents an 'uncouthe' place inhabited by lions and wolves, who tear up human flesh but fortunately leave a harp undamaged (535–40). The suggestion is clearly that Orfeo was killed by these wild beasts, but Orfeo himself is careful to avoid saying as much explicitly.[20] This allows his audience to invent as lurid a death as they wish without requiring him to traduce his own actual experience of life in the wilderness. Yet, despite this silence on the subject, ten years in the wilderness have left their mark and, while Orfeo may be able to reclaim his wife and his kingdom without undue difficulty, his physical appearance retains a vestige of his sojourn beyond the bounds of human society. He is, we are told, 'y-clongen also a tre' (508), gnarled to the point of being not only no longer human, but not even animal. Indeed the exclamations of the people upon seeing him enter the city at the end of the poem recall the image of the wild man of the woods more fully than any previous description has done:

> 'Lo!' thai seyd, 'swiche a man!
> Hou long the here hongeth him opan!

> Lo! Hou his berd hongeth to his kne!
> He is y-clongen also a tre!'
>
> (505–8)

That last exclamation points to an aspect of Orfeo's exile hitherto overlooked. Gradually he has become more a part of wilderness than civilisation and this goes some way to explain the silence surrounding him until that moment in line 315 when his laugh and speech reassert his civilised, court mode. Significantly, his strange appearance calls forth remark only on the human streets; his entry into the fairy court drew no such comment. There the only surprise was that any human being should voluntarily venture into that land. Such lack of comment suggests that even at this point the wilderness, fairy world and human civilisation are on a par and apparently interchangeable. It is only when Orfeo invokes human codes of conduct in order to force the Fairy King to honour his agreement that the alignments are finally fixed with human and fairy being united in opposition to the wild. The fluid movement between human, wilderness and fairy realms thus ceases and Orfeo is free to return to his proper habitat.

It is worth tracing some of the ways the text exploits the fluidity of boundaries between the three realms it establishes. Within the poem Orfeo has entered each realm, each time prefacing his entry by putting on humble clothing and taking up his harp. In consequence, each space is at different times the unknown entered by Orfeo's strange presence as he moves from human court to wilderness to fairy realm and back to human court. It is possible to extend this parallelism and say that each of these realms at some point invades at least one of the others, albeit to varying degrees. Thus the fairy king enters the human world, each time abducting Heurodis,[21] and evidently Orfeo is completely human when he enters the fairy realm. The ladies hawking expedition offers a moment when the fairy world enters the wilderness, even if the previous visions of the fairies have suggested a more ghostlike passing over rather than full entry into this realm. Orfeo's human entry into the wilderness is uncontroversial, and it is he, too, who suggests that he be read as a figure of the wild entering the human, not because he looks like a gnarly tree but because, as he puts it 'Icham an harpour of hethenisse' (513). Most glosses give 'hethenisse' as 'heathendom', with little further comment. The usual assumption must be that Orfeo is presenting himself as outlandish in religion as well as origin, a reading which endorses both the classical roots of the story and the Christian elements of the medieval version. However, it is equally plausible that he is presenting himself here as a denizen of the heath itself, very literally a heathen man. Or rather, he is describing himself as one who can sing stories about the heath, the otherwise undescribed wilderness. It is perhaps not necessary to be entirely a thing of the heath in order to talk about it, indeed it may be that only someone who is somehow part of both the wilderness and the human is able to give the wilderness a voice in the human realm. In this context, it is worth pausing again on that description of Orfeo as a gnarled tree and reflect that, if we accept the possibility that Orfeo is in some way representing the wilderness, it is significant that the analogy is with a tree, not an animal. Had Orfeo resembled a beast he would not only have been closer to the figure of the wild man but also would have become one of the creatures gathered to listen to the harping rather than a harpist himself. Indeed some correlation between the harp and the tree has already been suggested by Orfeo's choice of a hollow trunk as protective storage for the instrument during the hard months: a choice made all the more appropriate by the fact that the harp's frame would have been made of wood. The latent possibilities of Orfeo's claim are thus extreme and also deeply disconcerting in a text which has allowed for, and indeed sought, parallels between human and fairy worlds, but rested on the absolute difference of wilderness from either.

In the end, though, such a reading does not finally convince and it may be that the poem cannot afford for it to do so. However far it may have ventured into the non-human, the poem clearly seeks to return to the safety of the human at the end, and moreover to a human social world in which harpists and poets command respect. It is thus significant that trees in this poem have tended to stand on the edge of the human and fairy worlds, as Heurodis found to her cost when she slumbered in the orchard under the grafted (ympe) tree.[22] So, in a peculiar way, Orfeo's gnarled appearance is as much a poetic parallel to this initial grafted tree as it is a reference to the wilderness in which he has spent the intervening years. Certainly this is a more comfortable way to read this likeness to a twisted tree, though of course the most comforting of all is as a simple, graphic and realist detail – a recognition that no one can spend ten years in the wilds without it leaving a mark.

Be that as it may, the poem remains consistent in silencing the wilderness to the end: we are not privileged to hear Orfeo's harping and Orfeo himself is quickly reabsorbed into the human world following the steward's recognition. The process of thorough going rehabilitation is signalled by Orfeo being washed, shaved and clothed in kingly attire and then being joined by Heurodis, led back into the mortal world for a second time with music. The fact that the two are given a second coronation serves to set the stamp of the solely human on these two who have in different ways become a part of other worlds for a time.

It seems right that the wilderness should be denied and resist easy embodiment, especially in a poem which has been able to suggest it only through absence, finding more to say about what it is not than what it contains. In the end it is precisely this unknowable, unspeakable and marvellous aspect of wilderness that *Sir Orfeo* maintains, even as it averts its eyes and returns us to the human world. Much the same might be said of *Sir Gawain and the Green Knight* for here, too, we have a man who voluntarily enters the wilderness but who returns to court in the end. Indeed the pattern of the two poems reveal a general similarity of form as both take us from an indoors human court to a wild outdoors terrain, to another, possibly supernatural court and back to the initial human court again. However Gawain's relation to the natural world is markedly different from Orfeo's. The preparations he makes are a ritual adoption of the role of representative of the court of King Arthur, not a public shedding of court identity, and he enters the wilds with the intention of passing through them, not of living in them. Yet despite this apparent lesser interest in the wilderness, *Sir Gawain* engages more directly with the natural world and at greater length, than does *Sir Orfeo*. It does this in a variety of ways: from the depiction of the landscape, the description of the seasons and the detailed descriptions of the three hunting scenes to the figure of the Green Knight who, with his green skin, green horse and holly branch clearly represents nature in some way.[23] If *Sir Orfeo* shies away from embodying the wilderness, *Sir Gawain* manifestly does not and it is only right that any green reading of the poem should begin with some consideration of this figure.

It is surely impossible to conceive of a greener person than this knight who so suddenly rides into Arthur's court. The poet is at pains to ensure we understand exactly how thoroughly green he is, from the hair on his head to the enamelling on his stirrups and including the colour of his steed. This Green Knight does not get his name from the colour of his dress alone: this is the embodiment of green. As the phrase has it, 'overal enker-grene' (150).[24] The point is stressed through the three following stanzas which ensure that whenever we might find ourselves visualising colour we are reminded that that colour is green. Even the gold becomes a version of green expressed in precious metal whose function is to bring out the greenness of everything else, as, for instance, in the embroidery on his silk which is 'gay gaudi of grene, the gold ay inmyddes' (167). Yet, although this person is beyond doubt *a* green man, he is not strictly speaking *the* Green Man. As both Kathleen Basford and William Anderson have demonstrated, the Green Man is a figure directly associated with vegetation and often made out of it.[25] Where he is not actually composed of vegetation, he is wreathed in leaves and branches, or devours or disgorges them. The figure we encounter in *Sir Gawain and the Green Knight* is neither of these; on the contrary he is, we are assured, human: 'Bot mon most I algate mynn hym to bene' (141). Yet the terms of that assertion admit some question. The rather over-emphatic 'algate' ('anyway') suggests uncertainty even as it seeks to be most sure, and although 'most' grammatically belongs to 'mon' (thus emphasising the knight's exceptional height) the impulse to read it as 'must' persists, as if the poet is somehow constrained to call this creature a man, despite his hunch that he is in fact something else. Paradoxically then, this line both denies and endorses the fleeting suggestion that this knight is supernatural, raised by the earlier term 'half etayn' (half giant) in line 140 and finally fixed by the coutiers' use of 'alvisch' (elvish) in line 681. Moreover, without actually being composed of vegetation, his clothing and accoutrements go some way to suggest that he might be. He carries a holly branch as well as an axe, and his dress is intricately ornamented with birds and insects which decorate a costume which covers, we must remember, the green-skinned background of the Knight himself. The image invites us to regard the Green Knight as part of the tapestry, almost as if he himself is the plant amongst which these birds and insects roost or live, and surely invokes the figure of the Green Man, even if it does not quite fulfil his usual specifications.[26]

The timing of his entry into Arthur's court also suggests connections with the folkloric Green Man who embodies the principle of new life returning after the dead of winter. His appearance thus answers Arthur's call for 'some marvel' but also and perhaps more disconcertingly, hints at the distance humans have put between themselves and the rest of the natural world, to the extent that the simple processes of nature have become imbued with an air of the supernatural. Anderson refers to the way the figure of the Green Man developed within a context of 'the rise of the intellectual and objective attitude to Nature characteristic of the progress of Western thought and science' (Anderson 1990: 21). The point is that as human culture and religion (particularly in Anderson's view, Christianity) increasingly divided the human from the rest of nature, and as the rational, intellectual and scientific were privileged more and more, the only place left for other modes of apprehension and being, indeed for otherness in general, was that of the supernatural, yet a supernatural conceived of most readily in human form. Thus the Green Man becomes an acknowledgement of forces beyond the human, but also a way of containing those forces, of making the idea safe. His disruptive character and his ability to survive death reassert the power of natural life forces and cycles, which is particularly welcome in the depths of winter, but by making his manifestation human he is also available to be brought within the bounds of human culture. Thus he may be found adorning churches, or interrupting a feast to declare a seasonal challenge.

Rightly, then, the Green Knight, like the Green Man, is both welcome and disconcerting. The energy he brings initiates the process of new growth and in doing so disrupts the suspended feeling of the enclosed court which fends off winter privations with feasting. Rightly, too, it is this same disruptive figure who at the end of the poem urges a return to court and feasting as a sign of the due completion of the beheading game. The invitation he extends seems to offer the chance for Gawain to return to his castle[27] and see it as it really is, stripped of the trickery and game playing which are apparently over. Wisely, Gawain refuses. In doing so he seems to be defining the relationship between the two courts as not just oppositional but actively antagonistic, regardless of (or rather, thoroughly in keeping with) the kinship relation between them, since just as Camelot is the court of his uncle, so this other castle, it is now revealed, is that of his aunt, Morgan le Fay. By this stage in the poem, we are inclined to forget about the figure of the Green Knight and have in mind instead that of Bertilak, the hale and hearty host of Fitts III and IV. Gawain is seen to be rejecting a mocking sham of cultured virtue in favour of returning to the real thing and the absorption of the Green Knight into Bertilak simply enhances the extent to which true civilisation is seen to triumph. Such readings appeal to many in part because they endorse the view that *Sir Gawain* exemplifies 'the great contrast . . . between nature and culture' which Jaques Le Goff so influentially described;[28] the tendency being to interpret Bertilak's castle as somehow representing the world of nature, fittingly enough, perhaps, given that it is placed deep in a forest. However, we need to pay more attention both to the text and to Le Goff's words, for the opposition as he describes it is 'between what was built, cultivated, and inhabited (city, castle, village) and what was essentially wild (the ocean and forest, the western equivalents of the eastern desert), that is, between men who lived in groups and those who lived in solitude' (Le Goff 1998: 58). Bertilak's castle is just as much a built and cultivated environment as Arthur's court. It is this that makes it so welcome to Gawain; but it is also this that makes it so easy to read as a challenging alternative to Camelot. The opposition becomes a competition between like powers rather than a contest between contrasting realms. It is only when we refocus our reading to concentrate on the green elements within it, that we notice how this inclination to mark the opposition between the two courts overwrites the initial opposition between the built and the 'essentially wild'. The Green Knight of the first fitt is all to easily replaced by the effusive Bertilak of the third and fourth. However, the ease with which both poem and readers accept the substitution of Bertilak for the Green Knight is just the final sleight of hand in a poem full of ruses. For, by shifting the focus finally on to the courtly elements of the text and appealing to the tradition of Morgan le Fay's hatred of Arthur, the poem reasserts human concerns and interests over those of the rest of the world. It becomes easy to say that the values of human culture triumph over those of ungoverned nature, and it goes unnoticed that the natural world has been subsumed into the human, not so much by being personified by the Green Knight but by being finally located in an alternative court (Bertilak's castle) governed, we are told, by a woman (Morgan le Fay) who is part witch, part goddess and entirely held within the human domestic relation of being Arthur's half-sister.[29]

This process of substitution is not limited to the poem alone: much critical argument surrounding it has likewise ended up focusing on human affairs, even when the initial interest was in the representations of the natural within it. After equating the Green Knight with the Green Man we are easily led into arguments over civilisation, grandeur, power, display, Celtic and folkloric elements and so forth, all of which revolve round human concerns. The poem in general and this figure of the Green Knight in particular thus elicits our profoundly anthropocentric habits when viewing nature, making it a spectacle and, beyond that, wishing to make it spectacular.[30] This is one step beyond the kind of anthropomorphism Plumwood defends as being possibly the most effective way humans can admit life, consciousness and worth to non-human elements (2002: 56–61). However, figures like this Green Knight result in the very incorporation into the human that Plumwood fears, as the non-human is explicitly brought into human schemata, and elements that do not fit are rendered invisible, although, be it noted, are not actually eliminated. This Green Knight is literally superhuman: he is bigger, more kingly, more courtly and more indestructible than the best of the human court, but his direct challenge of that court and its values bring him within the human realm as surely as he has ridden into Arthur's hall.

However, just as Ingham's postcolonial reading of the poem reminds us that incoming power often retains an element of the colonised (Ingham 2001) so, here, the movement is not totalising. Nature may have been made human in order for it to become visible to us, but it still displays its otherness and this is done not only through the Green Knight's appearance and dress but also through his refusal to play by human rules. Not only does this 'aghlich mayster' (136) refuse to die when his head is cut off but he also refuses to give either his name or his origin, both when requested to do so by Gawain before dealing the blow and again afterwards, when instructing Gawain to find him the following year. In the first case he teasingly prevaricates, suggesting that he will give Gawain his name after receiving the blow, and that if he is unable to tell him then Gawain need not worry; the implication being that he will have killed the Green Knight in which case it is no longer necessary to know who or what he was (399–412). In the second he offers not his name, but the sobriquet by which he is known 'the knight of the grene chapel men knowen me mony' (454). The Green Knight's refusal to identify himself is a significant evasion of the usual courtly exchange of names that precedes combat. Nor can such evasion be attributed to ignorance, because the Green Knight has previously demonstrated his knowledge of precisely this code of conduct when he demanded that Gawain gave his name and status before allowing him to continue with the challenge: 'Fyrst I ethe the, hathel, how that thou hattes' (379).

From the start, then, it is clear that in this Green Knight we have a laughing and indestructible figure who flaunts his knowledge of human rules and also his ability to flout them. His demeanour is thus a mixture of mimicry and mockery and it is perhaps partly in recognition of this that Gawain's clothing also features birds when he sets out, nearly a year later, to fulfil his challenge. The silk band that covers his neckline is emboidered with 'bryddes on semes / As papjayes paynted pervyng bitwene,/ Tortors and trulofes' (610–12). Significantly, Gawain's decoration features unusual birds and extraordinary foliage. His armour is not only a protection against the non-human natural world but also a deliberate exoticising of it. In an ironic gesture, the birds chosen for remark are parrots, known not only for their display but also for their powers of mimicking human speech. This little detail of clothing thus exemplifies the extraordinarily complex relations with the non-human world that human culture sets up and that the poem so deftly explores. These most exotic birds are also, paradoxically, some of the most humanly accessible, because of their ability to produce words, yet they are here carefully contained within the purely decorative and silent sphere of clothing and appear within the poem at the time that Gawain is being armed explicitly as a representative of Arthur's cultured and human court. The embroidered parrots thus tacitly indicate a desire to assert and preserve the difference between human and non-human. If the embroidery on the Green Knight's clothing showed what he represents, then that on Gawain's shows simultaneously what he seeks to conquer (non-human nature) and the strategies humans use to contain non-human nature within the human world – exoticism and domestication.

As the rest of the arming of Gawain passage shows, Gawain's preparations are very much in terms of protection against what he might find, in contrast to Orfeo's preparations which signal an intention to live within the wilderness he has chosen to enter. The contrast is an informative one, as it highlights Gawain's insistence on his separation from the non-human natural world, and on his conception of his opponent as a knight. Thus the 'Knight' aspect of the still unidentified challenger is stressed over his 'Green' aspect. Likewise, Gawain is explicitly seeking a Chapel, some kind of building, rather than considering the phrase 'Green Chapel' as a whole and admitting the possibility that his destination is some kind of natural landscape, not an artefact. Here we, like Gawain, are subject to the trickery of the poem, which, like a good conjuror, directs our attention to one place in the hope of detecting the truth of the trick, when in fact the action is all happening somewhere else. Usually that somewhere else is still in view, the knack lies in making us ignore what is under our noses. Even more cleverly, this strategy is finally made explicit in Bertilak's laughing explanation to Gawain of what has been going on in his castle. We are offered the notion that the attempted seduction and the exchange of winnings constitute the actual testing of Gawain and, later, that the beheading trick has been a creation of Morgan's. Yet although the strategy is thus exposed, the real sleight of hand remains hidden, because in fact the testing of Gawain is not strictly related to the original challenge, which required only that he deal a blow and be prepared to receive one in his turn a year later. The explanations are thus further acts of trickery, designed once again to distract us. Yet amongst all this substitution and sleight of hand, the neatest trick pulled off by this poem is that it both gives us direct encounters with the natural world and leads us to overlook them.[31] Nature is thus regarded as mere setting, or as correlative of Gawain's state of mind rather than as an active force within the text, still less as an autonomous entity – and this regardless of the overt invitation to see nature as a force offered by that initial entry by the Green Knight. The poem thus performs a kind of disappearing magic of the 'now you see it, now you don't' variety while advertising its concern with the difference between what is seen and what is recognised through phrases such as 'to quat kyth he becom knwe non there, / Never more then thay wyste from quethen he was wonnen' (460–1). In focusing on questions of place (rather than kindred or species) to express their bewilderment Arthur's courtiers are following a lead suggested by the Knight himself, when he told Gawain 'thou schal seche me thiself, where-so thou hopes / I may be funde upon folde' (395–6). Moreover, although Camelot knows nothing of this place, the Knight asserts that others do – 'The knight of the grene chapel men knowen me mony' (454) – thus implying that explicit directions are not needed and totally ignoring his earlier promise to provide his full name and abode after Gawain's blow.[32] Apparently, the Knight, like the natural world, is easily found by those who wish to seek it out or who, like Gawain, are compelled so to do.

Gawain directs his search to the most inhospitable lands around, those of North Wales and the Wirral. In doing so he is following the letter of those rather less than adequate directions to seek the Green Knight wherever he believes he will be found and so betrays his (and our) assumption that the wilderness is the appropriate place to look. Moreover, Gawain does not commence his search until November, which seems a perverse decision since it commits him to a rough journey at a bad time of the year. However, it also suggests that a search for the embodiment of Green is best conducted in desolate places at the time of year when green is generally scarce. It is in the winter that we are most likely to notice evergreen foliage or the new shoots of the earliest buds; by the time spring is well under way, the colour green is so pervasive as to be unremarkable. Bearing this in mind, the famous passage of the seasons passage that open Fitt II may remind us of how much the seasons affect our sense of well-being as much as mark the passing of the year before Gawain must set off. This section is one of the best examples of the tradition so thoroughly explored by Tuve (1933) and its very accomplishment means it is often praised in isolation from the rest of the poem, but it is worth considering how this passage of 31 lines reflects and develops some of the attitudes of the poem as a whole.

First there is the pertinent reminder that although we tend to think of the natural year as a repetitive cycle, in fact no year is the same as any other, more precisely, it does not yield the same:

'yeldes never lyke' (498). 'Yield' suggests an agricultural framework and reminds us that there is no guarantee that one good year will be followed by another: the 'spring re-birth' that Spiers pinpointed as the sign of the 'assured knowledge, that there is life inexhaustible at the roots of the poem' (1971: 221) is a regeneration, not a repetition or immortality. For twenty-first-century readers that knowledge is becoming less and less assured. The assumption that spring regeneration is inevitable and reliable is challenged by the perceptible shifts in seasonal variation and the increasingly vociferous debates about global warming and climate change. The assurance Spiers can confidently cite is exactly the attitude that allowed Lovelock's Gaia to be understood as an essentially benign as well as indestructible organism; endlessly renewing, healing and forgiving. Doubtless this attitude was evident to some degree in the fourteenth century as well, but this is one case amongst many where a latter-day reading of the poem, informed by current environmental concerns, is bleaker and more discomfiting than one of as little as thirty years ago. Yet even without a green slant, this passage is less comforting than Spiers suggests. The principle of change, which is highlighted as the force commanding the seasons ('forthi') is not quite the traditional one. This cycle begins and ends in winter and, while that reflects the simple narrative action of the plot, it also serves to foreground the weariness and hardship associated with the season. We are given little time to rejoice in the new life of spring, the warmth of summer or the plenty of autumn, instead we are hustled on to the cold of winter, where the narrative spends most of its time. Moreover, the seasons themselves are lightly personified as competitive forces, as each 'serlepes sued after other' (501). The adverb 'serlepes' unites the separation of 'ser' (as in 'sere', severally) with that of jumping, 'lepe'. In terms of meaning alone the 'lepes' is unnecessary, lending only an emphasis akin to that found in 'anlepi' – 'only'; however here it combines with its verb, 'sued', to suggest pursuit, as each season takes over from the previous one before it is fully done. This version of succession, which is really overlapping, accurately reflects the mingling of seasons which actually occurs rather than the sharply delineated change over we like to imagine. The text here is thus not only showing us the progression of the seasons but also slyly showing up our habits of anthropomorphism and anthropocentrism as we easily pick up the hints of an actively hostile relation between the seasons which is surely simply human projection. The slight anthropomorphism in play then becomes a more subtle but still present animism as 'the weder of the world with wynter hit threpes' (504). 'Threpes' carries connotations of rebuking within its primary meaning of contending and quarrelling and such tetchiness extends the atmosphere of unease into spring. Here in the line 'Bothe groundes and the greves, grene ar her wedes' (508) it is not the latent characterisation that creates the sense of unease, but the associations the poem has already established with anything that is entirely green. The fact that 'greves' spells both groves and military greaves, together with the equally double 'wedes' (both clothes and weeds), encourages links to be made between this scarcely personified landscape and the highly personable Green Knight who was described as greener even than grass – 'As growe grene as the gres and grener hit semed' (235). After a brief respite in the description of summer, which contains the straightforwardly anthropomorphic Zephyr, we are once again presented with terms of contest and unease, heralded by the use of 'Bot then' (521) to introduce autumn, rather than the less confrontational 'And' which we might expect. The verbs 'warmes', 'dryves', 'wrastles' carry forceful effect, while the 'leves laucen fro the lynde and lyghten on the grounde' (526). These leaves do not just fall, they voluntarily loosen themselves from the trees, again creating the light personification that characterises this seasons passage and holds it somewhere between accurate, evocative description and anthropomorphism.

The beginning of Fitt II is by no means the only place the poem reveals what Winney terms its writer's 'feeling for winter' (1996: 145 n.726–32) and a shrewd insight into how humans conceive of the non-human world. The actual landscape of the Wirral elicits a bravura performance across 51 lines of evocative description (701–52) which builds on those earlier hints at the hostility of the non-human world. The forces of real landscape and human imagination meet in the creation of the wilderness in winter through which Gawain rides in the belief that here, if anywhere, is where he will find his mysterious opponent. In contrast to *Sir Orfeo* this poem can realise the wilderness and, importantly, it is not devoid of life, even in mid-winter. Not only are there people, but also serpents (or dragons, 'wormes'), wolves, bulls, bears and boars, as well as wildmen (Wodwos) and giants, all of whom seem to come under the heading of 'foe' for Gawain. There are also birds, mentioned later (746–7) as peeping sadly among the bare and significantly tangled branches, linked to Gawain in their shared misery at the weather. The setting and the inhabitants are no more than we would expect: inhospitable, cold, devoid of comfort, confused and confusing. There is no half-personification of the elements here to lend a shred of comfort, just winter weather, with its sleet and cold streams which are so far from animation that they freeze into icicles. In short, this is no place for humans, but it seems it is very much a place we need to imagine.

Frequently, this inhospitable and bleak landscape is read as a reflection of Gawain's state of mind, both as an individual, who is projecting his own feelings of misery on to the landscape, and as an everyman figure, whose woeful journey is taken to stand for the trials of life generally. In either case the upshot is that the wilderness itself fades out of focus, as interpretative efforts are brought to bear on the explicitly human concerns that the landscape is thus seen to represent. This compulsion to superimpose human reactions onto landscape is particularly marked in the case of wildernesses. As Harrison has pointed out, the 'wilderness, in its unappropriated otherness, represents a kind of external reflection of the soul's inner abstraction' (1999: 670). Harrison is referring explicitly to contemporary 'ordinary' Americans, but his observation holds true for anyone working within the western tradition, which has established retreat to the wilderness as a mark of holiness.[33] The effect of this association with the wilderness is to make it somehow a more real landscape than any other, where 'real' carries with it assumptions of an unchanging expanse, which carries no mark of life (where 'life' inevitably means human life). Significantly for this discussion of *Sir Gawain*, Harrison goes on to draw attention to 'the belief that the real antecedes history and is recoverable only through a radical and systematic abstraction from history' (670–1). The difficulty with acting on this belief (of which, incidentally, Harrison is highly sceptical) is that the areas we designate wildernesses are visible to us only by contrast the other kinds of landscape. Thus, even if we concede the somewhat debatable notion that there are actual areas of land which remain unaffected in one way or another by the passage of human history, such places are none the less brought into relation with human history by our desire to mark it off as an area essentially different from all others.[34] This veneration for the unappropriated, which is often taken to mean the untouched, is thus revealed to be an assertion of humankind's distance from the rest of the natural world, even as those who seek out the wilderness in the name of enlightenment assert that it brings them closer to nature.[35] Something of this compulsion to both divide the wilderness off from human history, while yet retaining it within its general framework can be seen in *Sir Gawain* which begins and ends with a summary reminder of the apparent history of Britain. Tellingly, that history begins after 'the sege and the assaut was sesed at Troye' (1, 2525) methods of human warfare that rely on surrounding a marked area and then, after an interval, invading it. The wilderness of Wirral that lies at the heart of the poem is thus visible only in contrast to the human civilisations that surround it and can be entered only by travelling though those humanly appropriated areas.

Seen like this it is no wonder that this wilderness includes everything that humans would rather avoid on a daily basis, be that wild animals or creatures of the imagination; bears or Wodwos. However, focusing on the non-human animal life of the wilds is simply another way of avoiding having to confront the actuality of this environment. Once again our habit of sliding off the subject is revealed by the skill with which the poet juxtaposes the real and imagined animal life of the wilderness with the geography of an actual region and its winter climate. It is the latter that most reveals our inadequacies. We can fight or run from animal threats, but the landscape and elements are unrelenting and, worse, indifferent. Our response tends to be to overlook them, or relegate them to being either just backdrops to human affairs or objective correlatives to our emotions. We can see this process at work within the poem in Gawain's reaction to his predicament. The initial description of the weather and landscape as he crosses the Wirral in Fitt II has linked the harshness of winter sleet with the hardness of rocks and frozen ground:

> When the colde cler water fro the cloudes schadde,
> And fres er hit falle myght to the fale erthe.
> Ner slayn wyth the slete he sleped in his yrnes
> Mo nyghtes then innoghe in naked rokkes,
> Ther as claterande fro the crest the colde borne rennes,

And henged heghe over his hede in hard ysse-ikkles.
(727-32)

Although there is no explicit personification here, it is habitual to refer to such conditions as hostile and indeed it is easy to perceive in such words as 'slayn' and 'claterande' a degree of intention and animation that adds to the sense that those hanging icicles are deliberately menacing Gawain. The same thing happens again, this time more explicitly, in the final fitt as Gawain travels to the valley that contains the Green Chapel.

> Thay bowen bi bonkkes ther boghes ar bare,
> Thay clomben bi clyffes ther clenges the colde.
> The heven was up halt, bot ugly therunder;
> Mist muged on the mor, malt on the mountes.
> Uch hille had a hatte, a myst-hakel huge.
> Brokes byled and breke bi bonkkes aboute,
> Schyre schaterande on schores ther thay doun schowved.
> (2077-83)

The bareness of the branches is simply neutral, but 'clenges' acts much as 'claterande' did in the early passage, suggesting but not requiring a degree of animation. Then the ugly look of the sky introduces some open anthropomorphism, as the hills are given hats and cloaks, which then fades into the background again with the boiling brooks. The effect is perhaps most familiar to us now through Walt Disney films such as *Snow White* in which the trees and rocks slip disconcertingly between being just inanimate things and having sneering faces and tugging fingers.

One thing that emerges from such descriptions of the landscape is our inability to let it be as it is, without attributing some kind of attitude to it. However this poem takes that process a step further. In each case the actual landscape is swiftly displaced by a more explicitly human one, created by a deliberate act of vision on Gawain's part. The first example is the clearest as the frozen rocks are dismissed in favour of the castle that suddenly becomes visible; literally, the answer to a prayer. This magnificent fortification with its paper cut-out pinnacles is significantly described as proof against the elements – 'The walles wer wel arayed – / Hit dut no wyndes blaste' (783-4). Moreover, it is set in a wood and is surrounded by a fenced park. We have left the tangled misery of the wilderness and happened upon humanly ordered landscape. It is only in such surroundings that Gawain feels able to act. Similarly, when confronted with the confusing landscape of the valley in lines 2160–88 (which, we are told, he finds 'wylde' (2163) and devoid of human habitation, 'no syngne of resette') Gawain is able to act as a challenging knight should only after he has substituted a humanly comprehensible construction for a natural phenomenon. The terms used to identify the overgrown crevice move it increasingly towards being a human construction: 'lawe' (2171), which might be a natural knoll, but might also be the result of human digging, becomes 'berw' (2172) a barrow, which could also be just a mound and finally, in Gawain's words, 'the grene chapelle' (2186) within which the devil might say his matins (2188). Gawain elaborates this description further and then displays himself in full knightly mode on its roof, as if advertising his readiness to engage an enemy. His words and actions successfully insist on the primacy of 'chapel' over 'green' in the phrase 'grene chapel'.

Yet Gawain has come to a place where 'green' is the operating term, whether he acknowledges it or not and indeed he finds greenery when he inspects the crevice, but, like most of us when reading the poem, he fails to take note of it. The entrance to the hole is 'overgrown with gresse in glodes aywhere' (2181) but Gawain seems bent on ignoring such direct encounters with the natural world and instead accounts for the adjective 'grene' in 'grene chapell' by associating the place with the devil, whose colour was traditionally green. Rather than recognising the place for what it is, Gawain thus superimposes on the natural rocky landscape a form more comprehensible to himself, more plausible as a site for knightly encounter and less accommodating of the actual environment. He reasserts both his desire for some kind of building and his need to push the non-human world out of sight, and thus, one suspects out of mind. Attendant to his desire, the Green Knight appears for the second time in the poem, once again apparently called up by the wishes of a human. It is becoming clear that here, as in *Sir Orfeo*, people prefer to work within an opposition of human and personified non-human, than to tackle the non-human natural world in its own various forms. More than that, it seems that in order to be comprehensible and so to command any respect, the non-human world must take on some kind of human guise. Hence the attraction for us of the

Green Man as well as the Green Knight.

There are two more substitutions within *Sir Gawain* which likewise reveal our habits of thinking about the natural world. First, the Green Knight tells Gawain that his name is Bertilak, a revelation that means that the Green Knight who seemed to personify vegetative nature is now identified with the hale and hearty hunting lord of the castle. This identification is significant, for it exposes the division humans tend to make between animal and non-animal worlds, and also shows that it is this division that has been the most active within the poem as a whole. Just as the weather and the landscape cause Gawain most hardship, so the Green Knight, Bertilak, merrily hunts down animals. Yet, by personifying the vegetative world and by having him hunt, the poem enacts a perfect assimilation of the Green Man into the human world, rendering him safe by in effect covering up the more discomforting elements of this bit of nature. However, although it is easier to deal with something human-shaped, we are unwilling to lose much of what this force of nature represents to us, such as the promise of enduring greenness and regenerating life even in the bleakest winter landscape. Marvellously, the poem preserves this for us too, initially through the phrase describing the final exit from the text of this 'knyght in the enker-grene' as being 'whider-warde-so-ever he wolde' (2477–8). Both the evergreen principle and the mystery are reasserted in a way that allows us to believe that this laughing and disconcerting power of nature has departed free of any human agency.

The final substitution in the poem may also be read as a way of preserving this idea of regeneration, but it is a more ambiguous act of assimilation than any of those associated with the figure of the Green Knight. Like the Green Knight, the green girdle is subject to several shifts of identity both in the poem and in its critical reception. Proffered as a love token it is accepted as a protector against death. Its colour, as much as it origin, links it irrevocably with the Green Knight and thus also makes it an insignia of the natural world. This in turn means that when he is wearing it Gawain, too, becomes a figure of regeneration and also of the assimilation of the natural world into the human sphere. The parallel is continued in the way Gawain rides into the Green Chapel much as the Green Knight rode into Arthur's hall, and again when Gawain returns to Camelot at the end of the poem.

However, having proved its powers of preservation (after all, Gawain does not die) the girdle is then subject to several acts of redescription. First, but only fleetingly, it becomes a sign of female treachery – a move that neatly offers an alignment of female and nature, complete with the assumption that both exist to be mastered by men. Then when this version of events is laughed off by the male embodiment of nature, the girdle becomes a token of male/male chivalric bonding – of truth upheld, debts paid and a challenge duly met. It is this symbolic meaning that is seized upon and loudly asserted by Arthur and his court as every knight in Camelot adopts the wearing of a green garter as a sign of the triumph of human valour against the unknown and, above all, as a badge of knightly community and courtly conduct. Yet strictly speaking it is not the girdle that is the sign of the fulfilment of the original New Year bargain, but the scar on Gawain's neck. Camelot's general adoption of the green belt hints at a deeper desire on their part to somehow domesticate that otherworldly green that entered their world so abruptly at the beginning of the poem. This communal move is in the teeth of Gawain's desire to retain it as an individual emblem and perhaps he is the only one who is in a position to recognise that encounters with the kind of nature personified by the Green Knight cannot be communal, since the introduction of a human community necessarily destroys a defining element of a wilderness untouched by humans. Gawain's apparently assimilative act of making the girdle into an emblem is thus also a commemorative act which asserts the uncomfortable relations between human and vegetative nature and particularly between human and climate. Arguably it offers the possibility of non-combative, non-destructive interaction with the environment, but in fact this does not seem to be how Gawain himself views it. Part of his achievement has surely been to learn how to survive unmediated encounters with the natural world, but this is not a lesson he puts to use. Not only does he return to court, but, significantly, his return journey through 'wylde wayes' (2479) includes lodging in houses as well as sleeping out of doors (2481) and, while it contains many adventures, he is now victorious in all, with no hint of running away from giants (2482). Moreover, it must be admitted that although Gawain's return to Camelot bearing something green in some way echoes that initial entry of the Green Knight, a silk belt, however beautiful, is no match for a holly bough as a token of enduring natural life. Only its colour hints at the connection with whatever lies beyond assimilable nature and the wilds that we seek to preserve.

Sir Gawain seems to show that however different nature may appear to be, as long as we can in some way give it a physical body it becomes accessible to us and thus it becomes possible for us to deal with it. It does not matter what form that body takes, from superhuman knight to wild animal or even one of the harder to define creatures that inhabit the borderland between real and imagined creature – dragon or Wodwo. We have developed ways of dealing with all of these, of making them visible in forms that we can assimilate into our human perception of the world. Yet in *Sir Gawain* as in *Sir Orfeo* there remains the fact that the wilderness itself is resistant to such assimilation and, it appears, we like it that way. If we value the wilderness for its standing as an untouched, regenerating force, we are also wary of too much direct contact with it. In order for it to retain its standing as synonymous with the unknown it cannot be brought into the human realm entirely. Thus, although the green girdle seems to be the new sign of the non-human world, it is in fact the badge of human relations, while the green knight himself melts back into the unseen, just as the wilderness inhabited for so long by Orfeo remains unspoken.

Harrison is surely right when he points out how much people rely on the idea of wilderness as both antecedent to the human historical moment and utterly resilient to it. Humans have a vested interest in believing in such indestructibility, since it relieves us of both anxiety and responsibility. We see all of this at play in *Sir Gawain*, a text which flaunts its pseudo-historical setting before sending us off into the enduring and actual wilderness. *Sir Orfeo*, likewise, is at pains to offer a double historical identity in Greek Thrace and British Winchester before the wilderness sets both aside. However, current ecological thinking is now at pains to make us believe that our hopeful belief in this resilient, perpetually regenerative force is misplaced, and perhaps the Green Knight embodies just such misplacement as he enters the poem bearing both the holly bough of evergreen life and the axe that lopped it off. *Sir Orfeo* is nearer the mark in showing that the wilderness cannot be brought into the human realm and that those who enter it must be prepared to be silenced. This, finally, is to be the greatest challenge the wilderness poses to humans – to simply let it be. It seems we do anything rather than that, preferring to make it a canvas for our wildest imaginings rather than leave it alone.

This impetus to project on to the wilderness has two main consequences. The most obvious is that the wilderness expands to become rich in associations, both negative and positive. Thus time spent there can be reminiscent of Christ's forty days in the wilderness, complete with forms of temptation, or it can be more straightforwardly a form of penance, or holy retreat. It can be a place of refuge, without necessarily carrying religious associations, or it can be a place of testing – again without necessarily carrying Christian or any other religious overtones. It becomes a place of strange beasts, ranging from the actual animals who surround the harping Orfeo to those nearly-but-not-quite-human creatures, like the Wodwos mentioned in passing in *Sir Gawain*. Importantly, the wilderness also becomes the kind of place where one might encounter the supernatural, either in the form of fairies, as in *Sir Orfeo* or in the figure of the Green Man, or even in the form of a vision, a possibility hinted at in the sudden appearance of Bertilak's castle as an answer to Gawain's prayer. However, although all these elements can be associated with the wilderness, and may even be regarded as part of it, they are not integral to actual wilderness itself, which brings us to the second main consequence of this urge to project – the over-writing of the physical place by such imagined projections. The richer the nexus of associations, the harder it is to perceive the actual landscape and to resist the impulse to read allegorically. Given the overtly Christian context of *Sir Gawain*, it is not surprising that this impulse has not been resisted; *Sir Orfeo* is a slightly different matter, however, as, although it is a Christianised story, its roots are classical. None the less, it, too, is prone to allegorical interpretation; Henryson's explanation of the story (which is as long as the actual story) is simply part of an ongoing tradition, still detectable today in critical responses to the poem.[36] Both poems and their reception thus illustrate a continuing challenge for humans in the face of wilderness: the difficulty of abiding in patience before it without succumbing to the temptation to impose human meaning upon it, whether in terms of mystery or as a testing ground for human values.

Primarily, however, wilderness functions as a place that is utterly other and is assumed to be inhospitable more because it is simply indifferent than because it is explicitly hostile. Paradoxically, this apparently most disconcerting concept is a great source of comfort, as it asserts the warmth of human community in the face of such universal disinterest. So it might seem that we retain a concept of the strangeness of the wilderness in order to bolster our concept of human society as homely, but the substitution is more far-reaching than that, as wilderness is eventually transformed into a version of home. Wade Sikarski's Heideggerian approach offers a rather glib example of this attitude towards the wilderness: 'In going into the wilderness . . . we are going home because wilderness is the place where we recover the things that are most ourselves, but that we have denied, repressed, forgotten. (Sikarski in Bennett and Chaloupka 1993: 29)'. Like Harrison, I am sceptical of such interpretations of the wilderness, which in effect reduce it to being an aspect of the human psyche and nothing more, but the terms Sikarski employs bear some comparison with Chaucer's juxtaposition of home and wilderness, which becomes tantamount to a union in his lyric 'Truth'. His invocation of wilderness is simultaneously despairing and evocative of the comfort of home. 'Truth' amply demonstrates both our emotive attachment to the wild as unknowable other and our habitual sliding away from accepting that concept by recasting it as both mortal human home and religious refuge:

> Her is non hoom, her nis but wildernesse:
> Forth, pilgrim, forth! Forth, beste, out of thy stal!
> Know thy contree, look up, thank God of al.
>
> ('Truth' 17–19)

The agonised cry that the 'hoom' of this world is no home at all, but a wilderness serves to make both the home alien and the wilderness homely, for we are familiar with 'here', whatever 'here' may be. The unheimlich comforts by necessarily asserting the heimlich; a conceptual relation heightened by the images of pilgrim, beast and stabling, each of which combines everyday and religious connotations. Such slippage and recombining of association allows the actual wilderness to melt away from the text, leaving us again with the familiar terrain of human constructs.

David Graber has pointed out that this paradoxical relation with the wilderness has progressed to the point where wild spaces are carefully managed by humans in order to appear free of human contamination.

> It now functions to provide solitude and counterpoint to technological society in a landscape that is *managed* to reveal as few traces of the passage of other humans as possible. Contemporary wilderness visitors are just that. Unlike the hunters and gatherers who preceded them on the land, moderns who enter wilderness do so not to live on the land, or to use it, but rather to experience it spiritually. The ecosystem is defined in its own terms, but this wilderness is a social construct. (Graber 1995: 124)

Graber's moderns are similar to medieval knights, who overlook those who live their lives in the wilderness and, by defining their own, court-based existence as the norm, define any wilderness dweller as radically other, possibly not even human. Even when such people enter the wilderness to hunt, they do so in the knowledge that the meal will be consumed within a humanly defined social space, so that hunting itself, as Orfeo recognises, is an assertion of the human over the wild. Perhaps most telling, however, is the parallel here between the wildernesses constructed as part of American national parks, which is what Graber is describing, and the wilderness of literature. Each has a connection with actual wilderness habitats, but each is also a way of over-writing that actual landscape and substituting instead a more humanly accessible one. The upshot is that the wilderness continues to elude definition, and in this may lie its greatest strength.

Notes

1 Grendel and his mother, who inhabit the foul mere in *Beowulf*, are clearly also of this kind.
2 Traces of this association with entry into the wilderness as a process of transformation is to be found in our latter day attitudes towards wilderness and wild places. Most of the debate here is conducted with reference to national parks, particularly in America. Wilderness as enshrined in such parks is largely a myth, of course, since it takes much careful land-management and policing to ensure that the area remains 'unspoilt', but the power of the idea is evident in the efforts taken to preserve them. Good discussions of the standing of national parks and the questions they raise may be found in Graber and in Nabhan (both in Soulé and Lease 1995); the concept of

Wilds, wastes and wilderness

wilderness is explored in some depth by Oelschlaeger (1991) and differentiated from wildness by Evernden (1992: esp. pp. 120–4). A Heideggerian twist can be found in Sikarski and an intelligent scrutiny of Thoreau's retreat to nature is offered by Dizard (both in Bennett and Chaloupka 1993). Buell 1996 remains the primary source for American views of wilderness.

3 All quotations from *Sir Orfeo* are taken from the TEAMS text, *The Middle English Breton Lays* edited by Anne Laskaya and Eve Salisbury, Kalamazoo: Western Michigan University Press, 2001.

4 Perhaps the greatest exponent of this trope is in fact Ywain, whether in the version given by Chrétien de Troyes or in the Middle English romance *Ywain and Gawain*. Importantly, however, Ywain first goes mad and then, as a result, runs into the wood: his flight is neither premeditated nor into the wilderness. None the less, comparisons are often drawn between Orfeo and Ywain: see, for example, Saunders (1993: 137).

5 See Gros Louis 1967: 245–52.

6 I cannot help but wonder if there is an implication that the lords have been snakes of a different species, but if so the satire is latent and generic: there is no hint that Orfeo's courtiers have been in any way slippery.

7 Several critics, most notably Penelope Doob (1974: 158–207) have followed the lead of this description and sought to read Orfeo's ten years in the wilderness as a form of penance, seeing his appearance as evidence of his role as a form of holy wild man. However, for such readings to work thoroughly there would have to be some kind of external acknowledgement of the ten years as penance duly performed and accepted, as well as some indication of why Orfeo is required to perform penance at all. The latter of these two exceptions may be met by referring to the tradition of the just man being tested; that is, Orfeo need not have done anything wrong, instead it is the very fact that he appears to be fulfilling his duties properly that attracts the divine or supernatural test. However, even if this is granted, there is no clear sign that such testing is taking place, nor that Heurodis is a reward. *Pace* Gros Louis, Heurodis is not in fact brought to Orfeo; he simply happens to see her among the hunting ladies.

8 Henryson's precise dates are unknown, but it seems he was writing in the middle of the fifteenth century: see Fox 1981: xiii–xxv. The lay is likewise difficult to date with confidence, but it appears in the Auchinleck manuscript which is generally thought to have been compiled from about 1330–40, with *Sir Orfeo* being regarded as one of the earlier pieces within it; see Laskaya and Salisbury 2001: 15–16 and Bliss 1966: ix-x.

9 All references to Henryson are given by line number and taken from Fox 1981.

10 Andrea Babich suggests that Orfeo is at fault for not recognising the power of music from the start, preferring to attempt to protect Heurodis by force of arms rather than more magical, musical means (Babich 1998: 481). As a whole this article is an illustration of our ingrained habit of assuming that the human way is the best way of acting within the world. Thus she assumes that the Fairy King is seeking to emulate Orfeo, without pausing to consider why he should wish to do this.

11 Although they are working on early modern literature, the discussions of how the boundaries between human and other species are set up and transgressed found in Wiseman (1999) and Fudge (2000) are of interest here.

12 For an exploration of the link between times of day and the supernatural see Friedman 1966.

13 The commonly used prologue is not found in Auchinlek, the earliest manuscript to contain *Sir Orfeo*, but a missing leaf suggest that there was one there originally. Later manuscripts contain one, as do the other lai within Auchinlek, so most scholars assume that *Sir Orfeo* would have had some kind of introductory section and reconstruct accordingly. Fuller discussion of this may be found in Laskaya and Salisbury (2001: 24) and Bliss (1966: xlv–xlviii).

14 Seth Lerer's article (1985) particularly interesting in reading the poem as a whole as a demonstration of the power of artistry.

15 The whole area of speech and lack thereof is fraught with prejudices and assumptions, many of which are most easily seen in people's attitudes towards other humans who do not speak, further heightened in regards to those who are also deaf. This is in marked contrast to the respect often accorded those who can speak, but choose not to.

16 Plumwood's subtitle to her book *Environmental Culture: The Ecological Crisis of Reason* signals her belief that we too readily value reason as a human faculty to the detriment of other faculties, which adds to the ease with which other species are undervalued. Ambivalence about reason itself can also be found in medieval debates on reason, imagination and knowledge, as discussed in Rudd 1994.

17 A useful assessment of ecofeminism is Guttman's article 'Ecofeminism in Literary Studies' in Parham 2002: 37–50. Plumwood touches on the problems attendant on using human speech to represent non-human communication in her discussion of the role of anthropomorphism; see Plumwood 2002: 60.

18 This habit of disappearing into the unknown is similar to the Green Knight's exits at the beginning and end of that poem 'to quat kyth . . . knwe non there' (*SGGK* 460) and 'Whiderwarde-so-ever he wolde' (2478).

19 Here, again, there is a similarity with *SGGK* in which Gawain acts as the focalizer for the text, as see Stanbury 1991: 2–4 and 105–7. Stanbury's refinement of focalization to include that idea of 'eyewitness' could also be applied to *Sir Orfeo*.

20 In this invented story of Orfeo's death we can see traces of the Classical version of the myth in which Orfeo is indeed torn to pieces, not by lions or wolves but by Bacchae who, significantly, mistake the grief-ridden man for a wild animal.

21 Babich (1998) poses and answers the pertinent question: why does the fairy king bother to return Heurodis the first time instead of just making off with her?

22 The fact that 'ympe tre' seems to indicate a grafted tree simply adds to the resonance here, as it means that the tree itself is the result of human manipulation and can be regarded as a kind of hybrid of natural and human forces. This has given rise to speculation that such trees are easily regarded as

Wilds, wastes and wilderness

gateways to the supernatural world. See the discussion of grafting in Chapter 2.

23 Much critical and scholarly effort has been devoted to showing how the Green Knight can or cannot be the same as the folkloric Green Man who figures on so many church roof bosses, yet surely there cannot be a reader of the poem who does not make precisely that association to some degree. Sadowski (1996: 78–108) offers a chapter on the greenness of the Green Knight which is a useful overview of the main responses to this figure's colour both within the poem and in critical discussion.

24 All quotations of *Sir Gawain and the Green Knight* are taken from the Everyman edition by J.J. Anderson (1996) and cited by line number.

25 Kathleen Barsford's *The Green Man* appeared in 1978 (most recently reprinted in 2002) and remains the most informative and fascinating guide to the figure of the Green Man generally and the motif of the foliate head in particular in medieval art. Anderson's study *Green Man: The Archetype of Our Oneness with the Earth* (1990) discusses the figure across a longer time-span and, as his title suggests, takes a particular view of what it represents.

26 Although it passes without comment and usually without notice, it is significant that no mammals figure in the Knight's dress, either as heraldic beasts or as part of the natural world depicted on his clothing. Their omission and the inclusion of birds and insects which rest on foliage (166) emphasise the vegetative essence of this figure and is part of the distinction between animals and plant non-human world that often operates in our thinking about nature and which is firmly marked by the poem.

27 Habitually critics refer to Bertilak's castle as 'Hautdesert', pointing out that the name means 'High Desert' or Wasteland. However, we do not know that Hautdesert is in fact the castle. The term occurs only as part of Bertilak's name – Bertilak de Hautdesert (2445) – and may as easily be a country as a court. If so, Bertilak is declaring his identity as a denizen of the wilderness even as he seems to be identifying himself as a human lord.

28 Le Goff points out the difference between this, medieval, opposition and that of antiquity, which was typically between city and country, where 'country' was inhabited and cultivated, that is also subject to human intervention (Le Goff 1998: 58).

29 Patricia Ingham (2001) shows how the poem uses this process of domestication to render safe the potentially rebellious forces of alternative power-bases. Her argument takes a post-colonial stance and focuses on the tensions between English and Welsh elements, but the principles of substitution are similar to those I outline here.

30 In different ways Pearsall and Salter (1973: 148–53), Burrow (1971: 69–75) and Stanbury (1991: 96–115) all show how the poem's interest in visual detail lends an air of spectacle to everything it describes. This is particularly true of the depictions of the natural world, whether as landscape or in the embodied form of the Green Knight.

31 An example of the poem's persuasive powers is Saunders's placing of Bertilak's castle in the Wirral wilderness, despite the fact that Gawain explicitly rides out of the wilderness into a forest to reach it and despite Saunders's own acknowledgement of the distinction in this text between the typical,

conceptual forest of romance and the Wirral landscape (Saunders 1993: 149–51).

32 There is, as so often in this poem, room for some ambiguity in the Knight's assurance in lines 406–8 that he will reveal his identity once Gawain has struck his blow. The phrase 'quen I the tape have' is usually taken to mean 'when I have received your blow', but it could mean 'when I have struck you'. The context leads us to take the former reading, but in the event the poem carries out the latter. The Green Knight reveals his name as Bertilak only after striking Gawain, in other words, only once all the exchanges of the game has been completed.

33 Doob (1974) offers the most succinct consideration of the western spiritual tradition with particular reference to literary works.

34 There is another argument to be made here about the rather arrogant human assumption that we are the only species with a notion of history. The recorded ability of elephants to return to watering holes that are present only under certain, rare, conditions, or to which they have recourse only in the extremest droughts, sometimes at intervals exceeding the life-span of any given member of the herd, is just the most accessible evidence of another species's possession of history.

35 The version of this veneration, which avers the existence of a prenatural soul in every person, lies at the root of Harrison's scepticism.

36 Fox's edition provides the text of Nicholas Trivet's commentary on Boethius which underpins the 'moralitas' of Henryson's text (Fox 1981: 384–92). See also his introduction to the poem for information about Trivet and medieval tradition of interpretation of the Orpheus myth. Although less fully allegorical, Bliss, Babich and Doob all tend to regard the landscape of the poem in particular in a metaphorical light.

4
Sea and coast

If the wilderness defies literary containment, the sea, it appears, defies expression. R.W.V. Elliott's careful lexical studies of middle English alliterative poetry uncovers a revealing aspect of the phrases typically used to describe the sea: 'words denoting open sea are less common, and the interesting fact emerges that poets often used "inland" "water" words like northern *borne* or the widely current *broke* or the more specific *dam* to describe the sea'.¹ Although it could be argued that this quirk reflects the knowledge typical of the writers that feature in Elliott's study rather than a more general sensibility, it is nonetheless striking that descriptions of the sea are often lacking even in the very texts one might expect to find them. This phenomenon is remarked upon by (amongst others) Jonathan Raban in his introduction to *The Oxford Book of the Sea* (1992), where he comments that surprisingly little is written about the sea for a seafaring nation, the focus being more often on what is to be found across the waters than on the waters themselves.² A case in point is Chaucer's telling of the story of Custance in his Man of Law's Tale. Given that the heroine journeys from Rome to Syria, to Northumberland and back to Rome, two of which voyages were the result of being put out to sea in a small boat without captain or crew, one might have expected some space to be spent describing the sea itself. In fact we get next to nothing. We are told 'Yeres and dayes fleet this creature / Thurghout the See of Grece unto the Strayte / Of Marrok' (463–5) until 'She dryveth forth into oure occian / Thurghout oure wilde see' (505–6) but are given no details about what distinguishes the sea, or the conditions she encountered. Where we might expect heart-rending accounts of the trials attendant upon drifting over the oceans in a rudderless boat, we get stanzas urging us to consider the God who looked after her as he did Jonah (itself a rather ambiguous comparison). The only indications of what the sea itself is like lie in that repeated word 'thurghout', which hints at trackless expanse and the rather cursory 'wilde' applied to 'oure' sea. The second enforced sea voyage is treated even more concisely as Custance merely 'fleteth in the see, in peyne and wo / Fyve yeer and moore' (901–2) and here the analogies are completely free from any maritime connections, as we are encouraged to compare Custance with David and Judith. Chaucer does show his geographical knowledge in specifying that Custance drifts through the Gibralter straits, but such precision is immediately undermined by the ensuing emphasis on Custance's lack of control over her direction 'dryvynge ay / Somtyme west, and somtyme north and south, / And somtyme est' (947–9). It is part of Custance's almost saintly persona that she is entirely at the mercy of the winds and waves, but it is none the less telling that her helpless situation is not highlighted by a detailed description of the sea itself and its perils.

That link with saints' lives is worth pursuing a little further. Voluntarily going to sea, frequently in rudderless boats, in order to display their trust in God was the northern European equivalent of undertaking a sojourn in the desert. Adomán's sixth-century Life of St Columba makes this parallel clear by repeatedly using what seems to be a recognised literary trope equating the sea with the desert. Thus in the space of one paragraph we read of Báitán 'qui cum ceteris desertum marinum appetens enavigaverat' (who sailed out with others, looking for a desert in the sea), who is again 'cum ceteris in mari herimum quaesiturus' (with others seeking out a desert place in the sea) and 'qui ad quaerendum in ociano desertum pergit' (who goes on to seek the desert in the ocean). Later we are told of Cormac who 'etiam secunda vice conatus est herimum in ociano quaerere' (even for a second time attempted to find a desert place in the ocean) and to whose group Columba refers as 'desertum in pilago intransmeabili invenire obtantes' (desiring to find a desert place in the sea that cannot be crossed).[3] Such phrases endorse Le Goff's claim that the sea and wilderness occupied a similar place in the western European medieval imagination (1998: 51) and point in particular to the notion of huge expanse that underlies many of the associations of the sea and ocean. These connotations of immensity and boundlessness add a twist to Elliott's observation that much of the vocabulary used by the alliterative poets refers to water lying within known boundaries; lakes, streams and so forth. We are thus brought to a central contradiction in our concept of the sea. It is both an immense, even boundless, expanse which is to be rightly feared as it is capable of producing unknown creatures from its depths and a navigable tract to be crossed, a route to safe haven, adventure or even riches: simultaneously a refuge and a place of trial.

The one story that must surely spring to mind as encompassing all these associations is that of the Flood. It is easy to see here many of the associations of the sea at work. For Noah and his companions on the Ark (human and animal) the waters are a place both of safety and of trial, as it is both proof and test of faith to be floating on floodwaters for a hundred and fifty days after forty days of persistent rain. From within the Ark the waters constitute refuge, but significantly that is because they are afloat. For those unfortunates left outside the waters are fatal. Here most clearly we see the concept of the sea as cleanser at work, but both the Wakefield master and the Chester playwright make it clear that the flood is also a force of fear. The God of the Wakefield play of Noah is perhaps the most explicit:

> Therfor shall I fordo   all this medill-erd
> With floddis that shall flo   and ryn with hidous rerd;
> I have good cause therto   for me no man is ferd.
>
> (100–2)[4]

Since it is lack of proper fear in humankind that has angered God, the remedy is to instil fear and the chosen method is Deluge. The flood here is explicitly an agent of dread as well as a purifying force. In the Chester version it is not only humankind but also 'Beast, worme, and fowle' (10) that have incited divine anger through their neglect of God, explaining why they, too, must be done away with. The plays thus establish the principle of the flood as unstoppable force that will literally wash all away before it, but of necessity their focus is on the humans in the plot. There is almost no description of the expanse of the water, nor of what it is like to be adrift for a total of 190 days. It is easy to accept this omission as a consequence of the genre, allowing that weeks of aimless drifting do not make for very good theatre, but as this chapter will make clear, the omission goes deeper than that. It appears that we resist focusing on the sea itself, always preferring to fix on something smaller and more manageable instead. At the best of times it seems to defy our imagination, and when it comes to the notion of flood, it is so big as to be invisible.

This observation holds true even for *Cleanness*, a poem in which we might reasonably expect the waters of the Deluge to command some attention. Indeed *Cleanness* is often praised for its dramatic and effective description of the flood,[5] but the aspect that draws such praise is the depiction of the distress of those left outside the Ark. The section describing their desperation (lines 363–408) is without question excellent and is all the more remarkable for including animals among those running, uselessly, for safety (391–2). Nor does the poem shirk the appalling nature of death by inches, as it traces the waters rising first from the rivers, through valleys and up mountains, until it laps over the feet of those standing on the highest points and finally covers even the highest peak with fifteen cubits of water (369–70, 397–406). Likewise our attention is drawn to the mud that holds the rotting carcasses (407–8) and, later, to the stench that greets the raven set free from the Ark by Noah when the water begins to subside (461–4). All these details make the Deluge and its effects all too real, but when it comes to describing the waters themselves the poem is comparatively reticent.

We are treated to a vivid account of the beginning of the flood:

> Then bolned the abyme and bonkes con ryse;
> Waltes out uch walle-heved in ful wode stremes.
>
> Was no brymme that abod unbrosten bylyve;
> The mukel lavande logh to the lyfte rered.
> Mony clustered clowde clef alle in clowtes,
> Torent uch a rayn ryfte and rusched to the urthe,
>
> Fon never in forty dayes, and then the flod ryses,
> Overwaltes uche a wod and the wyde feldes
>
> (363–70)

The most noticeable motif here is that of breaking boundaries. The abyss boils up and the banks of rivers rise up as the fountains shake off the connotations of containment in 'wall-heved' to become mad torrents ('ful wode stremes'). Then comes the rain, driving down through rents in the clouds. This continues for forty days and it is only then that the floods rise, subsuming woods and fields. It is a dynamic passage, but it does not describe the sea.

Forty lines later (413–24) the poem again turns its attention to waters, now dwelling briefly on the Ark weathering the storm. Nicolas Jacobs (1972) has illustrated that storms at sea was a favourite literary topos for the alliterative poets and indeed it seems to have persisted as a preferred topic for those treating the sea down the ages.[6] The verbs here enact the ungoverned motion of the boat, utterly at the mercy of wind and waves.

> The arc hoven was on hyghe with hurlande gotes,
> Kest to kythes uncouthe the clowdes ful nere;
> Hit waltered on the wylde flod, went as hit lyste,
> Drof upon the depe dam – in daunger hit semed
>
> (413–16)

> flote forthe with the flyt of the felle wyndes;
> Whederwarde-so the water wafte, hit rebounde.
> Ofte hit roled on rounde and rered on ende
>
> (421–3)

The movement is unruly: heaving, hurling, cast, weltering, driving, rebounding and rolling. For most of the time the Ark is the passive subject of all this motion, emphasising its helplessness, which of course is exactly the thing that ensures its safety: 'Nyf oure Lorde hade ben her lodesmon, hem had lumpen harde' (424). The Ark is saved precisely because those inside it do not attempt to exert control over their fate. Indeed one of its significant features is its lack of rigging or other steering gear.[7] However, once again, vivid as this passage is, it does not in fact focus on the water as much as it appears to. It is the ship that draws our attention as it is tossed around on the surface.

When the storm has passed and we do come to contemplate the waters themselves, it is their vastness that strikes home and here, too, we are brought up against a failure of the human imagination. The only way the extent of the flood can be indicated is through reference to the earth and the mountains covered, just as the wildness of the initial flooding was indicated by the bursting of banks and the water hurtling through houses seizing their inhabitants. It is this breaking of bonds that marks out the terrifying nature of the Deluge and makes us aware of the exceptional nature of this disaster, but it is the encroachment on the human environment that marks the reach of its devastation. This perhaps accounts for the lexical trait observed by Elliott, since referring to the apparently unbounded sea as, for example, a 'mere' (a term attributed to Jonah in *Patience* 112) keeps it within a human scope. This preference for land boundaries betrays our preference for comprehensible order and, beneath that, the often unacknowledged belief that all is 'right' with the world when it is working to human advantage. It is the fear that the non-human natural world might defy our notions of what is the proper state of affairs that raises our deepest fears. Some latitude is allowed, as long as we retain a sense of events being either controllable or only just out of our control. Thus floods and storms at sea can be accepted as part of the natural order as long as they are mainly survivable and are neither too long nor too fierce. Paradoxically then, the utter devastation of the Deluge is imaginable precisely because even that storm and consequent flood proved survivable by some. The recurrent theme is that of the waters exceeding their bounds and this reveals the root of both our fear and our delight in the sea. It seems to have no end, yet in order to think of it at all we must provide it with edges and shores.

It appears then that much of our view of the sea depends both imaginatively and literally on having a coast from which to view it. Once out of sight of land we are liable to become conceptually adrift, aware of a vastness which is so big as to be inconceivable. Moreover, because we tend to consider only the surface of the sea, the expanse of a calm ocean is extremely hard to envisage: there are no differentiating factors to lend perspective or offer a focal point. This again helps to account for the popularity of storm descriptions – they offer something to describe; without them we tend to shy away from attempts to look at the sea itself. That is not to say that the sea does not exert a powerful influence. The effects of the sea on those who live close to it have drawn comment from the ancient times and were not always considered beneficial. Clarence Glacken summarises Cicero's misgivings in terms which are particularly apposite for this chapter's discussion of *Patience* and Chaucer's Franklin's Tale: 'a maritime location causes men's mind to go wandering; they have hopes, dreams, temptations, desires for luxury, incited by the commerce of the sea' (Glacken 1967: 102).⁸ Embedded in this assertion that proximity to the sea encourages restlessness is a recognition of the constant change that seems to lie at the heart of our understanding of the sea. The pattern of tides, waves and currents allows us to think of the seas as perpetually renewing themselves, as each tide washes away traces of the previous one. Yet, comforting as this pattern of repetition is, a disturbing degree of unpredictability remains, as the extent of each tide is affected by weather conditions far from the shore we inhabit. Part of our image of the ocean thus reflects our awareness that weather conditions can change rapidly and have a direct and often frightening effect on the waters. Perhaps this accounts for the dominance of tempest scenes in what little writing there is dealing with the sea directly. It is only when the waters become thus dramatic that we are forced to focus on them, rather than skim their surfaces. It is also worth recalling that it was only with the advent of motor engines that the fear of a dead calm at sea was removed. Until then being becalmed was to be dreaded as much as encountering a tempest. All this should make us humans wary of the oceans and conscious of how little control we can have over them, but Cicero's warning reflects both our persistent belief that we can harness the seas, at least to some extent, and our habit of transmuting that element of dangerous unpredictability into the potential for beneficial change.

Certainly Averagus's decision in Chaucer's Franklin's Tale 'to seke in armes worshipe and honour' in England (FT 810–11) is based on the belief that crossing the seas can be a route to man's fortune, with the implication that prestige won abroad is somehow more convincing than that acquired at home.⁹ It is not only goods that form part of commerce, and dreams and desires come in many forms. However, the Tale does not follow Arveragus; instead it remains at home in Syria with Dorigen, a figure left gazing out to sea from the shore, thus occupying the place depicted by Cicero as so perilous to peace of mind.

Dorigen is up on the cliffs because her friends have taken her there in a failed attempt to shake her out of the malaise that has afflicted her ever since her husband, Averagus, left her to go to England. While Averagus thus proves Cicero right in one effect of coastal life, Dorigen exemplifies another: her mind goes wandering as she looks at the sea, or more precisely, first at the ships upon it and then at the rocks offshore. Unluckily for her, she falls prey to 'hopes, dreams and temptations' that are not directly associated with seagoing, but certainly spring from her reflections as she looks out from the clifftop. At first the sight of ships merely increases her misery, as she wonders at the number that can pass without any of them bearing a returning husband (853–6). This observation endorses the opinion that the prospect of prosperous sea trade encourages sea journeys and consequent lack of domestic stability. Indeed the Tale as a whole revolves around the desire for stability versus the desire for change, with the assumption that the two must be diametrically opposed. Yet, as we read and consider the story, we realise that it is the fixed things that cause the difficulties and it is the possibility of change that offers solutions; finally resulting in the teasing question 'who is the most fre?' where 'fre' denotes freedom of movement as well as generosity. Significantly, our answer to the question tends to alter depending on which player's perspective we take. Similarly our understanding of what 'stable' means undergoes some transformation, as it becomes evident that in certain circumstances flux is the thing to be relied upon and stability springs not from rigidly staying in one place but from knowing how sway with the tide.

Dorigen's argument is not with the sea per se but with the place where sea meets shore, and specifically with the rocks that mark the water's edge. It is these which attract her frustration, but that frustration springs from her own human and anthropocentric reasoning, epitomised when she upbraids God for the existence of the rocks which seem at such variance with human notions of an ordered world. Unable to imagine a rationale for their existence, she assumes there is none and does not consider that the fault might lie with her own restricted outlook, far less that the kind of reason she is employing here is itself inappropriate. To her the existence of these rocks defies the right ruling of creation:

> 'Eterne God, that thurgh thy purveiaunce
> Ledest the world by certein governaunce,
> In ydel, as men seyn, ye no thyng make.
> But, Lord, thise grisly feendly rokkes blake,
> That semen rather a foul confusion
> Of werk than any fair creacion
> Of swich a parfit wys God and a stable,
> Why han ye wroght this werk unresonable?

For by this werk, south, north, ne west, ne eest,
Ther nys yfostred man, ne bryd, ne beest;
It dooth no good, to my wit, but anoyeth.
Se ye nat, Lord, how mankynde it destroyeth?'
(Franklin's Tale 865–76)

Here idleness is implicitly placed in opposition to action and making, and so the rocks, which are capable of wreaking destruction without having to exert any effort of movement, are the confusion of the perfect wisdom of an eternal and stable God. Dorigen's speech recognises a paradox which she herself is unable to see: nature is regarded as inherently unstable and apparently irrational, and thus in need of control from the presumed rational and stable Creator, who is 'Eterne' and rules the world 'by certein governaunce'. Yet it is the very immobility of the rocks, their ultimate stability, that makes them 'semen rather a foul confusion / Of werk than any fair creacion' of a divinely ordered world. Dorigen's objections invoke the notion of nature as a unified entity, designed as a mode for educating humans. In Chaucer's text that notion is automatically couched in Christian terms through this appeal to the Creator God, but it is the same attitude as that which mistakenly makes Gaia into a coherent, nurturing and caring force. Tellingly, Dorigen cannot see any benefit of them to 'man, ne bryd, ne beest', which endorses the division between the animal and non-animal (here inanimate) worlds of nature we have seen surface in *Sir Gawain and the Green Knight*. However her real and thoroughgoing anthropocentric priorities emerge two lines later as she cries out, 'Se ye nat, Lord, how mankynde it destroyeth?' It is ironic that in this speech, with its too-ing and fro-ing as Dorigen struggles with the purpose of rocks, the only things which neither move nor change are the 'rokkes blake' themselves.

Of course the rocks are destructive only to those who do not know how to negotiate them, and Dorigen, to her detriment, proves to be an inexpert navigator. Rather than accepting both the physical fact of these rocks and that sailors have navigated them successfully for years, she brings them into the realm of romance, thus making them symbolic and, ostensibly, negotiable, where 'negotiable' comes to mean 'eradicable'. By striking the bargain with Aurelius, she (perhaps inadvertently) makes it possible for these rocks to disappear: it is, after all, in the nature of such bargains that the apparently impossible becomes possible. Moreover, as so often, the very terms of her demand carry within them the way of fulfilling her requirements:

> 'Looke what day that endelong Britayne
> Ye remoeve alle the rokkes, stoon by stoon,
> That they ne lette ship ne boot to goon –
> I seye, whan ye han maad the coost so clene
> Of rokkes that ther nys no stoon ysene,
> Thanne wol I love yow best of any man'
>
> (Franklin's Tale 992–7)

Initially, the rocks need be removed only in so far as they present an obstacle to the safe passage of boats (992–4). Yet this objection to them exists only in Dorigen's mind, as becomes clear when we realise that Averagus arrives home safely some two years before the clerk/magician apparently makes the rocks disappear. Dorigen's second articulation (995–7) is the significant one, as the requirement becomes merely that the rocks vanish from sight, leaving open the possibility of them remaining in place, hidden from view by the tide, rather than actually removed. This loophole betrays Dorigen's shortsightedness, since rocks lying below the water can pose more danger to shipping than exposed ones. Her view is very much one of a landlubber who looks out over the water rather than venturing out on its surface, but it also betrays an assumption that nature is subservient to human whim. Literally so here, since, if Dorigen gets her way, these rocks will disappear entirely from the actual shoreline which they help define and become merely props in her own tale; there for the sole purpose of being removed. This point in the text thus brings together the force of folk-tale (or lay) tradition, the common belief in the natural world as a means by which God makes his purpose known and, in ecocritcal terms, the undesirable habit of humans to appropriate nature. It is this last that remains unaddressed by the plot of the Tale and so leaves green readers with that sense of unease in resolution that seems to me to be a mark of ecocriticism. That sense of unease begins with this address to God and leads us to circle one of the central conundrums of the story – do those rocks actually disappear?

In making her bargain Dorigen not only overlooks the tradition that the apparently impossible task is inevitably completed but also ignores the actual (as opposed to romantic) setting of the rocks and one of the most basic observable aspects of coastal landscapes. Seas are in constant motion and it is the nature of both rocks and waves that occasional freak high tides will cover even those rocks which seem to be furthest out of reach. As is well established, such a possibility is latent in the tone in which she delivers her promise, as Dorigen speaks 'in pleye', thus admitting the concepts of game and trickery into the agreement and with them the action of the random or chaotic, the unstable and irrational: the very things to which she objects so vehemently in her accusatory speech to God.[10] While one aspect of a green reading would here focus less on her heedlessness of her own fate, and more on her wilful ignorance or deliberate dismissal of the rocks as actual objects, another would see in her words a familiar alignment of gender associations and the natural phenomena.

Dorigen's introduction of a place for the irrational and unstable opens the way for an ironic use of the typical gender associations of male with rational stability and female with emotional (and so irrational) instability. Changeability is traditionally associated with women, so it is surely no coincidence that the principles of flux should prove so central to a plot which is ostensibly governed by a woman: not only is Dorigen here creating the terms of the agreement with Aurelius but it has been established from the start that she has an unusually 'large reyen' (735) in her marriage with Averagus.[11] However we must be careful not to jump to conclusions here, for Dorigen's desire to see the 'irrational' rocks removed may be a testimony to her male position at this point in the story. Certainly her view of the natural world is not only anthropocentric but specifically androcentric, as she seeks to master and subdue the environment to what she perceives as the greater good. It is thus in keeping with the tenor of the Tale that Aurelius (feminised in his relation to the dominant Dorigen) seeks help in the first instance not from Neptune, god of the sea, but from Lucina, goddess of the changing moon and creator of the tides. Importantly, he does not petition Lucina directly, but appeals to her brother and controlling male, Apollo, asking him to command the moon, who will in turn influence the tides (1031–79). Aurelius's speech reveals his knowledge of the actual workings of the natural world, as he prays for a freak spring tide that will last two years. Unlike Dorigen, he is seeking not to act against the order of the natural world but rather to exploit its capabilities for his own ends. In this his actions and prayers are entirely in keeping with his gender, as he tacitly acknowledges the assumption that the sea, like every other natural resource, is there to be used for man's benefit. Despite this conscious attempt to invoke these rules, he has no luck. It requires a magician to help him achieve his end, one who deals in illusion and who can apparently change reality because of his greater knowledge of what is actually real. A strange conjunction is thus made between scientific knowledge and magic, in which the dual powers of careful observation and illusion are acknowledged and put to use. The 'poor clerk' who is called in to make the rocks disappear is not only magician but also a scientist and philosopher, well versed in both 'monnes mansyons' and, it is implied, in 'other magyk natural'. The Tale leaves it ambiguous as to whether the disappearance of the rocks is due to magic or to an abnormally high tide, which the philosopher's astronomical skills allow him to predict accurately, whereas Aurelius could only hope for it to occur spontaneously.

While these possible immediate causes of the vanishing of the rocks may seem to be diametrically opposed (magic versus science) in fact the distance between them is not so great as, crucially, both are regarded in the text as natural. It is this natural quality that Dorigen fails to recognise as she accepts with horror Aurelius's claim that the rocks have gone:

> Allas, . . . that evere this sholde happe!
> For wende I nevere by possibilitee
> That swich a monstre or marvielle myghte be!
> It is agayns the proces of nature.
>
> (1342–5)

Dorigen's words betray our tendency to describe abnormal events as unnatural, and also act as an object lesson in the dangers attendant on changing the local environment in order to satisfy a passing desire. It is surely part of the process of nature that such changes could occur spontaneously, however extraordinary they appear to us; something that Dorigen fails to consider as the plot, the process of the narrative, takes over events. Indeed, so swept away is she by the very possibility that the one thing she regarded as impossible has happened that she never actually goes to see for herself, thereby breaking one of the first rules of both good science and nature observation. This is the final proof that Dorigen has long since left the world of observable natural phenomena and immersed herself in the world of human stories.

The triumph of the clerk/scientist is that he knows how to make use of the very attitudes towards the natural world that Dorigen (and Aurelius) merely express. If, like her, we fall into the habit of regarding rocks as hostile to humans and also as immovable, and forget both that people have navigated rocks for years with some success (Averagus being the obvious case in point here) and that freak high tides do occur, then we, too, are open to being made to believe that, once those rocks are no longer visible, they are no longer there. The Tale thus plays with our habitual way of regarding the rest of the natural world and with our attitudes towards the sea in particular, as we are easily tempted away from considering the sea itself into sharing Dorigen's preoccupation with the shore.

Dorigen's habit of thought has a further consequence: the denial of that important third option, that the rocks are simply covered for a while, holds her within an essentially dualistic conceptual framework which privileges the rational and stable over the emotional and fluid. Ecocriticism troubles such embedded dualism by suggesting that we regard ourselves as being part of an eco-system in which we are no more (or less) important than any other constituent. This in turn should alter not only how we regard our relations to the world but also how we think about it, questioning, amongst other things, the kind of 'reason' we use. Dorigen furnishes us with an object lesson in the dangers of persisting with dualist thinking which relies on the opposition of reason and nature. Her insistence on seeing herself as of greater consequence than the rocks, on asserting that they pose a threat to her happiness, and indeed on assuming that she has a right to pursue personal happiness at all costs, results in her designating those rocks an unreasonable 'foul confusion of werk'. Since she is operating a thoroughly anthropocentric view of the world, her wish to see these now offending rocks removed is legitimised, yet the plot of the Tale plays out the adverse logic of using this kind of reasoning. By seeking to impose her desires on the rocks she endorses the notion that nature is there to be used and altered according to humanity's preferences, and so inadvertently lays herself open to being similarly manipulated via her own correlation with the managed natural world, as mediated through her gender. The Tale has already hinted that Dorigen is both safer and happier in the more traditional settings for a romance heroine – by rivers, wells and in a formal garden (FT 895–905) – and the denouement of the plot further declares that she would be better off within traditional gender-relations as well. The fundamentally dualist and masculinist assumptions of the Tale thus triumph at the end, as two strands of literary convention unite to displace Dorigen from the Tale's centre and subordinate her to the working out of social relations between its male actants. The narrative's restoration of the 'right' balance of power is thus revealed as one which suppresses human anxieties in the face of natural forces by focusing first on the static forms of the rocks, rather than the fluctuating expanse of sea, and then shifting attention away from the question of how humanity regards the world, on to the far more familiar, and altogether less threatening, topic of how men relate to each other. This places great power in the hands of those who know how to manipulate our concepts of our world, a fact figured in this text by the educated clerk, who, in the end, is the one who controls the fates of both the rocks and Dorigen.

For green readers, then, the fate of Dorigen illustrates the dangers inherent in allowing a dominant habit of thought to prevail. Having begun well by refusing a simple inversion of gender-roles in her marriage which would leave the binary opposition intact, she then fails to imagine that there is another way of relating to the natural world than the one most frequently offered to us. The problem is not that she invokes the concept of a rational order, but that the reason she employs is exclusively anthropocentric. As Val Plumwood puts it:

> It is not reason itself that is the problem . . . but rather arrogant and insensitive forms of it that have evolved in the framework of rationalism and its dominant narrative of reason's mastery of the opposing sphere of nature and disengagement from nature's contaminating elements of emotions, attachment and embodiment. Increasingly these forms of reason treat the material and ecological world as dispensable. (Plumwood 2002: 5)

Dorigen's desire to have the rocks removed is a plain case of treating the natural world as dispensable.

The clerk, on the other hand, with his conscious use of our domineering habit of reading the environment in terms of its perceived relations with man, might perhaps offer a better role model. His reputation for wisdom, gentilesse and apparent ability to control the natural world rests on his skilful use of predominant perceptions, without actually requiring him to alter the environment at all. However, the use to which the Tale allows him to put his skill is that of commenting on human social relations, as he, like Dorigen, is inevitably subject to the plot in which he finds himself. At the end of this Tale, then, the realm of nature is rendered safe not through taming it or burning it out (as in The Knight's Tale) but through removing the actual, physical natural world from the plot altogether and substituting our common conceptions of it before marginalising even those in favour of a game of homosocial relations.

Looking out from the cliff top, Dorigen exemplifies the difficulties of rethinking our relation to the rest of the world. For her those rocks are literally 'the impediments to emergence of environmental imagination from environmental unconscious' just as her reactions to them are 'the very templates on which it relies for expression' (Buell 2001: 250). She cannot conceive of the rocks as anything but dangerous, despite all the evidence to the contrary, and she seems incapable of contemplating the sea itself at all. Additionally she brings to the fore our complex reactions to the ideas of change and changelessness; process and stasis. A tale by its very nature relies on process to carry its plot from beginning to end in however convoluted a line. We ought, then, to like the idea of change and development and in some contexts we clearly do, as for instance where the turn of the seasons is concerned. The medieval lyrics discussed in Chapter 1 show how we depend upon the certainty of movement in order to be assured that spring will follow winter; without that promise we would find the dark months impossible to survive. However, when it comes to apparently unpredictable events, those we typically term 'natural disasters', the case is very different. Then, it seems, we would rather deal with a nature that is consistent, even one that is prone to anger ascribable to a definable cause, than with a nature that is random and unconcerned with human actions. The security that this concept of nature affords is the assurance that humanity is the most important species on the planet: hostility reaffirms our pre-eminence; why else would the natural forces combine against us? As much of this book demonstrates, humans are deeply disconcerted when that affirmation is lacking and our standing as central to creation is challenged. The engima of the 'erthe toc of erthe' lyric is rooted in its refusal to endorse that pre-eminence unambiguously.

Dorigen's inablility to deal directly with the sea is tantamount to a refusal to actually see it. Rather than focus on the waters, she looks at either the ships on its surface or the rocks and cliffs that mark its shore. Her literal looking over the sea thus neatly becomes an actual overlooking of it: a deliberate, if scarcely acknowledged, refusal to grant it entity.[12] Such wilful blindness seems to be diametrically opposed to Jonah's decision to escape God's command by embarking on the waters, but the two reactions spring from the same source: an association between the sea and the invisible. The connection is a complicated one, as it has to do with a notion of vastness – of breadth as well as unplumbable depths which themselves may hide unknown, immense creatures. Those who are on the sea pass beyond sight and thus beyond the immediate ken of those left on shore, and so themselves become part of the expanse of the unknown, for the duration of their voyage at least.

We find this belief in the sea's ability to render people invisible at work in *Patience*'s version of the story of Jonah. In the Biblical version Jonah's immediate reaction to the divine command to go to Nineveh is to flee to Tharsis. Both the Vulgate and the Wycliffite versions repeat the phrase 'into Tharsis, from the face of the lord' ('in Tharsis a facie Domini'; 'in to tharsis: fro the face of the lord') and thus suggest that Tharsis itself is somehow out of God's sight, while also allowing that it could be Jonah's flight which is from the sight of God. The Biblical ambiguity is resolved in *Patience*, where it is the sea itself which is thought to be beyond divine sight. The poem's expansion of the succinct Biblical phrase includes two lines that make the implications of Jonah's flight to sea explicit:

> He wende wel that that wyy that al the world planted
> Hade no maght in that mere no man for to greve.
>
> (*Patience* 111–12)

Not only does the use of 'mere' bear out R.W.V. Elliott's observation on the poet's use of inland water vocabulary for the sea, but these two lines also reveal our habitual opposition of land and sea, with the concomitant preference for land. Thus God, acting as a true husbandman, has 'planted' the world, but is presumed to have no power over the sea. Or, more precisely, has no power to harm a man on the sea. This is intriguing, offering as it does the conclusion that, although God is able to contain the waters within defined bounds, the seas themselves yet remain somehow beyond his control. Conceivably this reflects the prior nature of the waters of the deep, which, unlike the earth, were not called into being, but already existed at the pre-creation expanse of Genesis 1: 1–3. It was over these that the spirit of God moved before dividing them into the waters of earth and the waters of heaven on the second day. The creation of the seas as such took place only on the third day, when the dry land was separated from the waters:

> god forsoth seide / getherd be(n) waters· the wich ben under heven in to o place: & apeere the drye / & made it is so / And god clepide the drye erth: & the gatheringeth of waters: he clepide seese / (*Wycliffite Bible* Genesis 1: 9–10)

Seas, then, are created by holding waters within limits in a process which makes the land seem precarious. If land appears only when the waters are moved away, it is all too easy to imagine that it could be subsumed again when they move back, which is of course exactly what happens in the Deluge. Two lines from *Cleanness* express the point perfectly: 'For when the water of the welkyn with the worlde mette, / Alle that deth moght dryye drowned therinne' (371–2). The fact that the flood is brought about through rain, rather than simply having the seas, lakes and rivers miraculously break their bounds, is more than straightforward climactic observation; more even than an example of God using the natural processes to His own ends. It is a direct reversal of the original process of Creation, made all the more disturbing for being so clearly imaginable. In this light, it is significant that the absence of the sea is the marker of the profound difference between our current, old world and the new one of the Apocalypse: 'and I saw new heaven and new earth, for the first heaven and the first earth went away, and the sea is not now' (Revelation 21: 1). Water remains necessary in this new world, but its kind is radically altered as the sea is replaced by a different kind of flood, that of the clear water that springs from under the seat of God and spreads out through this new creation, flowing always within defined banks.

The Wycliffite terminology reveals our dual concept of the oceans as both unbounded waters of the deep (the waters which in medieval global concepts literally encompassed the earth) and those held within bounds as seas, while also touching on a latent fear of an entirely submerged world. The implication is that the seas at some level defy order and control. Linked to this is perhaps the fact that, unlike the land, which is divided into countries, peoples and rulers, the sea is not governed by any human figure or nation. Instead it is an element that connects and surrounds all countries, allowing passage from one to another, but defying national boundaries itself. Custance's drifting from Syria to Northumberland relies upon exactly this aspect of the sea, and she shares with Jonah the belief that while on the waters she is outside the normal human world. The crucial difference is of course that she believes she is still fully within the sight and governance of God, while Jonah hopes that he is not. Jonah's choice of the sea as a refuge beyond the sight of God necessarily suggests that he is fleeing to a godless place (reminiscent of Gawain's Wirral) in which ungodly powers may be at work. For those who know the story (as the author of *Patience* surely assumed his audience would) this must immediately bring to mind the whale who will shortly swallow up Jonah as surely as the Deluge did those left outside the Ark. This whale in turn draws on the tradition of the Leviathon, that immense but undefined sea-creature, created at the dawn of time and due to arise at the end of it, when, according to early medieval Christian iconography, it will be the physical form of the Antichrist.[13]

All of these connections are possible because of our highly ambiguous relations with the sea, which in turn, arise from our knowledge that more things lurk in its depths than we can possibly envisage. When they are taken together it may mean that, as Buell puts it 'oceans are the closest thing on earth to a landscape of global scope' (2001: 199) but if so that 'landscape' (itself an ironic term in this context) is a far from comforting one.

Such connotations and associations cast Jonah's decision to flee to sea in a desperate light, and indeed the poem promptly highlights his folly, ensuring we do not labour under the same delusion as Jonah. The lines that follow the ironic report of

Jonah's belief that God is powerless to harm those on the sea make the folly of such a belief evident in no uncertain terms:

> Lo, the wytles wrechche, for he wolde noght suffer,
> Now has he put hym in plyt of peril wel more.
>
> (113–14)

Here, suffering, which the poem has initially allied with patient endurance,[14] is combined with the physical pain that Jonah has envisaged himself undergoing at the hands of irate Ninevehians and simultaneously closely connected to 'peril' in sardonic comment on Jonah's escape attempt. His 'plight' is now not just that of physical danger or possible storms at sea but also of an almost fatal misunderstanding of divine sight. However, it is important to acknowledge that it is the sea that allows the poem to thus link physical and spiritual peril. Our human associations of tempest, sea monsters and fear of drowning all unite to provide a fitting image for Jonah's position, and find a ready echo in not only the ocean storm, but also Jonah's later identification of the whale's belly with 'the hole . . . of hellen wombe' (306).

The poem may thus pour scorn on Jonah's hope that the sea will offer some kind of escape route, but that hope is merely another aspect of the concept of 'beyond' that seems to be so closely associated with the ocean. Like Dorigen, Jonah fails to focus on the sea itself; instead he sets his sights on Tharsis, a place which, crucially, is reached by sea, providing further contrast to the overland journey required to reach Nineveh.[15] *Patience*'s version of the Biblical story emphasises that when Jonah goes to Joppa his main aim is to get out of God's way as speedily as possible in the belief that out of sight will be out of mind. To this end he runs away to sea: the port for which he is bound is important because it is not the inland city he has been ordered to go to. However, once he has booked his passage, the poem brings in to play the effect of having a named destination to a voyage. Jonah is suddenly keen to set sail and replaces his desire to be safely hidden in Tharsis with a notion of being invisible while at sea. It is a nice touch that the word he uses for being thus hidden in Tharsis is 'lest' (88), which in this context must surely carry ironic connotations of the more literal being lost at sea he is about to experience.

This eagerness to contemplate arriving at another shore is

reflected in the keen interest he takes in all the paraphernalia of navigation and shows just how far removed his attitude is from that of the saints who undertook their voyages in rudderless boats.[16] It is therefore appropriate that Jonah takes particular pleasure in noting the details of the ship's rigging which seem to display human ability to harness the powers of the winds and thus assert some kind of control over our fate on the seas.[17] On the quay in Joppa it is specifically the various method of propulsion that catch his attention, as we might expect of a man eager to make his escape; later it is the steering gear that features, as it collapses under the force of the storm. As the ship leaves port all seems to be going well for Jonah, but the language of the poem hints at changes to come and this not only in the overt warnings that God sees all but also in the marine vocabulary that infuses the text. The juxtaposition of the happily sea-borne Jonah and the narrator's warning of disaster to come offers a case in point:

> For he was fer in the flod foundande to Tarce.
> Bot I trow ful tyd overtan that he were
>
> (126–7)

The 'flod' which is a source of relief for Jonah need not carry dire overtones of flood and disaster, but it nevertheless stirs up an undercurrent of danger in the common phrase 'ful tyd' and the word 'overtan', allowing an image of sea tides overwhelming Jonah to join the more prosaic and immediate meaning of non-specific events soon catching up with him. Such an image is entirely in tune with our human fear of the sea, its powerful tides and unexpected squalls, and all the more appropriate for a story whose protagonist is not only thrown overboard but also literally overtaken and swallowed by a sea creature.

The precise order of events in the storm sequence follows that set out by Nicolas Jacobs in his study of the storm topos in medieval alliterative verse, namely foul, windy weather, damage to tackle, perilous plight of sailors and finally the fate of ships (Jacobs 1972: 700). However the scene in *Patience* is more than a simple adherence to rhetorical rules: the demolition of the steering gear in particular once again invites comparison between the fugitive Jonah and the obedient Noah safe in his rudderless Ark, or the saints who sought the desert in the sea.[18] Likewise, the narrator takes care to mention that, once free of Jonah, the ship finds good currents and safe harbour despite its now useless tackle (233–6). The sailors who previously prayed to their own several gods now thank 'oure mercyable God, on Moyses wyse' (238) showing that they at least are aware of the implications of their miraculous survival.

Vivid as such human details are, what is particularly telling about this storm is that it is terrible enough to disturb even the fish seeking shelter in the depths of the ocean.

> The wyndes on the wonne water so wrastel togeder
> That the wawes ful wode waltered so highe,
> And efte busched to the abyme, that breed fysches
> Durst nowhere for rogh arest at the bothem.
>
> (141–4)

It is in fact forceful enough to disrupt the alliterative pattern of the verse, as line 144 thrashes around briefly, nearly establishing alliteration on 'r' before succumbing to the turmoil, and echoing the 'b' of 143. Poetically, this enacts the powerful undertow that follows the huge upsurge of the towering waves in the previous lines. Mimetically, it reveals how marine life seeks refuge in the depths from tempests that normally disturb only surface of the water, and so indicates the devastating force of this storm that make such refuge impossible. In terms of plot, this detail accounts for the presence of the whale passing fortuitously close to the ship just as the sailors tip Jonah overboard.

Having such a pragmatic explanation for the presence of this whale at such an opportune moment is slightly at odds with the Biblical version of the tale, wherein God quite deliberately 'made redi a gret fish', raising the possibility that this particular creature has not existed up till now. *Patience*'s 'wylde walterande whal' has been 'beten fro the abyme' (247, 248) and although this rising up from the depths may seem similar to the sudden appearance of the fiend conjured up at Saturn's behest in the Knight's Tale, the previous mention of the terrified ('breed') fish ensures that *Patience*'s beast is firmly part of the real world and that its actions are entirely credible. What follows is a remarkable act of inversion, in which the human – accustomed self-important exploiter of the sea and sea-life – becomes that most overlooked and exploited part of the marine economy – fish-food.[19] In swallowing Jonah the whale thus forces him to become a literal part of sea life, albeit an undigested one. In a reciprocal movement, the whale is interpolated into the human literary world by becoming a church, a representation of hell and the embodiment of the abyss, while Jonah is subsumed into the non-human world by becoming a piece of jetsom, dangled over the side of the boat like bait and eaten by the fish.

> The folk yet haldande his fete, the fysch hym tyd hentes
>
> (251)

True to the principle of inversion, the human aim is here to get rid of the bait and escape the fish, rather than catch it. This comic touch allows an odd shift in the narrative to go unremarked as the story-line doubles back on itself, repeating the act of throwing Jonah overboard to show it first as part of the sailors's desperate attempt to assuage the storm and then from the whale's perspective. The first telling is succinct as Jonah is speedily jettisoned:

> Tyd by top and bi to thay token hym synne,
> Into that lodlych loghe thay luche hym sone.
>
> (229–30)

Immediately the tempest ceases, calm descends and the ship is driven to safety by strong currents. However, it is not the business of this story to follow the ship, so the next section returns to Jonah, but it returns to him in his new position outside the anthropocentric view of the sea world. In order to establish this shift of position the poem recapitulates the moment Jonah crosses from one world-view to the other. From this point of view, Jonah is no longer a man 'schowved' from the ship, but a 'wyye that the water soghte' (249) where 'soghte' suggests that water is the natural place to be, as well as reminding us that Jonah did indeed seek the water in his attempt to escape having to go to Nineveh. Immersed in the sea, Jonah's position is critically different from his previous one as a refugee on the surface. Now he is regarded as merely another, smaller, life form thrashing about in the waves – fair prey for any passing predator. In this element humankind is not the dominant species, however much it may like to think itself so when sailing the surface.

Having established this radically different world-view, the

poem continues to use it, making the whale, not Jonah, the protagonist for a while:

> Ande ever walteres this whal bi wyldren depe,
> Thurgh mony a regioun ful roghe, thurgh ronk of his wylle;
> For that mote in his mawe mad hym, I trowe,
> Thagh hit lyttel were hym wyth, to wamel at his hert.
>
> (297–300)

Once again part of the effect is comic: Jonah is described as an irritant causing heartburn, inviting us to feel some empathy for the unsuspecting whale and share its relief when this indigestible morsel is finally spewed up on shore. Yet we should not allow the touch of the comedy to prevent us noticing the imaginative leap from human to whale that makes the incident so successful. Such details offer ways of adapting our current templates of environmental imagination for the kinds of alternative imagining that Buell asserts is so necessary if we are to see our surroundings through different lenses and thus evaluate them in more ecologically friendly terms. This example, unlike those cited by Buell, relies not on creating a domestic structure for the whale but on a more straightforward bond based on physical discomfort.[20] It is important to recognise that this whale is not solely an instrument of God; it is granted an existence beyond that, as it is shown to be a distinct entity which happens to be pressed into service before swimming out of the poem back to the invisibility of the deep. Thus while undoubtedly being an agent of divine will and an embodiment of 'ocean's mysterious, radical, ambiguous otherness' (Buell 2001: 203) it is also, by virtue of its actuality, part of the real marine ecosystem. When Jonah is swallowed he thus finds himself forced to recognise that he is an integral part of an environment he has hitherto taken advantage of, but spared very little thought for.

Just as part of the 'inexaustibleness' of the sea (Buell 2001: 201) rests on the belief that the food stock never runs out, so there is the concomitant belief that the sea can take in and neutralise whatever we care to throw at it. Superficially this seems to be another version of our belief in the purifying power of water, but in truth it is a case of 'out of sight, out of mind' as the dumped waste melts from our minds as soon as it sinks out of sight in the all-consuming depths. Here again we see the operation of the association of invisibility with the sea, tinged this time with a belief in the cleansing ability of water. The sailors who heave Jonah overboard are throwing out a pollutant in the hope that doing so will save their lives and without any thought of what effect it might have on the sea. Although it is possible to perceive here an echo of placatory offerings being given to the gods, their action continues their previous desperate jettisoning of goods and cargo (157–60).[21] The result is a curious blend of the concept of 'ocean as ultimate sanctuary' which Buell suggests was the dominant view up to the twentieth century (Beull 2001: 201) with sea as 'realm of evil' which also pervaded the medieval world-view (Wright 2001: 78). Jonah's position as he is dangled by the heels over the side of the boat is thus precarious indeed, for at that point it is unclear whether the sea will prove to be a purifying refuge or a source of consuming evil.

In the event it proves to be both, but the point of interest is not the allegorical readings of the whale as hell, or Jonah's rueful admission of the all-seeing power of God in his prayer from the whale's belly, but rather the radical overthrow of Jonah's position from being a human whose main concern is how to use the sea as a route to another area of land, to being one forced to recognise that he is part of a wider, interconnected, system. Within the whale's stomach he usefully portrays what Val Plumwood terms 'our ecologically embedded lives' (2002: 28) so much so that the narrative fleetingly identifies Jonah with the whale.

> Ande as sayled the segge, ay sykerly he herde
> The bigge borne on his bak and bete on his sydes.
>
> (301–2)

Most commentators read the 'his' of 302 as referring to the whale and allow the verb 'sayled' to convert the whale into a second ship, with Jonah once again cowering in its bowels. Strictly speaking, though, 'his' refers back to the 'segge', creating the more immediate experience of the waters beating directly on Jonah's own back and sides, and denying the actual, bodily presence of the whale in the process. Jonah's prayer continues this habit, describing his ordeal in terms of being directly immersed in the deep – 'The grete flem of thy flod folded me umbe' (309) while all the waters 'In on daschande dam dryves me over' (312). There is no mention of the fish here, rather Jonah portrays himself as sitting 'in the se bothem' (313) and 'wrapped in water to my wo stoundes' (317). 'The body that I byde inne' (318) may refer to the whale but equally easily, and more in keeping with the tone of the rest of the passage, it may refer directly to his own bodily existence, particularly as in the next line he claims that 'the pure poplande hourle playes on my heved' (319). Wilfully and almost incredibly, then, Jonah manages to deny the whale existence even as he sits in its belly.

This feat of denial is all the more ironically impressive when we consider that Jonah's position in the conceptual economy of the sea has been radically changed. From being a confidant purchaser of other men's sea-faring skills to traverse the surface of the water, he has become a part of the human detritus that is cast into it. In a way this ought to be the fulfilment of his desires, since he now occupies a space which is habitually 'disappeared or denied' as Plumwood puts it.[22] In Plumwood's argument the denied other is not 'waste' but resource, the material which is traded or the elements that make such material available in the first place. Jonah could be regarded as occupying this position both as a paying passenger and as food for the whale. However in each case, in each economy, he upsets the smooth running of the system: his presence on the boat endangers it and he irritates the whale's gut. In this Jonah becomes a type of humankind in general, especially in green reading of the poem. For him the sea is first only an intermediary way of getting somewhere else, then a usefully invisible arena, which will (he hopes) allow him to disappear from the sight of God, and only finally is it something to which he is connected as part of the created world as a whole. In this he evinces the attitude of 'hyperseparation' that Plumwood argues arises from the habit of regarding 'nature as a passive field for human endeavour, a malleable order that has no agency or autonomy of is own and imposes no real constraints upon us' (2002: 26). Such hyperseparation means that 'the others' contributions are thus relied upon but at the same time disappeared or denied' (2002: 27). In other words, the various intricate relations that go into sustaining a marine system are ignored, often by dint of simplifying what is going on.

Such simplification arises from a combination of ignorance and wilful blindness and requires a radical change in attitude to overthrow it. We might imagine that finding oneself at the other end of the economic and value system, contemplating life from the inside of a whale, would be precisely the kind of radical change necessary, and in one way it is. Jonah's prayer is not only an admission of his dependent position within the wider non-human natural world but also an acknowledgement that the sea is an integral part of the whole system. This acknowledgement is cast in the terms of the poem as a rueful assertion that there is nowhere in Creation that is beyond the sight of God. Tellingly, though, Jonah's insight proves fleeting. As soon as he is back on dry land his deep-seated anthropocentrism reasserts itself, proving again just how difficult we find it as a species to shift our imaginative paradigms and oust our accustomed habit of regarding ourselves as the centre of the universe, the species that gives all else meaning. The point is amply illustrated when Jonah is next at the mercy of the elements. This time he is at the opposite extreme in the desert plains above Nineveh, exposed to the harsh sun. He builds a kind of shelter, but it seems rather ineffectual; no wonder then that he capers with delight when he finds himself shaded by a luxurious woodbine that springs up overnight. We easily sympathise with his rage when the vine wilts, but the conclusions offered by this bit of the story are somewhat paradoxical for a green reader. On the one hand God's rebuke is another reminder of our species's persistent opportunism and lack of consideration.

> Thou are waxen so wroth for thy wodbynde,
> And travayledes ever to tent hit the tyme of an howre,
> Bot at a wap hit here wax and away at an other;
> And yet lykes the so luther, thi lyf woldes thou tyne.
>
> (497–500)

On the other, Jonah has shown his awareness and even appreciation of the non-human world by rejoicing in the appearance of the woodbine. He may not have tended it, but he did not treat it as 'a malleable order' either; did not, this time, relegate it to the realm of the 'disappeared'. Thus the poem brings us to what remains the central and divisive question of ecological thinking: when and to what extent (if any) should we deliberately interfere with the rest of the natural world? God's response to Jonah's complaint about the withered vine highlights the evaluative system we tend to use: the more we are involved with something, the more we care about it, especially where we feel the other thing bestows some benefit upon us. Simultaneously it suggests that humans need to recognise their place as merely one component among many of the divinely created world. This latter interpretation regards the incident with the vine as simply the last in a series of examples of 'God's using for a specific purpose, a component of divinely ordered nature' (Andrew and Waldron 1978: 196 n. 247). This is a common view, and one the poem certainly can be seen to endorse, but it should make a green reader uncomfortable, because it necessarily denies the whale, the woodbine and the worm autonomy and declares that the text's intention is to show that humankind should acknowledge itself part of creation and display that knowledge through prompt obedience to divine command and, it must follow, through giving up any pretence to autonomy ourselves. So the question still becomes: does God deliberately make the vine wither, thus making nature a tool for human education, or does he simply explain an inevitable process? While the former interpretation is clearly in keeping with much of the poem, we do well to note that alternative views are suggested, even if they remain latent.

One such alternative is that, *pace* Jonah's outburst, it is not the repentance of the people that wins a reprieve for Nineveh, but the recognition of the other species which would be affected by any retribution. When the king sends out the command for public repentance he specifically includes the beasts of burden, those animals who have been drawn into the human framework of life most fully:

> Ne best bite on no brom, ne no bent nauther,
> Passe to no pasture, ne pike non erbes,
> No non oxe to no hay, ne no horse to water.
> Al shal crye, forclemmed . . .
>
> (392–5)

The implication of such general and enforced penance is acknowledged in the reasons for mercy which form the last words of the Biblical book, as well signalling the end of the story in *Patience*: 'And als ther ben doumbe bestes in the burgh mony' (516). Nineveh is saved, it is implied, less because of the repentance of knowing humans than because the ignorant, the foolish and the non-human are suddenly rendered both visible and valuable.

Another alternative reading arises if we remember that not all nature is as quick to external bidding, divine or human, as some. The winds respond readily, blowing up the required storm and disturbing the whale, which also proves biddable to the command to regurgitate Jonah, although it is less clear whether the swallowing was a response to cetacean hunger or divine demand. The sea itself, though, remains powerfully autonomous, recalling the primary state of those deep, undivided pre-Creation waters. At the end of *Patience*, just as at the end of the Franklin's Tale, the text shifts its focus away from the sea on to land affairs. Jonah ends his story in the desert above Nineveh, as far from the memory of being surrounded by water as it is possible to get, while the voice of the narrator subtly suggests that for human beings it is better to be on land enduring privations 'in syght' (530) than to seek an alternative in the oblivion of the seas. In each text the net effect is to leave the sea untouched, outside the realms of human imagination and thus perpetually disconcerting in its ability to resist our attempts to describe, control or contain it. It remains instead a constant source of unsettling alternative world-views.

Much of this chapter's argument has dwelt on the paradox of our refusal or inability to envisage the sea, a paradox which seems to spring from the notion of the sea's vast expanse. However, although it defies sight, it is more perceptible to the ear. The sound of beating waves or the roaring of currents form a significant part of the literary seascape, just as surely hearing the sea is central to our actual experience of it. So it is that Jonah hears the rushing of the ocean from inside the whale ('ay sykerly he herde / The bygge borne on his bak and bete on his sydes' 301–2) and acknowledges the power of sound in his prayer, which specifically states that God can hear him even though he is at the bottom of the sea, cast out beyond sight (313–14). Unsurprisingly, the sound of roaring also features when storms brew up. The tempest that threatens Jonah's ship is heralded by sound: 'Anon out of the north-est the noys bigynes' (137) and continues with the sea itself creating noise 'The see soughed ful sore, gret selly to here' (140). *Cleanness* does not actually use vocabulary denoting sounds, but that is hardly necessary when the lines themselves can produce the required sound effects: 'The roghe raynande ryg, the raykande wawes' (382). The God of the Wakefield Noah is explicit in the use of noise as well as water to strike fear into the disobedient populace

> floodis that shall flo and ryn with hidous rerd
>
> (101).

What is noticeable here, though, is that the softer sounds of the sea are entirely absent. One would not expect to find lapping waves and gentle murmurings featuring in texts dealing with floods and tempest, nor even with a desire to remove rocks from a seashore, but it is remarkably difficult to find any reference to these more benign aspects of the sea. Instead we are left with sounds of roaring, much as we are with images of rising floods or tempestuous seas.

This green reading of these texts has brought to the fore our reluctance or perhaps inability to deal with the sea. Despite what may be our personal experiences, literature seems to find it easier to cast the ocean in a negative light, as a place of potential or actual danger, of trial and tempest, of rushing flood rather than calm waters.[23] At the same time ecocriticism's call to shift our focus away from the human and on to a more widely based and egalitarian view of the natural world and its value systems, allows us to appreciate more fully how these fourteenth-century texts skilfully evoke our often conflicted relations to both the world around us and the notion of divine control. When *Cleanness* and *Patience* are brought together with the Franklin's Tale we can see how they work with two dominant templates for imagining the sea: one based on what happens when we take to the water, the other based on the effects of looking out from the shore. What emerges is a broader understanding of the complexities that are in play in our concept of the sea. It is a refuge, a cleanser, an immense expanse which may crossed in a search for riches and reputation, or in the hope of escape; it is a source of potential unknown dangers and marvellous creatures and also, persistently, it is something that defies the imagination, something that again and again we strive simply to overlook.

Notes

1 Elliott 1984: 135. This volume is a collection of several of Elliott's essays and chapters on the theme of the topographical words in late medieval alliterative poetry, and the *Gawain* poet in particular. He is particularly concerned to

make the case for the *Gawain* poet being an inhabitant of the North-West Midlands and reflecting precise local knowledge of that landscape in his poems. Eagerness to prove this case dictates the focus of these studies, but they remain valuable nonetheless.

2 Despite the fact that Raban skips over the Middle Ages entirely (moving directly from *The Seafarer* to *The Faerie Queene*) his introduction nonetheless provides an engaging consideration of how the sea has been presented or literally overlooked in English literature. See especially pp. 3–6.

3 *Adomán's Life of Columba* ed. and trans. Alan and Marjorie Anderson (Oxford, Clarendon Press, 1991), pp. 46 and 166. Le Goff 1998: 51 cites the last of these examples in support of his passing comment that the sea and the wilderness are perceived in similar terms in the medieval West.

4 All citations from plays are taken from Happé 1987, unless otherwise stated.

5 Andrew and Waldron, Anderson and Stanbury all comment on the effectiveness of the flood description and indeed it seems to be regarded by many as the highpoint of *Cleanness* as a whole.

6 In his preface to *The Oxford Book of the Sea* Jonathan Raban comments on the difficulty of finding passages dealing with life at sea that do not dwell on tempests.

7 The lines that draw attention to this lack (417–20) come at exactly the point in the description of the storm where, as Jacobs demonstrates, rigging is usually shown to collapse (Jacobs 1972: 700). Ingeniously, the poet thus keeps to the pattern of the topos even though there is no actual rigging to describe.

8 Glacken makes no mention of either the Franklin's Tale or *Patience*, but his study shows that the association of seashore living with restlessness has proved one of the more resilient motifs in the western literary imagination.

9 Although we must allow Chaucer a certain patriotism here in implying that true honour is to be won only in England, there is a shadow of irony in the notion of going to England to win a name for oneself, given that the English magnates of the time had acquired their reputation for 'worship and honour' in arms in France or Spain.

10 This use of play offers an additional link between the Franklin's Tale and *Sir Orfeo*. Robert Cook (1994) suggested that the influence of *Sir Orfeo* on Chaucer might be detected in the clerk's conjuring up of the hunt scene as proof of his powers. It is possible to extend Cook's observation to point out that in both of these lays the context is one of game – 'revel' in *Orfeo* and 'pleye' in the Franklin's Tale. This in turn suggests that for each of these texts the spectacle of a courtly hunt belongs to the realm of illusion. The romances thus assert their status as alternative worlds by presenting the apparently normal human world as a form of illusion. Significantly, in each case the world inhabited by the romance is directly connected to the non-human natural world – Orfeo sees the hunt during his time in the wilderness and the clerk produces the vision of one in order to prove his ability to 'magic away' the offending rocks of Brittany. Both texts thus use a vision of a hunt to question, subtly, the usual, anthropocentric notions of what is real and what imaginary.

Sea and coast

11 It is important to note that Dorigen does not in fact rule the marriage. The opening of the Tale establishes a rare agreement of equality, as Averagus's promise to obey Dorigen is balanced by hers to be a humble and true wife to him.

12 Dorigen is not the only woman to deliberately overlook the sea. Raban cites a later example of the same phenomenon. 'To someone like Celia Fiennes, with her taste for titles and good houses, the sea was beneath her notice, one suspects, because it was irredeemably lower class' (Raban 1992: 7). It is tempting to attribute a similar attitude to Dorigen, particularly given the context of a Tale dealing with the concepts of right behaviour and class.

13 Rosemary Muir Wright (2001: 70–87) offers an example of this combination of elements and links them with the particular set of concerns one might expect of Irish monks, all too aware of the sea's ability to convey Norse invaders. Wright even goes so far as to assert that 'in the early Middle Ages it would seem that the sea was identified with the realm of evil' (78).

14 The narrator of *Patience* makes an explicit, if somewhat wearied, link between poverty and patience in line 45 of the poem and then goes on to say, resignedly, that since he (presumably) is saddled with both then it behoves him to put up with it.

15 Jonah could have opted to journey to Tharsis overland, but the sea route is evidently the more direct and was doubtless presumed the safer, even for those not eager to avoid the sight of God. The destination is less important than the choice of route.

16 There is also an implicit contrast with Noah's dutiful recourse to the Ark, which is usually described as having no steering gear. Noah's time on the flood waters is not in fact a voyage, as he has no destination; his boat is more strictly a sanctuary than an escape route.

17 I am here following Stanbury's suggestion that the details of the poem are at this point focalised through Jonah. The point-of-view changes once the action shifts to the boat at sea. See Stanbury 1991: 77–8.

18 Jacobs states that the motif of broken steering is found in Guido, but suggests that Ovid may be the true source. He does not mention the possibility of influence from the contrary example of saints' voyages, nor, indeed, the simple option of such details being a touch of realism.

19 Val Plumwood focuses on the way human economics persistently fails to take account of the most fundamental elements of the economic chain, whether it be an exploited and colonised human community or fish-food. She calls such miscalculations 'failures of ecological rationality delivered on a systematic basis by hubristic forms of rationalist economics' and points out how such forms rely on the (abusive and mistaken) assumption that one thing (more convenient to the human) can be substituted for another without any adverse consequence or effect on anything else. See Plumwood 2002: 26.

20 See Buell 2001: 250 where he casts the argument in terms of the obstacles to new ways of thinking posed by the fact that we necessarily work within established conceptual frameworks at the start. Buell perceives a shift between ancient and modern figurations of the whale through which 'the unnamed sea creature of the book of Jonah' becomes 'something like Shamu, Sea World's captive killer whale, or the winsome "Little Calf" ... whose early

life and adventures Victor B. Scheffer narrates in *The Year of the Whale'* (2001: 204). He notes that this shift in sentiment is being effected largely through depictions of whales that cast their habits in humanly familiar domestic terms, thus creating a notion of cetaceans being 'like us'.

21 The fact that Jonah is found asleep in the bowels of the boat when all others are helping bale, jettison or at the very least pray for deliverance emphasises that he has become useless even in the prevailing human economy. He regains worth only when he admits that he is the cause of the storm, at which point, interestingly, his value is evident in the fear he inspires as the sailors delay throwing him overboard, even though they had determined to do exactly that.

22 That being the position of the 'other' within an economy, which is fundamental to the power and position of 'self-made man' but is never acknowledged. See Plumwood 2002: 27.

23 This attitude finds its most succinct expression in Psalm 107, where the 'wonderous works of the deep' witnessed by those who go down to the sea in ships are explicitly the rousing and then calming of a storm (Psalm 107: 23–32).

5
Gardens and fields

Thus far the chapters in this book have focused on areas of the world that are regarded as outside human control albeit not beyond the effects of human actions. Although the notion of wild nature looms large in our imaginations, the majority of our actual physical encounters with the vegetative and animal worlds take place within more familiar and domestic domains, such as fields and gardens. One might expect these areas to be quintessentially different from the world of seasons, forests and wildernesses, but the notion of marvel, 'ferli', which has been shown to be so central to the mediation of the natural world in *Sir Orfeo* and *Gawain and the Green Knight* is also at work in the more everyday landscapes of *Pearl* and *Piers Plowman*. The spaces found in these two poems are linked by the thread of human cultivation, which is present to a greater degree in the gardens, parkland, fields and open country that figure in these two texts than in the most managed of forests. Both fields and gardens exist to create the conditions which will provide the highest yield for the plants we humans choose to put there, while simultaneously attempting to exclude any opportune and unwanted plants as weeds. Gardens are particularly interesting spaces, owing to the cluster of associations that gather within them, some at odds with others. The archetypal garden is an enclosed space, usually walled against the elements to create not only optimal growing conditions for the plants contained within but also a sense of refuge for those humans who are allowed entrance. This sense of retreat from the outside world and restoration of the spirit is enhanced by the traditional connection with Eden: 'since Paradise is a garden, a garden can, by transposition, be called a paradise' (Curtius 1953: 200 n. 32). That association, not always stated nor fully exploited, may operate at a variety of levels; Curtius's allusion is a case in point, as it rests at the moment of pre-lapsarian idyll, feeling no need to include snakes in the grass. Such paradisical gardens tend to subsume the more pragmatic kitchen garden, although the two functions were often united, as indeed they are again today. A carefully laid out and tended herb garden offered a restorative to the spirit as much through its design and the scents given off by the plants within it, as through the medicinal or culinary uses those plants were put to. A garden thus unites artifice and nature as the human skill and knowledge that creates and maintains it do so against a background of the less controllable world beyond its walls. The image that emerges is that of the *hortus conclusus*, an enclosed garden whose idyllic calm erases the labour that creates and maintains it (not least because such labour is usually done by unseen others) and also tends to overlook the change and decay that is a necessary part of any growing thing. A case in point is the quintessential garden of the *Romance of the Rose* in which all is held in a perpetual spring; even those who enter it must be spring-like as age, poverty, work and other undesirables are left outside.[1]

Perfect as this seems, scrutiny reveals that not all in this conceptual garden is necessarily lovely. Not only, according to Doob, is the restorative leisure garden liable to become a debased place of fleshly delight entered with more dubious intent than innocent recreation,[2] but its enclosure may also become a form of prison and its very lack of change a bar to development and growth. The first aspect is epitomised by the garden of Chaucer's Merchant's Tale. Here Januarie's locked orchard is both a sign of his desire to own the young and fertile May and the place that offers May and Damion their sexual opportunity. In contrast, the virginal Emelye of the Knight's Tale is first seen and desired when walking in the castle garden, but is actually available to the knights as a potential wife only when she and they are outside its walls.[3] Dorigen unites these two worlds: when her friends realise she is unable to find solace in the prospect of unkempt nature offered by a walk on the cliffs they decide to play in gardens 'ful of leves and of floures' instead (908). This is garden as place of solace, removed from everyday cares; a place of perfection, created by human skill:

> craft of mannes hand so curiously
> Arrayed hadde this gardyn, trewely,
> That nevere was ther gardyn of swich prys

Gardens and fields 167

> But if it were the verray paradys.
> The odour of floures and the fresshe sighte
> Wolde han maked any herte lighte
> That evere was born, but if to greet siknesse
> Or to greet sorwe helde it in distresse,
> So ful was it of beautee with plesaunce.
>
> (Frankin's Tale 909–17)

It is usual to equate Dorigen with the flowers of this familiar kind of garden, making her in this similar to Emelye. Both can be read as ladies of courtly romance requiring careful tending and segregation from the world at large, each a flower in a rarefied and contained area. Such readings align woman with nature, drawing on the tradition of flower comparisons and often pointing out the earthier side of the trope by pursuing it into the realms of plucking blooms as well as admiring them. Critics like Ellen Rose and Carolyn Merchant might well caution Dorigen and Emelye against being too readily aligned with elements of the natural world that are cultivated solely for the use and delight of humankind, while others, such as Ruether, might encourage them to reclaim this same alignment and make it the ground upon which to build to create a new world. Both lines of argument have much to offer medieval criticism and feminism and their very existence proves that ecofeminism is by no means an homogeneous school of thought,[4] but these kinds of debate run the risk of diverting attention away from the actual nature appearing in the texts, whether being deployed within literary analogy or depicted as part of the landscape. We should return to Dorigen's garden.

We would expect an idealised garden of this kind both to evoke and to fall short of the 'verray paradys', but the added detail that the only spirits it could not revive are those depressed by excessive sickness or sorrow is significant. Hearts so afflicted are 'helde . . . in distresse', imprisoned by their own grief impervious to the natural beauty around them. This almost throwaway comment betrays our deep-seated belief that being able to take due pleasure in the non-human world around us is a mark of mental well-being. Just how deep-seated this belief is is evident in Alan of Lille's use of it in his *De Planctu Naturae*.[5] After two sections describing the vivifying effect Nature's descent to earth has on the whole of creation, Alan opens the sixth section (Prose 3) with the statement: 'Hac igitur amenante temporis iuventute, nullis rerum exhilarata favoribus priorem virgo potuit temperare tristiciem' (Häring VI.1)[6]. Sheridan (1980: 116) renders it thus: 'Despite the fresh youth of the charming season, by no applause from created nature could the maiden be cheered and moderate her above-mentioned grief'. Things are bad indeed if not even Nature can rejoice in the beauties of the natural world: and that, of course, is Alan's point. Reading Alan of Lille it is impossible not to be struck by his thoroughgoing anthropocentrism,[7] of which this is a prime example. Nature's distress is caused by man's wilful disobedience of her laws and is not to be compensated for by the fact that all else proceeds as it should. Thus far it appears that man alone is at fault, but Alan's treatment of the idea is not entirely straightforward: it transpires that man's flouting of Nature's law was preceded by Nature's abandonment of the created world.

Having been appointed vice-regent to God ('tanquam prodeam, tanquam sui uicariam' *De Planctu* VIII.224) and overseer of the continued creation of species according to the original, divine, pattern, Nature later deserted her post, appointing Venus to take her place. The two reasons given for this desertion are cursory to say the least. One is the sheer volume of work that renders the use of a skilled subordinate necessary, the other is a desire to be in a better place. Significantly, the Latin syntax links the two reasons closely, using the '-que' suffix rather than giving each reason its own more distinctly marked clause: 'Sed quia sine subministratorii artificis artificio suffragante tot rerum species expolire non poteram meque in etheree regionis amenante palatio placuit commorari' (Prose 4.235–6). The effect is to make each reason look like a poor excuse, incapable of fuller explanation or defence. Sheridan calls this lack of explanation a 'fatal flaw' in Alan's argument, further asserting that other authors would not have allowed such a tenuous reason to stand unchallenged (Sheridan 1980: 147 and 40).[8] However, tenuous as it is, Alan's summary treatment suggests the way the concept of Nature represents two opposing notions of the ideal natural world. In one, the principle of transience dominates: individuals are rightly, naturally, subject to change and death, while the species is maintained by a constant stream of replicas. Alan provides a vivid representation of the sheer volume of creation that goes into maintaining this natural world in the description of Nature drawing on her tablet in Prose

2. The key phrase is 'velociter evanescendo moriens' (IV.5) which Sheridan renders 'quickly fading and disappearing' (108). However 'moriens' is strictly 'dying' and, while that may not suit the subject of pictures, it is absolutely accurate for the living things Nature depicts, which pass so quickly that they leave no mark on her tablet, thus both allowing and requiring Nature to draw again. In the other notion the natural world is static, envisaged at the peak of perfection, unharmed by ill-winds or decay. In *De Planctu Naturae* the ethereal region to which Nature retreats is clearly this second kind of natural space and, we may assume, it is a place in which she is required to do no work at all. This idea is expanded upon in the *Anticlaudianus* where Nature's realm is specifically a place free of decay – so much so that fine fabrics are excluded, despite their beauty, because they are liable to rot ('Non ibi materies, que sit demissior istis, / Jura tenet propriaque potest plebescere forma' I.117).[9] Such a description leads us to the paradoxical conclusion that Nature's idealised dwelling is in itself unnatural. That is to say, it is not subject to the principles of decay and renewal that are defining elements of the world over which she presides in *De Planctu Naturae*. The paradox is resolved if we think of this second space as supra-natural rather than unnatural; once we enter the realms of eternity there is a logic to envisaging the eternal world as one made up of things not subject to death and decay. Yet the ways in which that world is imagined betrays our deep attachment to the natural world we know and is perhaps again linked to that deep-seated belief that the human spirit is revived by being surrounded not only by beautiful things but by living ones. There is a tension, then, between the desire for an unchanging beauty, safe from decay, and the knowledge that death is inherent to the natural world. Flies in amber come to mind as artifice enters the equation, but, while such phenomena are to be admired and wondered at, they are not necessarily to be imitated. The trick is to know which world one is in and what is appropriate to it.

This tension between what is right for this world and what fit for the perfection of another forms the basis of *Pearl*. As is familiar to readers of the poem, the narrator moves from an actual garden into a dream landscape which is a form of Paradise on earth containing woods, a hill and a river, and thence to a sight of the city of the New Jerusalem (closely based on the description in

Revelation) before finally being returned to the original garden. Throughout, the text makes rich use of its landscapes, while also being filled with references to precious metals and stones, particularly, of course, to pearls, and we do well to remember that gems, gold and silver are as much a part of the natural world as flowers, rocks and trees: it is the human value-system that differentiates between them, creating categories of precious and mundane. Habitually the poem is described as becoming increasingly metaphorical in its use of landscape, preparing us for an increasingly allegorical understanding not only of the poem, but also of the general world around us. By moving gradually but persistently away from the secular, actual world of loss and bereavement towards the spiritual one, in which such emotions have no place, consolation and a humbler appreciation of God may be gained. Andrew and Waldron have summed up this mode of reading thus: 'But if the natural garden is a shadow of the Terrestrial Paradise, this in its turn is a shadow of the full glory of heaven' (1978: 31). Their phrasing reveals the habit of regarding the initial garden as inferior, yet it is to this place that we and the dreamer are returned. It is here, in the realm of death, but also of growth, that we must find ways to live. In similar vein Anderson comments that the 'poem drives home the point that the Christian view of things is at bottom alien to and contradictory of common human experience' (1996: xi). Without wishing to dispute the truth of such views, I want to show that reading ecocritically reveals a contrary and possibly contradictory movement embedded in the poem that seeks to take us away from the artificial and unchanging towards the natural and mutable.

The pearl with which this poem famously begins encapsulates the two worlds of nature and artifice. Unlike the gemstones that make up the walls of the New Jerusalem, pearls do not need to be cut or polished in order to achieve the lustre for which they are so highly valued. Nor can they be altered to improve the condition in which they are discovered: perfection in their case is found, not made. This holds true even if the pearl in question is a cultured pearl, rather than the more likely natural one.[10] Given this, the pearls we envisage as jewellery are in a way more natural than, say, rubies or diamonds. Such hard gems must be quarried and then polished, and perhaps also cut, before being incorporated into jewellery, clothing or objects. In the case of pearls, human artifice comes into play only when piercing them for threading or when setting them, at which point the skill is to create a jewel which is seen to enhance the natural beauty of the pearl without overpowering it. All this is evident in the first stanza of the poem where the pearl is said to be worthy of setting in the best gold, 'clanly clos in golde so clere' (2) because it is perfect, 'wythouten spot', the phrase which links all the stanzas in the first section of the poem. That concern with the right setting for such a valuable stone is still in play when the narrator bemoans the fact that, rather than being set in the gold it merits, his perfect pearl is surrounded by earth 'so clad in clot' (22). However, the ensuing lament 'O moul, thou marres a myry juele' (23) is more than regret at a clumsy piece of jewellery making, it is literally true that earth will eat into a pearl and gradually dissolve it. Moreover, while the concern with setting shows how the pearl is valued as a stone, an inert but valuable object, the concern with its dissolution reveals an apprehension of it as a more organic, if not actually living thing. This may reflect the fact that a pearl grows inside a living being (an oyster or other mollusc) or it may more simply reflect the fragility of pearls, with their easily chipped and damaged surface.

The narrator's distress at the pearl's current misplacement is further compounded by the belief that pearls were nourished by heavenly dew entering the open shell of the mollusc in which, it is implied, the seed lay ready. John Trevisa, translating Bartholomaeus Anglicus, *De Proprietatibus Rerum* at the end of the fourteenth century, describes the process thus:

> It bredith in fleissh of schellefissh and is somtyme yfounde in the brayn of the fissh, and is ygendred of a dewe of hevene the which dew schellefissh fongeth in certeyn tyme of the yere. (Trevisa 1975: 587)[11]

For readers of *Pearl*, this image of the pearl as an organic, if not actually sentient, thing which in effect descends from heaven, adds a further level of association between the stone and the maiden, who also descends from heaven in the narrator's dream. This understanding of how pearls are engendered makes even more sense of the development of the image through the poem's third stanza. Here the notion that a pearl lost in the ground will eventually rot away combines with the knowledge that bodies likewise rot, but is prevented from being merely morbid by the recognition that the result is superlatively fertile soil. The idea is literal as well as consolatory, as the pearl, now also understood as engendering, heavenly nourishment, gives rise to the plants whose scent comforts the narrator. The close association of what is in the ground affecting what comes up out of it is made three times in one stanza in terms which now reflect the knowledge of a gardener more than a jeweller (not that they need be mutually exclusive):

> That spot of spyses mot nedes sprede,
> Ther such ryches to rot is runne.
>
> (25–6)

> Flor and fryte may not be fede
> Ther hit doun drof in moldes dunne;
>
> (29–30)

> Of goud uche goude is ay bygonne;
> So semly a sede moght fayly not,
>
> (33–4)

It is often taken as proof of the value of the pearl that the plants that spring up from it are highly valued for their medicinal and culinary purposes, as well as aesthetically. It is less often noted that pearls, too, were used medicinally,[12] so, even in the choice of plants, the poem perpetuates its focus on the pearl. As it does so, it moves us into the garden and field, away from the courtly or mercantile concerns of jewels and their settings which infused the vocabulary of the opening stanza. At the same time the poem has established a way of working in two directions at once, a method that becomes a persistent habit as the poem progresses. Here, we are simultaneously looking into the ground to trace the pearl's descent and across the mound to remark the flowers growing on it – and the connection between the two is absolute: the plants spring up from the pearl which acts as both seed and fertiliser 'ther such ryches to rot is runne' (26).[13]

Having once entered this garden the poem never leaves it, for the narrator's body, like the actual pearl, remains there throughout: 'My body on balke ther bod in sweven' (62). Likewise, the actual nature within this literal garden is at work within the text, even when we might think it has been forgotten. That initial gar-

Gardens and fields

den deserves some attention therefore. To begin with, it is explicitly an 'erber' (38) and as such is a place set aside not only for the cultivation of medicinal and culinary plants but also as an area designed to restore flagging human spirits. Gordon points out that the spice plants listed here were valued as much for having the richest scents as for any precise kitchen use and are to be found decorating the landscapes of romance as much as growing in more pragmatic places. When we add to this his comment that the 'huyle' of the grave mound may be connected with 'hile' denoting a cluster of plants, we arrive at a picture of a densely planted area, perhaps a particular spot within a larger garden, where the scents of the plants conspire to provide an especially powerful result.[14] The affective force of this planting is evident in the phrase 'suche odour to my hernes schot' (58) which sends the narrator into 'a slepyng-slaghte' (59) and so into his vision. This sequence is echoed at the beginning of the last section of the poem when he is overcome by catching sight of the pearl-maiden amongst the company surrounding the Lamb: 'Delyt me drof in yye and ere' (1153). In each case there is a sense of real physical force ('schot', 'drof') as the narrator's senses are assailed by what he smells or sees. It is significant that the initial assault is set off by the weight of his body falling on the plants, thus releasing a sudden explosion of scent. In each case a dramatic physical action on the narrator's part returns him to the actual garden mound. However spiritual the poem becomes, and of course it is intensely spiritual as well as intellectual in its central debate, it thus forcibly reminds us of the power of the physical world. Tacitly it also offers the idea that comfort can be found here not only through intellectual or religious effort, but also physically through the effect of the plants with which we surround ourselves.

Regarded in this light, the original garden takes on an abiding importance in the poem, for although this is the most humble, it is also the most real of the landscapes at work in the text. Moreover, although the term 'erber' probably indicates a walled garden, this is not the self-contained, even self-obsessed place of the gardens of romance. Where the ornate and rarefied romance garden invites those who enter to leave behind all associations with the outside world,[15] the entry into this 'erber grene' (38) is accompanied by a reference to what is going on in everyday life:

> In Auguste in a hygh seysoun,
> Quen corne is corven wyth crokes kene.
>
> (39–40)

It is easy to see here an emotive connection between the cutting down of ripe corn and the death of a young girl, but this is also a specific reference to a precise activity, harvest, which contrasts sharply with the celebrations of spring, May and burgeoning new growth that typically preface garden walks and dream visions.[16] The brief enumeration of the plants thriving on the mound (pinks or carnations, ginger, borage, peony) again makes us look at an actual patch of ground with specific spices grown there for particular purposes. The effect is altogether different from the beautiful, but essentially literary, one of the typical romance setting in which the plants are often left unspecified.[17] The end result is an entirely credible, actual garden which not only is easy to envisage but is also a readily accessible place. It may have an air of privacy, but not of exclusion.

In fact this humble 'erber' is the only space in the poem which does not exclude the narrator in one way or another: he seems to be an interloper in the grand leisure garden of his dream[18] and is explicitly barred access to the grounds across the river and particularly to the city in which the Pearl-maiden dwells. Moreover, although in one way the path he follows in his dream is that of someone walking away from a grand house, through a walled garden, into the parkland beyond, in another it is typical of dream experience (actual and literary) in that elements of the waking world's geography appear in changed form in the dream. Thus the hill from which the narrator sees the heavenly city is the dream equivalent of the mound upon which he falls asleep, while the trees of the parkland in which he finds himself may echo the trained trees and vines of a bower within a garden, one of the available meanings of 'erber'.[19] Such references to the initial setting tend to be overlooked as readers are caught up in the impressive artifice of the dream world and the increasingly metaphorical tone of the poem. The intricacy of the text, with its ornate language and extensive descriptions of the wonders of the dream world in which the gravel is made up of precious stones, tends to lead to the assumption that the poem uses the contrast of natural and artificial as a way of pointing the argument about valuing what is eternal, rather than seeking to hold onto what is ephemeral. That assumption in turn requires the forced return to the garden at the end of the poem to be read as a moment of defeat, which either leaves the narrator inconsolable or finds him resolving to live henceforth by regarding this world as merely a place of preparation for the next. Both these interpretations relegate the actual garden to a secondary role, just as privileging the allegorical aspects of the text relegates vehicles of that allegory to the role of mere tool. Of course the poem is powerfully metaphorical, but we do well to acknowledge its literal levels as well and to resist the temptation to see the literal and metaphoric as being diametrically opposed.[20]

In its progression through its various landscapes, *Pearl* is more gradual than received wisdom leads us to believe. Section II with its concatenation on 'adubbement' (adornment) takes us into a forest of precious metals, with crystal cliff, silver leaves and pebbles of pearls and other precious stones. Yet, although it is true that by line 117 we seem to be in an entirely artificial landscape, we have arrived there through a series of stages, not a sudden switch. The first hint appears with the 'rych rokkes' (67) with their 'glemande glory' (70) which transmute to 'crystal klyffes so cler of kynde' (74). So far there is nothing that specifies abnormal materials, on the contrary 'of kynde' should remind us that rock can indeed shine naturally, whether because of water or because it has been polished by the winds. The 'holtewodes' with their dark trunks create a real, if exceptional, forest and due attention notes that the leaves of line 77 are like burnished silver, not actually made out of it. Too often our awareness of the narrator's identity as a jeweller (whether an actual craftsman or a merchant)[21] leads us to read this dream landscape as one made up of precious metals and stones. However, taking too quick a leap to an impressive but manufactured forest makes us blind to the actual pleasure park being described here. The enclosed space of the herb garden has been replaced by the far larger, but no less enclosed and humanly maintained arena of a leisure garden or parkland. The dreaming narrator's assumption that the waterways he sees are aesthetic boundaries used to mark out different areas within the park (139–42) and his expectation of finding the manor house ('mote' 142) further along the stream, show that he believes this is a humanly created landscape.[22] By now he is absorbed in puzzling out his surroundings and is taking more notice of what is around him than he did in the garden, where everything was linked to his grief and subordinated to it. We readers may have been struck by the beauty of that original garden, but for the dreamer every element within it had meaning only in so far as it referred back to the lost pearl. Now, in this strange dream wood, he is taken out of himself (literally, as his spirit springs from his dormant body) and is able to look at the landscape around him directly. Significantly, at the height of his description of this magnificent place, the dreamer is thrown back to the natural world, specifically the world as it appears when humans are at their least active. The only way to communicate the effect of the brightness of the stones in the riverbed is to refer the reader upwards, to imagine the stars on a winter's night:

> As stremande sternes, quen strothe-men slepe,
> Staren in welkyn in wynter nyght.
>
> (115–16)[23]

Yet, despite the detail of this description, the narrator reveals himself as relentlessly anthropocentric, if not simply solipsistic. The splendour around him must, he believes, denote some grand house in the vicinity and it is the hope of seeing this that draws him on.

Criticism of the poem tends to echo the narrator's own egocentricity. Stanbury explains how the description of the garden reveals the dreamer's spatial relationships by asserting that 'in the *erber*, . . . the narrator immediately establishes that the garden is a circumscribed space in which he is the central figure' (Stanbury 1991: 17). While this holds true in terms of the way he dictates the focus of the text, it is at least as accurate to say that in the garden it is the absent pearl (whether stone or child) that is the central entity, the thing that gives the garden meaning, and that much of the poem's impetus comes from the narrator's powerful wish to retrieve this lost focal point. The desire is necessarily a hopeless one and even the attempt to pinpoint the physical spot which holds the pearl is vain; the narrator himself acknowledges that the pearl is now dispersed into the ground and the flowers that spring from it. As Nick Davis puts it 'its place of interment is a spot of physical matter . . .; but its lack of a spot, as in the refrain, also latently implies the impossibility of making any physical discovery of it'.[24] It is the awareness of this impossibility and the concomitant loss of meaning for the garden space that is so disconcerting for our egocentric and anthropocentric narrator. He is more at home in the dream park of section III, even though, paradoxically, his own position there is close to that of an interloper. Its lack of familiarity lends emotional distance which allows him to take pleasure in the estate with its imposing trees and impressive streams. He stops being a mourning jeweller and becomes a man able to assess his surroundings. However, as sections III and IV progress, there is a growing sense of overload: adornment moves to excess, as 'adubbement' is replaced by 'more and more', highlighting the motif of over-decoration, which is also the kind of saturated reaction to the natural world we more readily associate with Keats. Here, though, part of the headiness comes from the belief that all this landscape is humanly designed and created, for the fleeting speculation that these are the environs of the earthly Paradise (137) is soon set aside for more concrete thoughts of human pleasure gardens and manor houses.

This habit of overlooking the ways of the natural world in a desire to concentrate on the humanly created one gradually emerges as a fundamental ill in *Pearl*, one which the text seeks to correct by repeatedly, but discreetly, asserting the natural processes of growth and decay over those of manufacture: in the mortal world mutability is to be preferred to stasis. This process of gentle correction begins with the appearance of the maiden, who almost immediately recalls the poem's initial landscape with the phrase 'this gardyn gracios gaye' (260). Her reference to 'cofer' in the previous line tactily acknowledges the role the first garden played as a graveyard for the narrator's pearl, but, rejecting that original notion as a 'tale mysetente' (257), she marks a distinction between the original 'erber' and the garden in which she stands. On her bank the grounds are evidently leisure gardens in which she will 'lenge fore ever and play' (262) but there is a suggestion of a boundary set and maintained in her use of 'this' (260) and 'hereinne' (262) which subtly emphasises that she is on one side of the river, the dreamer on the other. Despite being so close, they are not occupying the same space and it is possible to detect here the shadow of a hint that it may not be only on the matter of the death of the pearl that the narrator is mistaking the point. In this text different places mean different things, however similar they may appear.

Rather than elaborating the distinction at this point, the maiden turns to the root of the problem and promptly recasts the narrator's central symbol: 'that that thou lestes was bot a rose' (269). By redefining the lost object as a rose, not a gem, the maiden shifts the terms of the lament, placing it firmly in the realms of the material, natural and, above all, mortal, world. She thus brings him back from his speculation about parks and great houses to consider his actual known world: the one of cultivated gardens in which roses will bloom and, inevitably, die. Initially, the change of symbol serves to point the difference between the mortal and the eternal, as the dreamer is encouraged to rethink his loss in terms which will allow the lost one to retain her value, but which also include the appropriateness of death. As a rose, she becomes the chief of flowers, just as she was the best of pearls, and as a flower it becomes right that she bloom and fade. The aptness of the maiden's choice of image is increased when we remember that medieval roses, unlike the majority of our latter-day cultivars, had single, short-lived blooms. A garden was the proper place to grow the domestic plants, where they were trained against walls and tended carefully to prevent them reverting to wild roses.[25] This need for care adds to the appropriateness of the rose as the symbol for a young child and indeed that thread of fragility continues throughout Trevisa's entry on the rose, as he describes how the rosebud is protected by green leaves until it is ready, and these green leaves are themselves soft and so protected by greater, red ones.

> And for the[i] beth tendre and feble to holde togideres in the bygynnynge, therfore aboute thilke smale grene leves benethe the rede tendre leves and neisshe beth ysette al aboute, and in the myddel therof is seyne the seed. (Trevisa 1030)

Right at the centre of all these protective layers is not the flower but the seed of the 'smale rounde' fruit – and suddenly there is another connection between rose and pearl as the essence of each is revealed to be a small, circular object that grows inside another living thing. For the rose to germinate it must, of course, be seeded in earth and here the final move of the symbol reaches it cleverest and perhaps most moving part. For, understood in these terms, the soil that threatened to destroy the pearl in line 23 becomes the necessary catalyst for the fruit of the dead rose to become the eternal, heavenly, pearl. It is a masterly attempt at consolation through image, but is has a fatal flaw: however beautiful, a pearl is not a rose. The maiden's change of terms reveals an equally absolute change in matter: whatever the narrator thinks, this maiden, standing in the impressive grounds across the river, is not the same as the young girl buried in the spice garden – and the maiden knows it.

The maiden's rose image resonates throughout the rest of the poem, even though it was apparently introduced with the sole purpose of being set aside. In attempting to supplant the idea of losing a pearl with the concept of seeing a rose die in the natural course of events the poem has started a series of images and connections that continue to have a subliminal and subtextual effect, even when the poem itself enters into what appears to be the entirely metaphorical and intellectual realms of theological debate. One of the strands thus touched on is that of the 'raysoun bref' (268). In the context of the maiden's speech it is clear that it means 'trivial matter' and its collocation in parallel with the preceding term 'mad porpose' reinforces this interpretation. Yet given the wider context of the question of understanding, or at least coming to terms with, the processes of life, the phrase takes on a wider significance. In this context reason is at best a vital, but crucially limited, faculty. Crucially limited because to assume that a human faculty could encompass the mysteries of the whole world, is to be guilty of an act of extreme, even sinful, arrogance.[26] Alan of Lille dramatised this understanding of Reason as being incapable of going beyond a certain point in his *Anticlaudianus* and it is a view echoed in a wide variety of medieval texts, not least *Piers Plowman*.[27] This medieval acknowledgement of the limitations of reason finds an echo in latter-day challenges to the primacy of rationalist understandings of the world, of which the most appropriate for green readers are put forward by Val Plumwood (2002). Yet it may also be argued that reason is our main tool for understanding anything and it would be preposterous to cast it aside altogether (not that Plumwood is arguing this). A clue to how to resolve the difficulty may lie in the Pearl-maiden's choice of phrase: 'a raysoun bref' may be interpreted as a fleeting, short-lived, reason rather than a trivial one. If we adopt this reading then it becomes possible to say that such a faculty may be properly used in the equally short-lived, mortal world that the image of the rose is supposed to help us understand. There is a cross-current in the text here as, in setting aside an image of permanence in favour of one of mutability, the poem tacitly acknowledges that such mutable things have a value.

The point is, of course, that what is required is a proper understanding and valuing of the nature of each thing as itself, not as something else. The lost girl thus 'is' a rose who has been misunderstood as a pearl. It is only when she is transported beyond the mortal world that she becomes a pearl, but, as we have seen, that transportation is in the fullest sense a translation: a carrying over which effects fundamental change, requiring her to be understood in different terms. This insistence on understanding something as itself, rather than seeing it in different terms, casts some shadow over the glories of the parkland in which this debate takes place, for, while the initial 'erber' was described in simple terms, these more splendid grounds have been depicted mainly through simile. It is these comparisons that have led us away from the actual world of cliffs and leaves into the imagined one of beryl and silver. If we take the maiden's words to heart, we are mistaken in regarding this dreamscape as a more valuable setting. Rather, the humble but real and above all mutable garden is to be preferred to the impressive pleasure grounds, however skilfully wrought.

Although the plot of the poem takes us into increasingly metaphorical realms depicted in ever increasing degrees of artificiality, and even though we must bear in mind that 'artificial' was a term of praise not snide criticism in the Middle Ages, it nevertheless remains true that this early admonition to value the passing things of this world has made its mark. Hence, when the poem seems to be at its most literary and removed from the every day, citing the description of the New Jerusalem found in Revelations, this other mundane world erupts to the surface in the narrator's sudden outburst:

> I am bot mokke and mul among,
> And thou so ryche, a reken rose,
> And bydes here by thys blysful bonc
> Ther lyves lyste may never lose.

(905–8)

The narrator seems unaware of the extent of the challenge issued by his terminology and is immediately caught up in concerns about how the maidens are housed, retaining the mental geography of manor house surrounded by parkland that he adopted upon entering his dream. His language, however, reminds us of the waking world outside the dream, the one of common soil, fertile ground and transient roses. The contrast between the mutable and the eternal is suggested also by the description of the delights of this blissful shore which 'never lose'. The images are at odd with each other, for the rose was introduced as the epitome of ephemeral beauty and as such has no place in a land of eternal pleasure. By employing the maiden's terminology the narrator unwittingly challenges the delight of an eternity in which roses do not fade. It is possible to interpret his outburst as a sign of his continued misapprehension and to see in his adoption of the rose image (an image, we recall, invoked solely for the purpose of being immediately discarded) a second act of misplacement: when he was in a real garden he thought of her as a pearl; now, in this land of jewels, he calls her a rose. One might add that the narrator is doggedly, but mistakenly, asserting his human perspective, even to the extent of implementing a value-system that confers the greatest value on the rarest thing (fresh roses are as rare in heaven as perfect pearls are on earth). Yet although such readings meet the challenge in terms of the intellectual debate of the poem, it leaves untouched the more emotive question of whether permanence is in fact to be preferred to mutability. The dreamer's outburst reminds us that however splendid life on the further shore may be, it is not there that we do our living, but here, in the world of 'mokke and mul'. The actual, material, natural world is proving resistant to being overwritten by simile and metaphor, as the language of the text never quite forgets the real world in the way that its protagonist does. It thus comes as no surprise to the reader that the narrator's attempt to cross the river ends in disaster. By plunging into the water he treats this landscape as an actual physical place, running towards the river as if it were a real torrent complete with danger of being swept away.[28] However this is not a real river but a symbolic boundary, and his attempt to cross it returns him from imagined 'bonc' to actual 'erber wlonk' (1171).

It is hard not to share some of the narrator's disappointment at this point, despite the fact that the waking garden is now delightful ('wlonk') – an adjective previously applied to the dream's park (122). In part this sense of disappointment is essential to the poem, ensuring that we ruefully acknowledge the truth of the narrator's assertion that people always want to seize more happiness than they are due – 'ay wolde man of happe more hente / Then moghte by ryght upon hem clyven' (1195–6). Even so one is left, rightly, with a sense of abiding loss; for the poem is not denying that loss and grief at loss exist, it is just offering a way of mitigating bereavement. The very terms in which the narrator summarises the dream in the final stanza recall too vividly the loss that began the poem for any reader to believe that the loss itself has been forgotten:

> Over this hyul this lote I laghte,
> For pyty of my perle enclyin.
>
> (1205–6)

Here 'laghte' becomes a complex word, for although the sentence demands the meaning 'received', it cannot override the connotations of ensnarement suggested by the word's primary meaning 'catch' or 'trap'. There is thus a suggestion that the narrator is bound to his human lot by being on the grave mound that is the source of his grief, his dream and his poem, yet also that he recognises that he is trapped by it. He is still alive and part of the mortal world, and as such is denied access to the immortal realm glimpsed in his vision. Likewise 'pyty of my perle enclyin' revives not only the emotion but also the image of the man literally prostrate with grief. Thus, despite the apparent acceptance that comes with committing the pearl to God, a sense of unease remains, which is increased as the narrator puts aside the initial garden setting, and indeed the organic world as a whole, in a final choice of terms that seeks to transform him and by association all Christians into pearls: 'He gef uus to be his homly hyne/ Ande precious perles unto his pay' (1211–12).

Famously, that final line echoes the first and so returns us to the garden where the poem began. Yet this skilful closing of the circle of the text simultaneously creates a disconcerting sense of displacement which is enacted in the form of the verse itself. When the last and the first lines are put together it is clear that the link between them does not adhere fully to the pattern of the rest of the poem:

Gardens and fields

> Ande precious perles unto his pay.
>
> (1212)
>
> Perle, plesaunte to prynces paye
>
> (1)

The word 'pay' has been the final, *c* rhyming, word of the concatenating line of the final section; strictly, that word should appear towards the beginning of the first line of the next stanza with the new *a* rhyme appearing at the end of the line. Instead, the *c* rhyme-word of the final stanza, 'pay', becomes the *a* rhyme 'paye', while the word 'perle' lies in the position we expect 'pay' to be in. Having 'perles' present in the last line only adds to the sense of slight disorientation: all the elements required for the verse form to be maintained are present, they are just not employed in the way we have been led to expect. Although this effect is obvious only when we try to make the poem into a true circle by reading the first line directly after the last, the fact that the text does not actually comply with the expected circularity indicates that something has changed during the course of its narrative. We may be returned to its initial setting, but not to precisely the same emotional or intellectual starting point.

This impression of having progressed fits perfectly with readings that understand *Pearl* as a poem of human consolation, but the conclusion is less comforting for those taking a greener stance. The frustration of our technical expectations is paralleled by a similar misalignment in the outcome for the natural world. *Pearl*'s rhetoric seems to privilege the metaphorical world over the literal one: the central image of the pearl itself has moved further and further away from being an actual stone as the richness of its symbolic value has been exploited through the verse. Yet, throughout, the literal natural world has persisted in reappearing and so when 'this hyul' brings us back to the actual garden of the start of the poem we sense that we are being returned to a position where the literal landscape is once again uppermost. This reinstatement brings with it both relief at returning to a recognisable and comprehensible world, and unease at the way this world is immediately set aside as the narrator turns his attention to becoming himself a worthy pearl within a princely household. It can be said, perhaps rightly, that the narrator has finally understood the import of the maiden's teachings and, able now to see the pearl purely as a metaphor, is in a position to value such symbolic pearls in the proper way. Accordingly, the narrator casts his new understanding in terms of human social relations and the natural world is finally relegated to a secondary role. Yet an ending which so easily dismisses the only actual physical landscape in the poem should leave us with some qualms, for it is in the actual world that we and indeed the narrator must still live. In echoing the first line, and so reminding us of the original misconception of the lost pearl, the poem thus not only reminds us of the beauty of the initial garden setting but also tacitly admits the continued relevance of our natural world.

This final, fuller, understanding of the pearl (if such it indeed is) seems to come at the expense of appreciating the rose, yet earlier in the poem it the manufactured world and the natural one were inextricably linked and the narrator appeared to understand and indeed collude with the maiden's redefinition of herself as both rose and pearl. The moment occurs in section XVI of the poem (lines 913–72) where the jeweller/narrator calls the maiden 'flor' (962) thus indicating that he has accepted and understood her previous argument that what he lost should be understood as a flower; a rose which naturally dies. As the stanza goes on the natural and manufactured worlds blend in the rhyming words: the narrator uses 'bor' (bower, 964) for the maiden's current dwelling-place, a word that can mean both chamber and garden area, while the maiden uses 'tor' (tor or tower, 966) for the city in which she now lives. Significantly, most editors gloss 'tor' here as tower or stronghold, allowing the immediate context (the description of the New Jerusalem) to sway their interpretation; but there is no reason why we should not also have an image of a natural tor, particularly as it is common to find strongholds built on hills. Moreover, the landscape is explicitly hilly at this point: the maiden tells the dreamer to walk along the riverbank until he reaches a hill whence he will see a city, shining on another hill on the opposite bank. While one might argue that this stanza shows the harmonious blending of natural and artificial worlds is possible only in dreams or in the next life, I think it actually demonstrates the resilience of the natural world in this most artificial of poems. If we too, as readers, have acknowledged the resonance of that natural rose image and come to re-evaluate the worth of non-human, natural objects, then the dreamer's final words as we and he return to the hill in the last stanza must leave us a little uncertain of exactly where we now stand.

The difficulties of how we should understand our right relation to the world are explored in different, but no less allegorical, terms by *Piers Plowman*. Here the question is cast in the context of the wider world, of open fields and common experience, rather than in the enclosed setting of a particular garden and individual emotion; nonetheless here, as in *Pearl*, an abiding sense of unease surrounds the topic. The temptation to regard the non-human world primarily as a source for the metaphorical understanding of divine matters tussles with the actual experience of being in the world and having to acknowledge that humans are part of it. Langland's use of allegory scrutinises our relation to the material world around us and in so doing reveals how the terms in which we think affect our attitude towards the non-human world. There are many passages in this complex poem that would reward ecocritical reading but there is one section in which he examines two of the dominant images for how we think about our relations to the natural world. In Passus XI of the B-text Langland explores the ramifications of the ideas of seeing the world as a mirror and as a book. Each of these tropes depends on the notion of the natural world displaying the order of God and as such relies to a large extent on a predominantly allegorical habit of thought that is often regarded as the epitome of the medieval world-view. Gabriel Josipovici encapsulated this outlook and our latter-day view of it in his declaration 'Never has there been such faith in the phenomenal' (Josipovici 1979: 29). Yet while the spirit of that assertion is broadly sound, we must be careful not to allow the allegorical interpretation of the phenomenal to override its acknowledged material and affective presence. As Susan Handelman has usefully pointed out:

> Metaphor does not discard the particular, the letter, on the way to the universal; instead, metaphor exists within the tension of identity and difference, and metaphorical resemblance is at bottom, a unity of resemblance and difference.[29]

Handelman's use of the term 'unity' makes the position seem more comfortable than perhaps it is, but she is right to assert the abiding presence of the actual thing being used metaphorically, even in the most symbolic context. This is particularly true of Langland's complex use of figurative language which can move freely between direct observation, symbol, metaphor and fully fledged allegory but always retains an immediacy which demands his audience visualise the elements at play and considers them as physical as well as metaphorical entities. In addition, Josipovici's terms are particularly appropriate when considering Langland, who never allows the issue of faith to be far from the surface of his poem. In particular he is concerned about where a religious but uneducated person may find true guidance, and it is this concern that leads him to the two tropes of mirror and book, for each of them purports to be a way for the unlearned but earnest to learn something of God's ways.

The mirror trope is both the first explored and the one most swiftly found lacking. It is held up to Wil by Fortune who presides over an inner dream occasioned by Wil's argument with Scripture about the merits and demerits of untutored faith. Fortune carries Wil off into the land of longing

> And in a mirour that highte Middelerthe she made me to biholde.
> Sithen she seide to me, 'Here myghtow se wondres,
> And knowe that thow coveitest, and come therto, peraunter.'
> (B.XI.9–11)[30]

At this stage in the poem's general narrative Wil is engaged in a search for Dowel, Dobet and Dobest, as he seeks to learn how a person ought to live properly in this world. Initially it seems perfectly possible that Wil will learn something to help him from Fortune's mirror, since such knowledge might count as what he desires ('coveitest') and because he is already attuned to the notion of learning through wonders, having begun the poem in search of them: 'Wente wide in this world wondres to here' (B.Prol.4). However, the problem with looking in a mirror is that what we see tends reflect ourselves, either directly (if we hold it up straight in front of us) or indirectly, revealing what can be seen from our particular position depending on the angle at which we tilt the glass. An inescapable conclusion is that what we see in a world-mirror is necessarily dictated by what and where we are. Such a conclusion would fit well with the problem often raised in ecological discussions, that the human species is incapable of thinking itself out of centre place in the world. However hard we try, we are inevitably anthropocentric and narcissistic. Certainly Langland's Wil discovers this to be the case as what he actually encounters in Fortune's mirror are the familiar vanities of human life: power, social standing, riches and sexual conquests. The inner-dream becomes a nightmare, as Wil seems to grow old and feeble and, inevitably, finds himself deserted. The notion of the mirror being the natural world has been forgotten: this Middelerthe is entirely a place of human making.

Matters are not greatly improved when we explore the allusion to Alan of Lille that underlies Langland's mirror, even though Alan sustains the notion of the mirror being whole natural world. In the *Anticlaudianus* it is Reason who holds the mirror, which is golden-framed and tripartite, and allows her to see the relations of matter and form as they underpin the workings of the universe. In particular, in the third glass she sees the pure idea reflected somewhat dimly in the world, its copy:

> Qualiter in mundo fantasma resultat ydee,
> Cuius inoffensus splendor sentitur in umbra.
>
> (I.500–1)
>
> (Here it was possible to see how the image of the idea is reflected in the universe and the idea's pure splendour is sensed in its copy.) (Sheridan 1973: 65)

The choice of 'umbra' suggests this is a rather shadowy copy, and this coupled with 'sentitur' (sensed) indicates that this world hints at its original rather than faithfully recreating it.[31] Only Reason knows how to make proper use of this mirror, which implies that humans are obliged to use their reason to puzzle out the meanings of the examples presented to them by the rest of the world. Yet, as we have already seen, the human reason is also a limited faculty, incapable of reaching the heights of spiritual or religious understanding.[32] More to the point, both Langland and Alan seem to find the mirror motif limited and leave it behind in favour of other ways of exploring their chosen topics.[33] Langland presents a sceptical view of the benefits of regarding the world as a mirror, seemingly all too aware of the likelihood of it being used to reflect only human preoccupations and desires. For him mirrors distort: a statement that would be particularly true of medieval mirrors made of thicker and more uneven glass than our factory-produced ones or, more usually, of highly polished metal. Such materials meant one did indeed, with Paul, behold in a glass 'darkly' (1 Cor. 13: 12). Wil's experience in the world reflected by Fortune's mirror combines this sense of obfuscation with a familiar satirical version of the world as conceived from a self-interested human viewpoint. This is how the world appears to us all too often, if we look only for ourselves within it, and believe this earth to be solely ours. The world of natural phenomena has been utterly overlaid with that of human preoccupations.

That world is reintroduced some three hundred lines later and is once again given the name Middle Earth and once more associated with 'wonders'. This time, however, the world is displayed as a book and the figure presiding over that display is Kynde, whose very name associates him with nature, both in terms of the created world and individual character.[34]

> And slepynge I seigh al this; and sithen cam Kynde
> And nempned me by my name, and bad me nymen hede,
> And thorugh the wondres of this world wit for to take.
> And on a mountaigne that Myddelerthe highte, as me tho thoughte,
> I was fet forth by ensaumples to knowe,
> Thorugh ech a creature, Kynde my creatour to lovye.
>
> (B.XI.320–5)

The book of the world Kynde displays here is evidently an illustrated volume in which the creatures are living 'ensaumples', illuminating as well as comprising God's order. They are thus things to be observed and enjoyed as well as studied and explained, much as the pictures in a book could offer pleasure and even edification to those unable to read the accompanying words. Certainly this is the analogy found in Hugh of St. Victor's use of the topos in the twelfth century.[35]

> Universus enim mundus iste sensibilis quasi quidam liber est scriptus digito Dei, hoc est virtute divina creatus, et singulae creaturae quasi figurae quaedam sunt non humano placito inventae, sed divino arbitrio institutae ad manifestandam invisibilium Dei sapientiam. Quemadmodum autem si illiteratus quis apertum librum videat, figuras aspicit, litteras non cognoscit: ita stultus et *animalis homo*, qui *non percipit ea quae Dei sunt (I Cor. II)*, in visibilibus istis creaturis foris videt speciem, sed intus non intelligit rationem. Qui autem spiritualis est et omnia dijudicare potest, in eo quidem quod foris considerat pluchritudinem operis, intus concipit quam miranda sit sapientia Creatoris. Et ideo nemo est cui opera Dei mirabilia

non sint, . . . Bonum ergo est assidue contemplari et admirari opera divina

(For the entire visible world is like a book written by the finger of God, that is, created by divine goodness, and the individual creatures are, as it were, figures, not invented by human pleasure, but devised by divine judgement to reveal the wisdom of the God of invisible things. Moreover, just as when an illiterate man looks on an open book, he sees the shapes but does not understand the letters, in the same way he is an ignoramus and the 'simple man' who 'does not perceive those things which are of God' (1 Cor. 2); in the case of those visible creatures, outwardly he sees their appearance, but inwardly does not comprehend their rationale. On the other hand, one who is spiritual and able to distinguish all things, while outwardly considering the beauty of the work, inwardly recognises how wonderful the wisdom of the Creator is. And indeed there is no one for whom the works of God are not wonderful . . . Therefore it is good to contemplate them carefully and wonder at the divine works.)[36]

Despite employing the idea of the world as a book, it appears that Hugh is not concerned with its most obvious implication – that everyone has access to this particular volume. Confidant that he is addressing fellow intellectuals, Hugh moves swiftly over the notion of the world being something for all to gaze upon, educated and ignorant alike, into the greater understanding that he asserts is the province of the learned alone. His priorities are clear in his use of the Biblical citation (1 Corinthians 2) to endorse his point about the non-spiritual or natural man, thereby underlining the distinction between the unlearned and the learned. The educated are a couple of steps further away from the natural world than the 'simple' and it is implied that this is a better place to be.

Notably, Hugh omits any reference to Romans 1: 18–20, which asserts that what can be known about God is to be found manifest in the created world – surely a point germane to the subject in hand. The Wycliffite version of Romans reads:

For the wrath of God is shown from heaven on all unpiety and wickedness of those men that withhold the truth of God in unrightwiseness. For that thing of God that is known, is shown to them, for God has shown them. For the invisible things of Him that are understood, are beheld of the creature of the world by those things that are made, yea, and the everlasting virtue of Him and the Godhead, so that they mow not be excused. (*Wycliffe*, Cooper ed.)

The term 'creature of the world' retains the intimate connection between humankind and the rest of the world that lies at the root of the world/book trope. It may be this that deters Hugh from using it. Certainly, although he is careful to acknowledge that everyone, including the learned, ought to be open to the direct, affective, power of contemplating the natural world, Hugh's preference for an intellectual and broadly allegorical interpretation is none the less evident in his haste to move on to discuss the technicalities of reading by the spiritually educated, who are also intellectually trained.[37]

Although Hugh hurries on, we need not do likewise: moving too soon and too exclusively to allegorical translation does a disservice to both us and the text. Much of the appeal of the world-book topos is its suggestion that some apprehension of the divine goodness and power ('virtue') is available to all. The majority may not be able to move beyond apprehension to comprehension, but acknowledging the wonder of the created world goes some way towards appreciating the power behind it. Even Hugh, anxious to get on to higher intellectual levels, and away from the realms of thought shared with the ignorant, is aware of the validity and indeed importance of admiration when considering the earth.[38] Notice how the wonder of creation is emphasised ('miranda', 'mirabilia', 'admirari'); this is the right immediate reaction of ignorant and educated alike to the world around us, but it is the element most often overlooked. It is this sense of wonder and a concomitant acknowledgement of the beauty of things in themselves that Stephen R.L. Clark suggests we need to recover now when thinking of the earth (Clark 1993). Without it and the reverence that comes with it, he argues, there is little hope of regarding earth, be it as soil, planet or creation, in a way which will compel us to treat it with respect. Significantly, in Clark's argument this admiration, available and indeed necessary to all, is expressly not based on an allegorical understanding of the world: such attitudes perpetuate a sense of division between human and rest-of-world, privileging the human much as a clumsy reading of allegory privileges the interpretation over the vehicle. Instead 'we must . . . stop treating phenomena as episodes in some familiar fable' (Clark 1993: 31) and 'wake up to a real recognition of the world as something other than our obedient shadow' (22). Such an attitude is both unmediated and religious, requiring that we regard the world as 'something or some things that we must recognize a sacred' (22) albeit not in a way which requires engagement with specific theological or philosophical debates.[39] This stance advocated here is closer to the generalised 'faith in the phenomenal' described by Josipovici than one might expect. Both demand an attentive awareness of the world around us and a direct appreciation of the earth as something which surpasses the human imagination, and which is, simply, at least as important as (for some more than) humankind. Langland's Wil looking into Kynde's book of Middelerthe enacts something of this attention. To this world, as Hugh acknowledges, the right reaction is marvel.

Hugh himself, however, falls victim to the very danger Clark seeks to avoid. By implying that the world is a book to be read by trained readers only, Hugh risks excising the element of wonder, which he seems so eager to retain ('et ideo nemo est cui opera Dei mirabilia non sint' for there is no one for whom the works of creation are not marvellous). There is no hint that the reader colludes with or is part of this text in any way and that risks setting humankind apart from the rest of the world by presenting the non-human world as a composition created for the sole purpose of being interpreted by humans. Hugh's confidence can thus give rise to increasing uncertainty on our part. Even if we accept the role of overseer bestowed on Adam by some parts of the tradition (springing of course from Genesis 1: 26), it is a perilous business to dissociate humankind from the rest of creation. To deny inclusion in the phenomenal world also denies, by implication, our connection to the spiritual one, for the role of steward rests on the belief that we are created by the same power that created the rest of the world. Lose that and we lose the literally God-given right to rule over the rest of the created world. Yet Hugh's use of this image of the world/book topos seems to encourage just such dissociation, particularly given his inclination towards intellectual debate and scholastic understanding. The trope itself, however, offers ways of retaining an appreciation of our position within creation, rather than somehow outside looking in and this is in play even within Hugh's discussion.

Arguably the point of a book is not just to be written but also to be read, and to be read by someone other than the author. The world contained within it can be brought to life and given meaning only through the reading process, that is, only with some input from a reader who seeks to understand what is going on, and thus participates in the book's world. Hugh seems to assume that the reader's prime aim is to discover the author's intention, a tricky enough aim at any time and necessarily impossible when dealing with the ineffable intentions of God. Yet the persistent unease evident in Hugh's circling of the notion of abiding wonder that all readers of the book of the world must feel, betrays an underlying sense that even for a twelfth-century theologian there was something to be said for being uneducated.[40] That thing may well be the sense of the unfamiliar that would accompany an illiterate's encounter with the written word. If familiarity breeds contempt, lack of it might give rise to admiration and thence to a desire to understand spiritually as well as, or even rather than, intellectually. The implication is that the best readers retain something of this unskilled response, even as they embark on their scholarly interpretations. It is becoming increasingly evident that a degree of wonder is crucial.

Something of this juggling of the desire to understand intellectually with the value of apprehending affectively is also evident in Langland's poem and in his use of the world/book trope in particular. As those familiar with the poem will know, the reader follows Wil, the poem's dreamer and protagonist, through a series of dreams, inner-dreams and waking passages in his quest to understand more fully the tenets of his faith, the expectations of Church and Society, and the role of the individual in both. There is never a question about the validity of Christian belief itself (this is not a heretical poem) but there is a good deal of questioning of how such belief ought to be manifested in the life of a layman. Wil, then, is not one of Hugh's learned, but nor is he quite an illiterate. Indeed the image of Wil surveying the world from the vantage point of Middel-erthe's mountain (B.XI.323, see above) presents Hugh's putative scholarly reader as an actual lay viewer, applying the idea of reading the world in literal (as well as literary) terms. He knows what he has been taught, but is puzzled as to how it sits with the life he finds himself living. He also knows that there are others who claim greater knowledge and understanding and it is to these he turns repeatedly in the hope of finding reliable and comprehensible direction. In this combination of bafflement and enquiry Wil is very much like the dreamer of

Pearl and, like *Pearl*, *Piers Plowman* also provides guide figures who are not always as directly useful as we might wish.

At first it seems that Kynde is simply another such guide and we half expect a long exposition from him or perhaps an argument similar to the one with Scripture which triggers the events of Passus XI. However this expectation is disappointed as Kynde has no direct speech at this point. Having called Wil out of the despair occasioned by his sojourn in Fortune's mirror world of sensual gratification, Kynde places Wil in a position where he can look into the world and leaves him to draw his own conclusions. It is worth reminding ourselves of the exact terms Langland uses here. Wil is commanded to pay close attention, 'nymen hede' and to learn both 'thorugh the wondres of this world' and 'by ensaumples' (B.XI.321–5). As mentioned above, these 'ensaumples' fulfil the role of book illustrations, inspiring wonder as well as offering lessons – examples in that sense. By insisting on both due attention and admiration Langland ensures that the world book is an effective as well as affective tool for thought and religious investigation. Further, his careful geographical placing of his dreamer fends off the danger that the earth and all on it may be denigrated to the level of mere tools and thus denied any inherent worth. Although able to look down from a mountain vantage point, Wil is nevertheless inside the world, not apart from it. The mountain itself is Middle-earth, i.e. the mortal world between heaven (above) and hell (below). Moreover, at this moment he is standing next to Kynde, whose name reveals the intimate connection between God and Nature, as the word 'kynde' may mean character, genus, natural world, or may be used to denote Nature as regent of God, or even God in his role as Creator. The implication is that Wil is being drawn away from abstract discussion into direct understanding, governed both by his own human nature and by the force which we still often refer to broadly as 'Nature'.

However, Langland maintains some sense of a distinction between the power that creates and that which is created by using both the single word 'kynde' and, shortly afterwards, the phrase 'Kynde my creatour'. The possibility that in the image of Kynde himself showing Wil the world we see a picture of the divine artist displaying his work is one of which Wil seems unaware and it is closed down when he draws a shadowy distinction between

'Kynde' and 'Kynde my creatour'. What is clear, though, is that this first Kynde is an innate quality, it is, perhaps, human nature as it is supposed to be, that is, attentive and receptive to the wonders of the surrounding world and capable of perceiving the creative power that lies behind it. The hint that this is innate is signalled by Langland's phrase 'nempned me by my name', which carries with it overtones of intimate recognition and knowledge of the one being summoned. Wil is in effect being called to himself, out of over-intellectual debates into a more personal and affective mode. It is only when he is in this mode that he is able to look out at the world and learn from it.

This particular volume of the world/book is also an actual panorama available to anyone willing to climb the Malvern Hills and survey the view. While creating a sense of immediacy and emphasising the idea of Wil learning by looking directly at the actual world around him, this fact also raises the associated question of how much Langland's use of this apparently thoroughly literary topos is informed by a personal reaction to a precise geography. Surprisingly, R.W. Elliott, who is so convinced and convincing about the direct effects of the north-west terrain on the *Gawain* poet, is equally sure that there is no comparable effect of the landscape on Langland's writing: 'in *Piers Plowman* there is no such attempt to integrate landscapes into the texture of the poem' (1984: 20). I suspect Elliott's view is dictated by his concentration on topographically specific words and his belief that Langland is more interested in 'social and spiritual landscapes' (18) rather than physical ones.[41] Certainly here in B.XI we are returned to the Malvern Hills of the poem's opening and invited to reflect on what can be seen there. What Wil sees is a delicate mixture of straightforward observation and informed reflection. He begins with a sweep across 'the sonne and the see and the sond after' (B.XI.326) which moves outwards into a general view of birds and beasts, each, significantly, with its mate:

> where that briddes and beestes by hir make thei yeden,
> Wilde wormes in wodes, and wonderful foweles
> With fleckede fetheres and of fele colours.
>
> (B.XI.327-9)

As his eye moves on Wil sees 'Man and his make' and although 'make' is clearly 'mate' it is ironically apt that the next lines

Gardens and fields

mention poverty and plenty, peace and war, happiness and sorrow all together and all, arguably, made by humans (B.XI.330–3). An element of satire creeps in as a contrast is implied between human behaviour and that of the beasts and birds before him. Watching them, he is struck by the reason that governs the animals' habits, particularly regarding generation, as the males and females retreat to single-sex company after the mating season, leaving pregnant beasts untroubled by continued sexual attentions. Having tipped over briefly into social comment, Wil pulls himself up to look at the world in more detail. The birds' skill in nest building attracts his admiration, and he wonders who taught them their various tricks (344–61). Finally, his attention is drawn to the flowers in the grass and the variety of their colours as by now even the humblest parts of the vegetative world command his admiration (364–7). The whole is a series of precise observations, encompassing the sea, the stars and the ground, which combine sincere love of the world with a sense of unease. Repeatedly, words such as 'wonder' (346) and 'merveilled' (350, 359) are used as well as turns of phrase indicating wonder and admiration more generally as Wil enacts the very reaction to the pictures in the world/book outlined by Hugh. He can see the figures, but declares he does not know quite what to make of them.

Yet while Langland's Wil is not a scholar he is not an utterly ignorant man either, and thereby falls into the category in which most of us would place ourselves – a category Hugh simply overlooks. Wil sees the reason behind the wonders, but what he sees depresses and indeed angers him to the point where he takes Reason himself to task.

> Ac that moost meved me and my mood chaunged –
> That Reson rewarded and ruled alle beestes
> Save man and his make: many tyme and ofte
> No Reson hem folwede, [neither riche ne povere].
> And thanne I rebukede Reson, and right til hymselven I seyde,
>   'I have wonder of thee, that witty art holde,
> Why thow ne sewest man and his make, that no mysfeet hem folwe.'
> (B.XI.368–74)

Wil's mood has changed from one of peaceful wonder to one of argumentative debate. The trigger has been his awareness that somehow mankind is not fully part of this world picture. It seems that every animal and plant does what is best innately, or (it is implied) suffers the consequences. Only humankind seems to go along without having to obey any obvious rationale and thus, importantly, is not better off, but rather abandoned by the benign force that seems to govern the rest of the world. Put briefly, Wil's complaint is that if we are part of nature we ought to be treated like the rest and looked after properly, not allowed to stray into ever increasing error uncorrected. This complaint reveals one source of his underlying unease; a sense that in some way humankind is superior to everything else, even if it is related to a degree. Moreover, our species is set aside by our Reason, the very capacity that here is portrayed as letting us down. Far from endowing us with greater insight and understanding and thus assuring us of superiority, Reason here seems to be leading us astray. Wil's response hardly improves matters. Up to this point we have been able to assume that Kynde is standing next to him, in which case one might assume that Wil would refer his anxiety to him. But Kynde has apparently slipped away, or Wil no longer sees him, and the outburst is thus directly addressed to Reason, who may be a force within nature, but is also an intellectual capacity. Ironically, this anger at not being able to understand what he sees distracts Wil from looking: he is no longer viewing the world with wonder, he is embarking on argument. From this point onward Wil loses his sense of connection with the rest of creation and with it his hope of comprehending humanity's place in its scheme.[42]

The paradox is evident: thinking rationally seems to destroy our sense of connection with the world around us and with it our ability to respond affectively and effectively to what is going on in it; yet how else can we understand? Perhaps this is the challenge: to think through and with the earth rather than just in terms of contrast to it. Kynde's attempt to make Wil establish a more affective relation to the world, based on a sense of being part of it has foundered on the way acknowledging such a relation brings home to us our innate anxieties and a deep-seated desire to see ourselves as somehow essentially, not just accidentally, distinct. The effort to recognise that we are part of a book in which we appear alongside the rest of creation is thwarted by the apparent difference between our habits and those of the other inhabitants of its pages. Using the world/book trope has cast the issue of the relation of human to natural world in terms of those between reader and text. The analogy of reading remains useful because reading necessarily involves interpretation, understanding and, frequently, confusion, paradox and lack of resolution; all of which also arise in environmental or ecological discussions. Similarly, Wil's admiration of the non-human world leads to an attentive inspection of it, which in turn leads to a perceived injustice and so into seeking an intellectually satisfying rationale that destroys that initial sense of wonder. As admiration fades, a more atavistic reaction surfaces, and the angry outburst to Reason is fuelled by dreadful anxiety that there is nothing to keep an eye on humankind, to prevent us from going horribly wrong.[43]

As a whole, though, Langland's poem shows that humankind does indeed suffer the consequences of its (ill) behaviour, not last in terms of famine and social unrest. Wil, of course, is particularly concerned with spiritual salvation or damnation and the question of how people may ensure the former rather than the latter by doing the right thing, living the right kind of life (Dowel). In accusing Reason of not preventing humans from doing the wrong thing he is overlooking the fact that Reason does not seem to be preventing wrongdoing in the rest of the world either. He specifically follows 'sewen' (334) their actions and Wil's use of the same verb in his accusation 'why thow ne sewest man and his make' (374) tacitly acknowledges this. So, despite Wil's implication that Reason is not treating humans as he does the rest of creation, the problem is in fact that he is: those who do the right thing survive, those who do not, perish. It is the lack of warning, not the lack of consequence, that Wil bemoans.

However, Wil's very anger shows that in fact there is warning to be found, if we are willing to look. It has been his contemplation of the world, of this book of nature, that has led him to realise exactly how far out of step with the rest of creation humankind is. Here we might recall Romans 1: 18–20, that text so oddly omitted by Hugh, with its pertinent implication that creation issues warning to ill-doers, just as much as it reveals wonder. The rub seems to be accepting our position as simply a component of the world, not a special case within it. If the created world does indeed offer examples, we should learn from them that actions have consequences: reason follows, it does not lead. Yet at the same time, it is clear that merely vilifying the human species and its integral faculties, like reason, will not mend matters. In the end it is a question of paying due attention to what is going on around us. An optimist might assert that the very fact that we can read the warning signs gives us the chance to correct our behaviour that Wil seems to demand. A pessimist might point out that perceiving the signs is no guarantee that we take any notice of them. In either case the key to Langland's presentation of the relationship between humans and the non-human natural world seems to be to mix wonder with empathy. His two versions of using the world as something separate from us have led in their different ways to despair. Looking into it as a mirror led to self-centred overindulgence, where what we come to is a degenerate old age and death. Reading it like a book led to wonder, but also to frustration and a hopeless railing against the very faculty that allows us to regard the world as a book to begin with.

Fortunately, these two metaphors are not the only ways the human and non-human relate in *Piers Plowman* and too much emphasis on them results in too dispiriting a poem. Langland also offers a more integrated way of thinking of humanity's role, usually couched in a subtle, often allusive use of metaphor. The most famous example is probably the opening image of the dreamer who 'shoop me into shroudes as I a sheep were' (B.Prol.2). It is almost impossible to rid oneself of the latent image of sheep wandering the hills, regardless of how much one insists upon the use of woollen clothing by the poor, the reference to hermits in the next line, or indeed the allusion to shrouds in line two. Such rural imagery persists throughout the text, however much scholars seek to assert that Langland was in fact a London poet.[44] It is also important to retain the thread of wonder that is started in these opening lines. Wil 'wente wide in this world wondres to here' (B.Prol.4) and, although his 'ferly' (which in the context of this study must recall the 'ferli' of *Orfeo*) is a dream that encompasses both king's courts and legal courts, it never strays far from those initial Malvern Hills and the countryside one can still see from them. It is as a 'feeld of folk' that Wil first views the world and it is in the hedges that mark out those fields that the birds build their nests with the skill that causes Wil to marvel in B.XI. It is also those fields that are ploughed by Piers and his helpers in B.VI in a doomed attempt to create an ideal society.

Gardens and fields

It is not just the use of the field as a conceptual space that should draw the attention of the green critic to B.VI; Langland's criticism of the prevailing economic system could also strike a chord. It is both interesting and disheartening to note that Langland would have agreed with many of our latter-day thinkers concerning the cause of famine. His passage on the ploughing of the half-acre reveals that food shortage is as much a result of poor distribution as of poor production. R.W. Frank Jnr has demonstrated the significance of the phrase 'but if the lond faille' that occurs in Piers's promise to provide for his community in B.VI.17. Frank enumerates the various causes of hunger which might be taken to prove that the land had failed (Frank 1990: 88) but also points out that Langland indicates that lack of food for the general populace has less to do with failures in production and more to do with inadequate distribution and the selfishness of the rich, especially the wealthy monks. Anima makes the point very clear:

> Right so ye riche – ye robeth that ben riche,
> And helpeth hem that helpeth yow, and yyveth ther no nede is;
> . . .
> Right so ye riche, ye robeth and fedeth
> Hem that han as ye han – hem ye make at ese.
>   Ac religiouse that riche ben sholde rather feeste beggeris
> Than burgeises that riche ben . . .
>
>   (B.XV.335–6; 339–42)

The 'hungry gap' of Frank's title which fell almost annually in the weeks before harvest is dramatised in the arrival of Hunger in Piers's half-acre in B.VI, and here, too, there is a suggestion that the land could provide enough, were people prepared both to work properly and to be less greedy. By the time we reach the C text Langland is prepared to be more explicit, once again placing overt criticism in the mouth of Anima:

> Nother see ne send ne the seed yeldeth
> As they ywoned were; in wham is defaute?
> Nat in God, that he ne is goed, and the grounde bothe;
> And the se and the seed, the sonne ad the mone
> Doen her dever day and nyhte – dede we so alse,
> Ther sholde be plente and pees perpetuel evere.
>
>   (C.XVII.88–93)[45]

Although the famine referred to in this later passus is plausibly a spiritual dearth as much as a lack of actual foodstuffs, the Hunger that visits Pier's half-acre earlier is literal enough. Frank is right to state that Langland, like his contemporaries 'rarely managed to disentangle economics from morality' (Frank 1990: 99) and passages such as these indicate that the lack of disentanglement is not a failure of conceptual ability (as Frank's 'rarely managed' seems to imply) but a deliberate political point. Food production and distribution, like any other activity, has its moral dimension and in an ecocritical light that morality looms large.[46] Moreover, then as now, the questions of distribution and production have become particularly pressing because the prevailing climactic conditions have changed and our, human, response is not changing accordingly. Frank usefully points out how many harvests had been ruined by rain in the years surrounding the composition of *Piers Plowman* (1314–70) and parallels might be drawn with the persistent famines afflicting Africa and India in our own time. Here again, what Wil sees in the real world has a direct effect on how he interprets both the world and his place within it.

Equally striking for a green reading of the poem is the central image of the final and most nearly successful attempt at an ideal society, that of the barn of Unity in B.XIX. This barn is both a metaphorical building constructed from the timbers of the cross, held together with the mortar of Christ's blood and roofed with the Scriptures (B.XIX.321–30) and an actual cruck frame barn, a form of construction associated with peasant buildings.[47] Allusions to human soil cultivation continue to underpin the metaphorical cultivation of right religious understanding; the seed that Piers must sow in order to reap an appropriate harvest being a case in point. Thus when Grace chooses to accompany Piers in B.XIX they may go 'as wide as the world is' but they do so with a ploughman's intent 'to tilie truthe / And the londe of bileve' (B.XIX.335–6). It may then seem that by the end of *Piers Plowman* we have left behind the wider appreciation of humanity's common link with the rest of creation and have taken on a thoroughgoing anthropocentric world-view that sees the world only in terms of cultivation. Given that the recurring guide figure of Wil's dream is a ploughman, such an outlook is hardly surprising, but in the end it does not triumph. Instead we are left with Conscience abandoning the now corrupted barn of Unity and

Gardens and fields

declaring his intent to walk 'as wide as the world lasteth' (B.XX.382). Admittedly this is in the hope of finding Piers, but it is significant that Piers the Plowman is no longer to be found ploughing his fields and that Conscience's words echo Wil's opening wanderings in which he 'wente wide in this world wondres to here' (B.Prol.4). Like *Pearl*, *Piers Plowman* thus returns us from dream vision to waking world and although the elaborate allegory and spiritual intent of the poem must not be dismissed, nor must the attention the poem bestows on the phenomenal. Throughout his poem Langland links the search for a right way to live with moments of acute observation, much of which, particularly in the first half of the work, consists of straightforward appreciation of, and sheer delight in, the natural world. These moments are often left untouched by the tussles with social ills that follow and epitomise the kind of direct engagement with the material world sought in their different ways by Hugh of St Victor, Stephen Clark and Val Plumwood. Such moments are integral elements of Langland's vision and as such should not only be accorded due acknowledgement but should also be allowed to resonate throughout the poem. Perhaps the best example of this attention, and a fitting one on which to end this study of the abiding presence of the natural world in late medieval literature, is part of Wil's view from the mountain of Middle-erthe:

> And sithen I loked on the see and so forth on the sterres;
> Manye selkouthes I seigh, ben noght to seye nouthe.
> I seigh floures in the fryth and hir faire colours,
> And how among the grene gras growed so manye hewes,
> And some soure and some swete – slekough me thoughte.
> Of hir kynde and hir colour to carpe it were to long.
> (B.XI.362–7)

It is no mistake that neither Langland nor Wil expound on these lines further. We are left with the impression of wonder instilled by these 'selkouthes' and, as Hugh of St Victor indicated, two centuries before Langland, that sense of true admiration of and at the world is one we can ill afford to lose.

Notes

1 Famously, the garden in *The Romance of the Rose* has Idleness as its gatekeeper while various vices are depicted on the outside of the walls; among

these is found Age. Chaucer's translation highlights how such walled gardens were similar to fortresses: 'everydell enclosed' and 'walled well / With highe walles enbatailled' (*RR* 139–40).

2   'Walking about in gardens was often interpreted as a sign of moral fault' (Doob 1974: 174). Interestingly Doob is dealing with the Orfeo story here and notes that, according to the Boethian tradition, Eurydice's enjoyment of the garden is associated with the soul's mistaken delight in fleshly pleasures. The danger can go beyond mere moral fault: 'Overindulgence in the joys of nature implies neglect of duty to God, and sensual pleasures open the soul to the devil; medieval gardens and orchards might be dangerous as well as pleasant' (175).

3   Ann Haskell's thought-provoking treatment of Chaucer's women and the gardens with which they are connected in 'Chaucerian Women, Ideal Gardens, and the Wild Woods' indicates the range of associations available, but is too brief to develop the possibilities fully. See Dor 1992: 193–8.

4   Comparison of the views found in Ellen Rose, Rosemary Radford Ruether, Carolyn Merchant and Val Plumwood will give some idea of the options available. Karen Warren's collection *Ecological Feminism* and the essays collected in Carol Adams's *Ecofeminism and the Sacred* offer a good range of views, while Merchant's *The Death of Nature* traces the various ways women have been defined with nature and the detrimental consequences such alignments can have for both.

5   Both the *De Planctu Naturae* and the *Anticlaudianus* were highly influential, especially in their treatment of Nature. Their influence continues in that many current critics turn to Alan for examples of how medieval thinkers and writers conceived of nature. J.J. Sheridan (whose translations and editions I have used) suggests a date of 1160–65 for *De Planctu* and 1181–84 for the *Anticlaudianus*. See Sheridan 1980: 31–5 and 1973: 24–5 respectively.

6   Following Sheridan, I have used Häring's edition of *De Planctu* in which each metre and prose is numbered separately rather than in pairs, thus section VIII is Prose 4 of Sheridan's translation. All quotations of the Latin are taken from Häring and cited using his division and line numbers. References to Sheridan are by page number.

7   Not to mention his misogyny. Custom and syntax force him to have a female Nature, but he is clearly convinced that no female, not even a metaphorical one, should be left in control of a chariot, as Sheridan has pointed out (1980: 109 n. 3).

8   One begins to wonder if in Alan's eyes part of the problem is that a woman was left in charge to start with: this might answer Sheridan's objections to the lack of challenge to the inadequate reasons given for Nature's deserting her post and her failure to appoint a reliable deputy (Sheridan 1980: 34 and 147).

9   'Material, which is inferior to these and is subject to degeneration in its beauty, has no rights here' (Sheridan 1980: 48), *Anticlaudianus*. I quote Boussart's 1955 Latin text.

10 Freshwater pearls were found in mussels in Wales, Cumberland and Scotland, but these were relatively few in number and by the fourteenth century the vast majority of real pearls were imported and were the sea variety, the best coming from India or east of the Mediterranean (see Campbell 1991:

115–17). The fifteenth-century Peterborough Lapidary declares that the best pearls 'comen out of ynde & of old brytayn' (Evans and Serjeantson 1933: 108). There is some evidence of fake pearls being made in the fourteenth century: Campbell refers to a recipe for making pearls and suggests that the beads on Edward I's burial clothing may have been imitation pearls (Campbell 1991: 117).

11   Bartholomaeus Anglicus's encyclopaedia of knowledge *De Proprietatibus Rerum* (On the Properties of Things) was written in Marburg in the 1240s. It gained increasing popularity, being translated into several vernaculars, while copies of the Latin text remained widely available also. Trevisa's English translation was completed by 1398/9 and is a mark of its popularity, although Trevisa's own text seems to have had limited circulation, perhaps, as the Oxford editors suggest, owing to the expense of producing copies. None the less, the influence of the *De Proprietatibus Rerum* continued to be felt into the fifteenth and even sixteenth century, not least because of the continued popularity of lapidaries, which tended to be conservative documents, preserving the ideas of former ages. See Evans and Serjeantson 1993.

12   As were many gems and precious metals: part of the function of a lapidary was to give the medicinal powers of the stones it listed.

13   This is an example of what Nick Davis terms 'an excess of "phenomenon" over "interpretation" making for a dramatic sense of immersedness in ongoing events' and as such endorses his point that, in common with the other three poems, *Pearl*'s emphasis is on the 'sheer human responsiveness to a given environment'. See Davis, 'Narrative Form and Insight' in Brewer and Gibson 1994: 340.

14   See Gordon ed. 1980: 47–8 nn. 41; 43–4.

15   As already mentioned, the walled garden of *The Romance of the Rose* epitomises this role and Chaucer uses its associations in the Knight's, Franklin's and Merchant's Tales.

16   Opinion differs as to whether the 'hygh seysoun' is Lammas (1 August) or the Feast of the Assumption (15 August). Andrew and Waldron (1978: 56 n. 39) favour Lammas with its harvest associations; Anderson (1996: 281 n. 39) inclines towards the Assumption.

17   Mirth's garden in the *Roman de la Rose* contains a similar list, which, as Gollancz and Gordon suggest, may have influenced the poet here. However there, according to Chaucer's translation, the plants are valued specifically as digestifs (*RR* 1367–72).

18   Helen Barr describes the dreamer as 'an impressionable social outsider' (Barr 2000: 63) while Andrew and Waldren regard his attitude as 'that of a social inferior trespassing in the grounds of a castle' (n. 149–50).

19   See *MED* 'herber' n.1 where this meaning is suggested, with a citation of the Auchinleck MS of *7 Sages* offering the clearest example of this usage. The other examples in this section are less clear-cut, although all indicate that a 'erber' is a discrete area of a wider garden and several link it with vines or trees.

20   In similar vein, Helen Barr has made a case for a more historically informed understanding of the poem which will 'continue recent moves to break out of a closed hermeneutic system of juxtaposing the heavenly and the earthly, the

literal and the figurative, and the aesthetic and cultural.' (Barr 2000: 59).

21 Riddy (1997) points out that it is more likely that the narrator is a merchant than a craftsman.
22 Andrew and Waldron, Barr, Gordon, and Stanbury all make this point in different ways.
23 In the light of the suggested glosses for 'strothe-men' conglomerated in Andrew and Waldron's note, a green reader, familiar with Pogue Harrison's *Forest*, might be tempted to detect here a possible association with Harrison's notion of the earliest human civilisations arising in woods and being awestruck by the sky visible when looking up in clearings (see Harrison 1992: 2–6). Such an interpretation allows for a general innate connection between humans and woods that could add to the dreamer's feeling of being at home in such a landscape. This connection seems to me tempting, but surely spurious.
24 Davis's (1997: 337) discussion of the narrator's position, types of knowledge and the kinds of time in all four poems of the *Gawain* poet is relevant to many of the issues I touch on here.
25 See Trevisa 1029–31, who distinguishes three types of rose: tame, wild and 'verray'. This last is the result of the cultivation of a wild rose; it is not clear what, if any, difference there is between the tame and the 'verray'.
26 This is not to say that reason was regarded as the preserve of humans alone. Animals, too, possessed reason, but it was usually thought to be in a less fully developed form than that available to humans. For discussion of reason as a human faculty see Rudd 1994.
27 Alan's Reason is the close companion of Phronesis, or Prudence, but can accompany her only so far on her trip to heaven to beg a soul from God. Reason is left behind when the journey enters the realms of the heavens, from there up Faith and Theology are the guiding principles. Langland is more nuanced in his exploration of Reason, but he, too, acknowledges its limitations (see Rudd 1994: 44–57 and 119–34).
28 The river was equally real for the person who drew the pictures in the manuscript. It appears in all four illustrations of *Pearl*, despite not figuring in each landscape depicted (there is no mention of a stream in the original 'erber') and has always has fish in it, as if to emphasis its reality.
29 Handelman 1982: 23; see also Barr 2000: 60.
30 All references to the B-text of *Piers Plowman* are to the Schmidt edition (Schmidt 1982). This edition remains the most readily available scholarly edition of *Piers Plowman* B-text, but readers are referred to the invaluable comparative text edition, also by Schmidt, published by Longman (Schmidt 1995).
31 Sheridan notes the clear influence of Plato here.
32 See note 27 above.
33 Alan includes a second mirror in Book VI, this time given to Phronesis by Faith in order to prevent her being blinded by the excessive light of the higher celestial regions, but this is not a mirror of the world.
34 The *MED* entry on 'kynde' is long and offers much relevant material. Langland spends some time exploring and exploiting the term in intellectual terms through his use of 'kynde wit' and 'kynde knowing'. At this point in the

poem, however, Kynde is most clearly nature and force of creation.
35 As one of the leading mystic theologians of the day, Hugh is particularly concerned with the relative merits of intellectual and deductive understanding and more affective, mystical forms of apprehension. A useful overview of Hugh and his work may be found in Smalley 1983: 83–105.
36 *De Tribus Deibus* as given in Migne 1880: 814. This treatise is erroneously presented as Book 7 of Hugh's *Didascalicon*, as pointed out by Buttimer (1939: vii). The translation is my own, but I am grateful to Professor Niall Rudd for his expert help with it.
37 Hugh's attitude here is rather at odds with his impatience elsewhere with those who overlook the literal meanings of words. See Smalley 1983: 93.
38 Lorraine Daston and Katherine Park's intriguing book *Wonders and the Order of Nature* (2001) demonstrates how wonder was an integral part of knowing throughout the Middle Ages (indeed from late antiquity up to the Enlightenment and arguably still today).
39 Importantly, though, Clark (1993) believes that we should identify with the rest of the world, not figuratively but as equal and different elements of the world as a whole. Clark's book offers comparisons of various available ways of thinking about the earth and our human relations to it and the other species that form part of it, so to quote from it as I have here necessarily gives a rather partial and incomplete impression of his arguments as a whole.
40 Although Hugh does not seem to acknowledge it, it is important for us to retain the distinction between the illiterate and the uneducated. It was perfectly possible for someone educated to a very reasonable standard to be a hesitant reader of the written word. Similarly, those who could read could not necessarily write.
41 Elliott's argument is further undermined by his own points that words of geographical expanse abound in the poem and that movement through landscape is an important element of it (see Elliott 1984: 20–3; 25–6). I would argue that Langland's engagement with the actual and physical landscape is present throughout the text and underpins much of the more abstract theological and social debates. In many cases that engagement is expressed in terms of food economics, as R.W. Frank Jnr and Kathleen Hewitt-Smith (1996) have shown.
42 The point is made explicitly by Ymaginatif in B.XI.411–14, where he tells Wil that had he been more patient he would have learnt more.
43 This desire to believe in a force that will correct us is similar to that latent in Chaucer's 'Knight's Tale', making it credible that Arcite's death is at least in part the act of a vengeful nature. See Chapter 2 above.
44 *Pace* Skeat and more recently Caroline Barron, my own experience of Langland is as a fundamentally rural poet. Derek Pearsall also of this view: 'I have found it necessary to stress that Langland, though he is conscious of and minutely attentive to the economical and political life of the city, chooses agrarian models for his allegorical ideals of community' (Pearsall 1997: 185).
45 Quotations from the *Piers Plowman* C-text are taken from Schmidt 1995.
46 In fairness to Frank it should be noted that his article as a whole takes due account of this and directs readers to economists of famine, such as Amartya Sen, who argue this view strongly.

47 Cruck-framed buildings could be used for the houses of people who were relatively well-off and indeed the term 'peasant' does not necessarily denote impoverishment. See Dyer 1994: 133–66.

References

Adams, C., ed. (1994) *Ecofeminism and the Sacred*. New York: Continuum.
Adams, C.A. and Donovan, J., eds (1995) *Animals and Women: Feminist Theoretical Explorations*. Durham and London: Duke University Press.
Adomnán's 'Life of Colomba', eds and trans. Alan Orr Anderson and Majorie Anderson. (1991) Oxford: Clarendon Press.
Alan of Lille (1955) *Anticlaudianus*, ed. R. Bossuat Paris: Librairie Philosophique J. Vrin.
—— (1973) *Anticlaudianus; of the Good and Perfect Man*, trans. J.J. Sheridan. Toronto: Pontifical Institute of Mediaeval Studies.
—— (1978) *De Planctu Naturae*, ed. N.M. Häring *Studie Medievali* 3rd series 19.2, pp. 797–879.
—— (1980) *Plaint of Nature*, trans. J.J. Sheridan. Toronto: Pontifical Institute of Mediaeval Studies.
Anderson, Alan O. and Majorie, eds and trans. (1991) *Adomnán's 'Life of Colomba'*. Oxford: Clarendon Press.
Anderson, J.J. ed. (1996) *Sir Gawain and the Green Knight, Pearl, Cleanness, Patience*. London: Dent Everyman.
Anderson, William. (1990) *Green Man: The Archetype of our Oneness with the Earth*. London and San Francisco: HarperCollins.
Andrew, Malcom and Waldron, Ronald, eds (1978) *The Poems of the Pearl Manuscript*. York Medieval Texts Series. London: Edward Arnold.
Armbruster, Karla and Wallace, Kathleen, eds (2001) *Beyond Nature Writing: Expanding the Boundaries of Ecocriticism*. Charlottesville and London: University of Virginia Press.
Auerbach, Erich (1953) trans. Willard Trask. *Mimesis: The Representation of Reality in Western Literature*. Princeton: Princeton University Press.
Babich, Andrea (1998) 'The Power of the Kingdom and the Ties that Bind in *Sir Orfeo*', *Neuphilologus* 82:3, 477–86.
Barr, Helen (2000) '*Pearl* – Or 'The Jeweller's Tale', *Medium Aevum* 69:1, 59–79.
Barron, Caroline M. (1992) 'William Langland: A London Poet' in Hanawalt (1992), pp. 91–109.
Basford, Kathleen (1978) *The Green Man*. Woodbridge: D.S. Brewer, rpt 1996, 2002.
Bate, Jonathan. (1991) *Romantic Ecology*. London: Routledge.
—— (2000) *The Song of the Earth*. London: Picador.

Bawcutt, P. and Riddy, F., eds (1992) *Selected Poems of Henryson and Dunbar*. Edinburgh: Scottish Academic Press.
Benson, Larry et al., eds (1987) *The Riverside Chaucer*. 3rd edition. Boston: Houghton Mifflin Co. paperback ed. 1988 Oxford: Oxford University Press.
Bennett, J.A.W. (1957) *The Parlement of Foules*. London: Oxford University Press.
—— ed. (1963) *Essays on Malory*. Oxford: Clarendon Press.
Bennett, Jane and Chaloupka, William, eds (1993) *In the Nature of Things: Language, Politics and the Environment*. Minneapolis and London: University of Minnesota Press.
Berry, Edward (2001) *Shakespeare and the Hunt: A Cultural and Social Study*. Cambridge: Cambridge University Press.
Blair, J. and Ramsey, N. eds (1991) *English Medieval Industries: Craftsmen, Techniques, Products*. London and Rio Grande: Hambledon Press.
Bleakley, Alan (2000) *The Animalizing Imagination: Totemism, Textuality and Ecocriticism*. Basingstoke: Macmillan.
Bliss, A.J., ed. (1966) *Sir Orfeo*. Oxford: Clarendon Press.
Bloomfield, Morton, ed. (1981) *Allegory, Myth and Symbol*. Cambridge, Mass. and London: Harvard University Press.
Bossuat, R., ed. (1955) *Alan of Lille. Anticlaudianus*. Paris: Librairie Philosophique J. Vrin.
Brewer, D. and Gibson, J., eds (1997) *A Companion to the 'Gawain' Poet*. Cambridge: Brewer.
Budinasky, S. (1995) *Nature's Keepers*. London: Weidenfeld and Nicolson.
Buell, Laurence. (1996) *The Environmental Tradition*. Cambridge, Mass. Belknap.
—— (1999) 'The Ecocritical Insurgency', *New Literary History* 30:3, 699–712.
—— (2001) *Writing for an Endangered World*. Cambridge, Mass. Belknaps.
Burrow, J. (1971) *Ricardian Poetry: Chaucer, Langland and the 'Gawain' Poet*. London: Penguin.
Buttimer, C.H., ed (1939) *Hugonis de Sancte Victore Didascalicon – de Studio Legendi: A Critical Text*. Washington: Catholic University of America Press.
Campbell, M. (1991) 'Gold, Silver and Precious Stones' in Blair and Ramsey (1991), pp. 107–66.
Carson, Rachel (1962) *Silent Spring*. London: Hamish Hamilton.
Chaucer, Geoffrey. *The Riverside Chaucer*, eds Larry Benson et al. (1987) 3rd edition. Boston: Houghton Mifflin Co. paperback ed. 1988 Oxford: Oxford University Press.
Clark, Stephen, R.L. (1993) *How to think about the Earth: Philosophical and Theological Models for Ecology*. London: Mowbray.
—— (1996) *Animals and Their Moral Standing*. London: Routledge.
Cook, Robert. (1994) 'Chaucer's Franklin's Tale and *Sir Orfeo*', *Neuphilologische Mitteilungen* 95:3, 333–7.
Cooper, Helen (2004) *The English Romance in Time: Transforming Motifs from Geoffrey of Monmouth to the Death of Shakespeare*. Oxford: Oxford University Press.
Coupe, Lawrence (2000) *The Green Studies Reader*. London and New York: Routledge.
Crane, Susan (1998) 'May Time in Late Medieval Courts' *New Medieval Literatures* 2, 159–80.

References

Cummins, John (1988) *The Hound and the Hawk: The Art of Medieval Hunting.* London: Weidenfeld and Nicolson.
Curtius, Ernest R. (1953) trans. Willard Trask. *European Literature and the Latin Middle Ages.* New York: Pantheon Books.
Davies, R.T., ed. (1966) *Medieval English Lyrics: A Critical Anthology.* London: Faber and Faber.
Davis, Nick (1997) 'Narrative Form and Insight' in Brewer and Gibson (1997), pp. 329–49.
Daston, L and Park, K. (2001) *Wonders and the Order of Nature 1150–1750.* New York: Zone Books.
Diamond, Arlyn and Edwards, Lee R., eds (1997) *The Authority of Experience: Essays in Feminist Criticism.* Amherst: University of Massachusetts Press.
Dinshaw, Carolyn (1999) *Getting Medieval: Sexualities and Communities Pre- and Postmodern.* Durham and London: Duke University Press.
Doob, P. (1974) *Nebuchadnessar's Children: Conventions of Madness in Middle English Literature.* New Haven and London: Yale University Press.
Dor, Juliette, ed. (1992) *A Wyf Ther Was: Essays in Honour of Paule Mertens-Fonck.* Liège: Liège Language and Literature.
Douglass, Rebecca (1998) 'Ecocriticism and Middle English Literature' *Studies in Medievalism* 10, 136–63.
Duncan, Thomas (1995) *Medieval English Lyrics 1200–1400.* Harmondsworth and New York: Penguin.
Dyer, Christopher (1994) *Everyday Life in Medieval England.* London: The Hambeldon Press.
Elliott, R.W.V. (1984) *The Gawain Country: Essays on the Topography of Middle English Alliterative Poetry.* Leeds Texts and Monographs new series 8. Leeds: School of English.
Evans, J. and Serjeantson, Mary, eds, (1933) *English Medieval Lapidaries.* Early English Texts Society old series 190. London: Oxford University Press.
Evernden, Neil (1992) *The Social Creation of Nature.* Baltimore and London: Johns Hopkins University Press.
Fein, Susanna, ed. (2000) *Studies in the Harley Manuscript: The Scribes, Contents, and Social Contexts of British Library MA Harley 2253.* Kalamazoo: Medieval Institute Publications.
Firmage, George J., ed. (1994) *E.E. Cummings Complete Poems 1904–1962.* New York: Liveright.
Flores, Nona C., ed. (1996) *Animals in the Middle Ages.* New York and London: Garland.
Fox, Denton, ed. (1981) *The Poems of Robert Henryson.* Oxford: Clarendon Press.
Frank, Robert Worth (1990) 'The "Hungry Gap", Crop Failure, and Famine: The Fourteenth-Century Agricultural Crisis and *Piers Plowman*', *Yearbook of Langland Studies* 4, 87-104.
Friedman, John (1966) 'Eurydice, Heurodis and the Noon-Day Demon', *Speculum* 41, 22–9.
Fudge, Erica. (2000) *Perceiving Animals.* Basingstoke: Macmillan.
Fudge, E., Gilbert, R. and Wiseman, S., eds (1999) *At the Borders of the Human.* Basingstoke: Macmillan.
George, W. and Yapp, B. (1991) *The Naming of the Beasts: Natural History in the*

Medieval Bestiary. London: Duckworth.
Gifford, Terry (1995) *Green Voices: Understanding Contemporary Nature Poetry*. Manchester: Manchester University Press.
Glacken, Clarence J. (1967) *Traces on a Rhodian Shore: Nature and Culture in Western Thought from Ancient Times to the End of the Eighteenth Century*. Los Angeles and London: University of California Press.
Glotfelty, Cheryll and Fromm, Harold, eds (1996) *The Ecocriticism Reader: Landmarks in Literary Ecology*. Athens, Georgia: University of Georgia Press.
Gordon, E.V., ed. (1980) *Pearl*. Oxford: Clarendon Press, rpt of 1958 edition.
Graber, David M. (1995) 'Resolute Biocentricism: The Dilemma of Wilderness in National Parks' in Soulé and Lease (1995), pp. 123–35.
Gray, Douglas. (1972) *Themes and Images in the Medieval English Religious Lyric*. London: Routledge and Kegan Paul.
—— ed. (1985) *The Oxford Book of Late Medieval Verse and Prose*. Oxford: Clarendon Press.
Gros Louis, Kenneth R. (1967) 'The Significance of Sir Orfeo's Self-Exile', *Review of English Studies* 18:71, 245–52.
Guttman, N. (2002) 'Ecofeminism in Literary Studies' in Parham (2002) 37–50.
Hanawalt, B.A., ed. (1992) *Chaucer's England: Literature in Historical Context*. Minneapolis: University of Minnesota Press.
Handelman, S. (1982) *The Slayer Moses: The Emergence of Rabbinic Interpretation in Literary Theory*. New York: State University of New York Press.
Happé, P., ed. (1987) *English Mystery Plays*. Harmondsworth: Penguin Classics.
Häring, N.M., ed. (1978) *Alan of Lille De Planctu Naturae. Studie Medievali* 3rd series 19.2, pp. 797–879.
Harrison, C.M. and Burgess, J. (1994) 'Social Constructions of Nature: A Case Study of Conflicts over the Development of Rainham Marshes', *Transactions of the Institute of British Geographers* new series, 19, 291–310.
Harrison, Robert P. (1992) *Forests: The Shadow of Civilisation*. Chicago and London: University of Chicago Press.
—— (1999) '"Not Ideas about the Thing but the Thing Itself"' *New Literary History* 30:3, 661–74.
Haskill, Ann (1992) 'Chaucerian Women, Ideal Gardens, and the Wild Woods' in Dor (1992), pp. 193–8.
Hassig, Debra (1995) *Medieval Bestiaries: Text, Image, Ideology*. Cambridge: Cambridge University Press.
Hayles, Katherine N. (1995) 'Searching for Common Ground' in Soulé and Lease (1995), pp. 47–63.
Henryson, Robert. (1981) *The Poems of Robert Henryson*, ed. Denton Fox. Oxford: Clarendon Press.
Hewitt-Smith, Kathleen (1996) 'The Allegory of the Half-Acre: The Demands of History', *Yearbook of Langland Studies* 10, 1–22.
Honegger, T. (1996) *From Phoenix to Chauntecleer: Medieval English Animal Poetry*. Tübingen and Basle: Francke Verlag.
Huffman, Bennett, (1997) *The Aesthetics of Mortality in the Middle English Lyric*. Unpublished M.A. Dissertation, Liverpool University.
Hugh of St Victor. *De Tribus Deibus* erroneously presented as book 7 of the *Didascalicon* in *Patrologia Latina*, ed. J.-P. Migne (1880), vol. 176. Paris: Maine.

Ingram, Patricia (2001) '"In Contrayez Straunge": Colonial Relation, British Identity, and *Sir Gawain and the Green Knight*' in Wendy Scase, Rita Copeland and David Lawton (eds) *New Medieval Literatures* 4. Oxford: Oxford University Press, pp. 61–94.

Jacobs, Nicolas (1972) 'Aliterative Storms: A Topos in Middle English', *Speculum* 47:4, 695–719.

Jolly, Karen (1993) 'Father God and Mother Earth: Nature Mysticism in the Anglo-Saxon World' in Salisbury (1993), pp. 221–6.

Joseph, Laurence (1990) *Gaia: The Growth of an Idea*. Harmondsworth: Penguin, Arkana.

Josipovici, Gabriel. (1979) *The World and the Book*, 2nd ed. Basingstoke: Macmillan.

Justice, Steven and Kerby-Fulton, Kathryn, eds (1997) *Written Work: Langland, Labor and Authorship*. Philadelphia: University of Pennsylvania Press.

Ker, N.R. intro (1965) *Facsimile of British Museum MS Harley 2253* Early English Texts Society no. 255. London, New York, Toronto: Oxford University Press.

Kerridge, Richard and Sammels, Neil, eds (1998) *Writing the Environment: Ecocriticism and Literature*. London: Zed Books.

Keulartz, Jozef (1998) *The Struggle for Nature: A Critique of Radical Ecology*, trans. Rob Kuitenbrouwer. London and New York: Routledge.

Kiser, Lisa (1991) *Truth and Textuality in Chaucer's Poetry*. New Hampshire and London: Hannover.

—— (1996) 'Alain de Lille, Jean de Meun, and Chaucer: Ecofeminism and some Medieval Lady Natures' in P. Boitani and A. Torti, eds, *Mediaevalitas: Reading the Middle Ages*. Cambridge: D.S. Brewer, pp. 1–14.

—— (2001) 'Chaucer and the Politics of Nature' in Armbruster and Wallace (2001), pp. 41–56.

Kroeber, Karl (1994) *Ecological Literary Criticism: Romantic Imagining and the Biology of Mind*. New York: Columbia University Press.

Langland, William (1978) *Piers Plowman by William Langland: An Edition of the C-text*, ed. Derek Pearsall. London: Edward Arnold.

—— (1982) *The Vision of Piers Plowman: A Complete Edition of the B-text*, ed. A.V.C. Schmidt. London: Dent Everyman.

—— (1995) *Piers Plowman: A Parallel-text Edition of the A, B, C and Z Versions*, ed. A.V. Schmidt. London: Longmans.

Laskaya, Anne and Salisbury, Eve, eds (2001) *The Middle English Breton Lays*. TEAMS Middle English Texts Series. Michigan: Kalamazoo.

Le Goff, Jacques (1998) *The Medieval Imagination*, trans. Arthur Goldhammer. Chicago and London: University of Chicago Press.

Leicester, H. Marshall (1974) 'The Harmony of Chaucer's *Parlement*: A Dissonant Voice', *Chaucer Review* 9, 15–34.

Lerer, Seth (1985) 'Artifice and Artistry in *Sir Orfeo*' *Speculum* 60:1 92–109.

Lindley, Arthur (1996) *Hyperion and the Hobbyhorse: Studies in Carnivalesque Subversion*. Newark: University of Delaware Press; London: Associated University Presses.

Liszka, Thomas R. and Walker, Lorna E.M., eds (2001) *The North Sea World in the Middles Ages: Studies in the Cultural History of North-Western Europe*.

Dublin: Four Courts Press.
Love, Glen A. (1999) 'Ecocriticism and Science: Toward Consilience?', *New Literary History* 30:3, 561–76.
—— (2003) *Practical Ecocriticism*. Charlottesville: University of Virginia Press.
Lovejoy, Arthur O. and Boas, George (1997) *Primitivism and Related Ideas in Antiquity* Baltimore and London: Johns Hopkins Press. First published 1935.
Luria, Maxwell S. and Hoffman, Richard L. (1974) *Middle English Lyrics*. New York and London: W.W. Norton and Co.
McDonald, William J. (1967) *The New Catholic Encyclopedia*. NewYork: McGraw Hill.
Malory, Thomas (1971) *Works*, ed. Eugène Vinaver. Oxford: Oxford University Press.
Martin, Priscilla (1997) 'Allegory and Symbolism' in Brewer and Gibson (1997), pp. 315–28.
Marx, Leo (1976) *The Machine in the Garden: Technology and the Pastoral Ideal in America*. London and New York: Oxford University Press.
Matthews, Freya (1991) *The Ecological Self*. London: Routledge.
Merchant, Carolyn (1982) *The Death of Nature*. London: Wildwood House.
—— (1992) *Radical Ecology*. London: Routledge.
—— (1995) *Earthcare: Women and the Environment*. London: Routledge.
Migne J.-P., ed. (1880) *Hugh of St. Victor. De Tribus Deibus* erroneously presented as book 7 of the *Didascalicon* in *Patrologia Latina*, vol. 176. Paris: Maine.
Minnis, A.J. (1995) *Chaucer's Shorter Poems*. Oxford: Clarendon Press
Murray, Hilda (1964) *The Middle English Poem 'Erthe upon Erthe'*. Early English Texts Society original series 141 (1911) London: Oxford University Press.
Nehamas, Alexander. (2000) 'The Place of Beauty and the Role of Value in the World of Art', *Critical Quarterly* 42:3, 1–14.
Oerlemans, Onno (2002) *Romanticism and the Materiality of Nature*. Toronto, Buffalo and London: Toronto University Press.
Olwig, Kenneth (1984) *Nature's Ideological Landscape*. London: George Allen & Unwin.
Orme, Nicholas (1992) 'Medieval Hunting: Fact and Fancy' in Hanawalt (1992), pp. 133–53.
Parham, John, ed. (2002) *The Environmental Tradition in English Literature*. Aldershot: Ashgate.
Patience, ed. J.J. Anderson (1996) Sir Gawain and the Green Knight, Pearl, Cleanness, Patience. *London: Dent Everyman*.
Pearl, ed. J.J. Anderson (1996) *Sir Gawain and the Green Knight, Pearl, Cleanness, Patience*. London: Dent Everyman.
Pearsall, Derek, ed. (1978) '*Piers Plowman*' by William Langland: An Edition of the C-text. York Medieval Texts second series. London: Edward Arnold.
Pearsall, Derek (1997) 'Langland's London' in Justice and Kerby-Fulton (1997), pp. 185–207.
Pearsall, Derek and Salter, Elizabeth (1973) *Landscapes and Seasons of the Medieval World*. London: Paul Elek.
Pepper, David (1996) *Modern Environmentalism*. London: Routledge.
Pevsner, Niklaus (1958) *The Buildings of England: Shropshire*. Harmondsworth: Penguin. Rpt 1989.

Phillips, Dana (1999) 'Ecocriticism, Theory and the Truth of Ecology', *New Literary History* 30:3, 577–602.
Phillips, Helen and Havely, Nick, eds (1997) *Chaucer's Dream Poetry*. London and New York: Longman.
Plumwood, Val (1993) *Feminism and the Mastery of Nature*. London: Routledge.
—— (2002) *Environmental Culture: The Ecological Crisis of Reason*. London: Routledge.
Pocock, Douglas, C.D., ed. (1981) *Humanistic Geography and Literature*. London: Croom Helm.
Raban, Jonathan, ed. (1992) *The Oxford Book of the Sea*. Oxford: Oxford University Press.
Rackham, Oliver (1976) *Trees and Woodland in the British Landscape*. London: Dent.
—— (1986) *The History of the Countryside*. London: Dent. Rpt 1995, 1996, London: Weidenfeld and Nicolson.
Reiss, Edmund (1972) *The Art of the Middle English Lyric: Essays in Criticism*. Athens: University of Georgia Press.
Riddy, Felicity (1997) 'Jewels in *Pearl*' in Brewer and Gibson (1997), pp. 143–55.
Robinson, D.W. (1962) *A Preface to Chaucer: Studies in Medieval Perspectives*. Princeton: Princeton University Press.
Rooney, Anne (1993) *Hunting in Middle English Literature*. Woodbridge: Boydell.
—— (1997) 'The Hunts in *Sir Gawain and the Green Knight*' in Brewer and Gibson (1997), pp. 157–64.
Rose, Ellen Cronan (1994) 'The Good Mother: From Gaia to Gilead' in Adams (1994), pp. 149–67.
Rowland, Beryl. (1971) *Blind Beasts: Chaucer's Animal World*. Ohio: Kent State University Press.
—— (1973) *Animals with Human Faces: A Guide to Animal Symbolism*. London: Allen & Unwin.
Rudd, G.A. (1994) *Managing Language in 'Piers Plowman'*. Woodbridge: D.S. Brewer.
Ruether, Rosemary Radford (1992) *Gaia & God: An Ecofeminist Theology of Earth Healing*. London and New York: HarperCollins.
Russell, Colin A. (1994) *The Earth, Humanity and God*. London: University College London Press.
Sadowski, Piotr (1996) *The Knight on His Quest: Symbolic Patterns of Transition in 'Sir Gawain and the Green Knight'*. Newark and London: University of Delaware Press and Associated University Presses.
Salisbury, Joyce E. (1994) *The Beast Within: Animals in the Middle Ages*. London: Routledge.
—— ed. (1993) *The Medieval World of Nature: A Book of Essays*. New York and London: Garland Press.
Salter, David (2001) *Holy and Noble Beasts: Encounters with Animals in Medieval Literature*. Woodbridge: D.S. Brewer.
Saunders, Corinne (1993) *The Forest of Medieval Romance: Avernus, Broceliande, Arden*. Woodbridge: D.S. Brewer.
Schmidt, A.V.C., ed. (1982) *William Langland, The Vision of Piers Plowman: A Complete Edition of the B-text*. London: Dent Everyman.

—— (1987) '"Latent Content" and "The Testimony in the Text": Symbolic Meaning in *Sir Gawain and the Green Knight*', *Review of English Studies* 38:150, 145–68.

—— ed. (1995) *Piers Plowman: A Parallel-text Edition of the A, B, C and Z Versions*. London: Longmans.

Seymour, M.C., general ed. (1975) *John Trevisa 'On The Properties of Things': Trevisa's Translation of 'De Proprietatibus Rerum'*. Oxford: Oxford University Press.

Sheridan, James J., trans. and commentary (1973) *Alan of Lille, 'Anticlaudianus or the Good and Perfect Man'*. Toronto: Pontifical Institute of Mediaeval Studies.

—— trans. and commentary (1980) *Alan of Lille, 'The Plaint of Nature'*. Toronto: Pontifical Institute of Mediaeval Studies.

Sikarski, Wade (1993) 'Building Wilderness' in Bennett and Chaloupka (1993), pp. 24–43.

Silverstein, Theodore, ed. (1971) *English Lyrics before 1500*. York Medieval Texts. N.p.: Northwestern University Press.

Singleton, C.S. (1954) *Commedia: Elements of Structure*. Dante Studies 1. Cambridge, Mass. and London: Harvard University Press.

Sir Gawain and the Green Knight, ed. J.J. Anderson (1996) Sir Gawain and the Green Knight, Pearl, Cleanness, Patience. *London: Dent Everyman*.

Sir Orfeo, in *The Middle English Breton Lays*, eds Laskaya, Anne and Salisbury, Eve. (2001) TEAMS Middle English Texts Series. Michigan: Kalamazoo.

Smalley, Beryl (1983) *The Study of the Bible in the Middle Ages*, 3rd ed. Oxford: Basil Blackwell.

Soulé, Michael and Lease, Gary, eds (1995) *Reinventing Nature? Responses to Postmodern Deconstruction*. Washington D.C.: Island Press.

Spiers, John (1971) *Medieval English Poetry: The Non-Chaucerian Tradition*. London: Faber and Faber.

Stanbury, Sarah (1991) *Seeing the 'Gawain'-Poet: Description and the Act of Perception*. Philadelphia: University of Pennsylvania Press.

Stone, Gregory (1998) *The Ethics of Nature in the Middle Ages: On Boccaccio's Poetaphysics*. Basingstoke and London: Macmillan.

Strohm, Paul (1989) *Social Chaucer*. Cambridge, Mass. and London: Harvard University Press.

Sweeting, Adam and Crochunis, Thomas (2001) 'Performing the Wild: Rethinking Wilderness and Theater Spaces' in Armbruster and Wallace (2001), pp. 325–40.

Thomas, Keith (1987) *Man and the Natural World: Changes in Attitudes in England 1500–1800*. Harmondsworth : Penguin rpt of 1984 edition.

Trevisa, John (1975) *On the Properties of Things: Trevisa's translation of 'De Proprietatibus Rerum'*, general ed. M.C. Seymour. Oxford: Oxford University Press.

Tuve, Rosemond (1933) *Seasons and Months: Studies in a Tradition of Middle English Poetry*. Cambridge: D.S. Brewer, rpt 1974.

Vinaver, Eugène, ed. (1967) *The Works of Sir Thomas Malory* edited in three volumes, 2nd edition. Oxford: Clarendon Press.

—— ed. (1971) *Malory: Works*. Oxford: Oxford University Press.

—— (2000) *On Art and Nature and Other Essays* Whitstable: Elizabeth Vinaver.
Wager, Sarah J. (1998) *Woods, Wolds and Groves: The Woodland of Medieval Warwickshire*. BAR British Series 269. Oxford: John and Erica Hedges, Archaeopress.
Wall, Derek (1994) *Green History: A Reader in Environmental Literature, Philosophy and Politics*. London: Routledge.
Warren, Karen, ed. (1994) *Ecological Feminism*. London and New York: Routledge.
Wenz, P. (1996) *Nature's Keeper*. Philadelphia: Temple University Press.
Williams, Raymond (1973) *The Country and the City*. Rpt 1985. London: Hogarth Press.
Winney, James, ed. and trans. (1996) *Sir Gawain and the Green Knight*. Peterborough. Ontario: Broadview Press.
Wirtjes, H., ed. (1991) *The Medieval Physiologus*. Early English Texts Society. London: Oxford University Press.
Wiseman, Susan (1999) 'Monstrous Perfectibility: Ape-Human Transformations in Hobbes, Bulwer, Tyson' in Erica Fudge, Ruth Gilbert, Susan Wiseman, eds, *At the Borders of the Human: Beasts, Bodies and Natural Philosophy in the Early Modern Period*. Basingstoke: Macmillan, pp. 196–214.
Woolf, Rosemary (1968) *The English Religious Lyric in the Middle Ages*. Oxford: Clarendon Press.
Wright, Rosemary Muir (2001) 'The Rider on the Sea-Monster: *Quid gloriaris in malitia* . . .' in Liszka and Walker (2001), pp. 70–87.
Wycliffe, John and Purvey, Forshall, trans. (1879) *The New Testament in English*, eds J. and F. Madden. Oxford: Clarendon Press.
Wycliffite Bible. The Earlier Version of the Wycliffite Bible. MS Bodley 959: Genesis – Baruch 3.20, ed. Conrad Lindberg (1959). Stockholm: Almqvist & Wiksell.
The Wycliffe New Testament (1388): An Edition in Modern Spelling. W.R Cooper, ed. London: The British Library, 2002.
Yamamoto, Dorothy (2000) *The Boundaries of the Human in Medieval English Literature*. Oxford: Oxford University Press.
Young, Charles R. (1976) *The Royal Forests of Medieval England*. Leeds: Leeds University Press.

Index

Note: 'n' after a page reference indicates the number of the note on that page.

Alan of Lille
  Anticlaudianus 169, 179, 187, 202n5
  De Planctu Naturae 167–8, 202n5
allegory (also metaphor and symbolism) 11, 57, 73–4, 77–8, 170, 174–5, 178–9, 185
  dangers of 26–7, 29, 183–4
Anderson, J.J. 170
Anderson, W. 110, 111, 131n25
Andrew M. and Waldron, R. 170, 203n18
animals, general 39, 41, 48–50, 54–8, 60–1, 62, 73, 94, 96, 99–100, 106, 119, 120, 123, 126, 127, 130n20, 131n26, 132n34, 135, 136, 141, 159, 194–6
  birds 38–9, 40–2, 47n13, 104, 110, 114, 119, 195
  boars 54–6, 94
  deer 48, 57, 60, 66
  fish 39, 153, 154, 204n28
  horses 64, 66
  pigs 15, 49
  sheep 15, 198
  whale 150–8, 160, 163n20
  worms 43–5
anthropocentrism 5, 14, 30, 36, 41–3, 50, 53, 66, 68, 74, 100, 113, 117–18, 140, 143, 145–6, 154, 158, 162n10, 168, 176–7, 186–8, 200
anthropomorphism 6 37, 53, 56–7, 61, 72, 88n8, 130n17, 117–18, 121
  see also personification

appropriation 58–60, 120, 142
  see also assimilation; incorporation; substitution
Arcite *see* Chaucer, G., Knight's Tale
Ark *see* flood
assimilation 123–5
  see also appropriation; incorporation; substitution
Aurelius *see* Chaucer, G., Franklin's Tale
Averagus *see* Chaucer, G., Franklin's Tale

Babich, Andrea 129n10, 130n21, 132n36
barn of Unity (Langland) 200–1
Barr, H. 203n18, 203n20, 204n22, 204n29
Basford, K. 110, 131n25
Bate, J. 6, 18n2
Bennett, J.A.W. 68, 89n21
Berry, S. 88n9, 88n11
Bertilak 112–13, 115, 123, 131n27, 132n32
book, world as 185–92, 196, 198
Buell, L. 10, 147, 150, 163n20, 155–6

Carson, R. 6–7, 18n3
Chaucer, G. 11, 80, 82, 87
  Book of the Duchess 70–4, 89n22, 87
  'Former Age, The' 12–16
  Franklin's Tale 138–48, 160–1, 162n10, 163n12, 203n15

General Prologue 42
Gentillesse 89n22
Knight's Tale 50–67, 147, 153, 166, 203n15, 205n43
Legend of Good Women, The 52
Man of Law's Tale 133–4, 150
Merchant's Tale 74, 166, 203n15
Pardoner's Tale 46n6
Parliament of Fowls 67–70, 71
'Truth' 127–8
Wife of Bath's Tale 74
Clark, S. 19n8, 190–1, 201, 205n39
Cleanness 136–8, 149, 160–1, 162n5
cliffs *see* rocks
coast 138–9, 140, 142–3, 145, 161
Cummings, E.E. 38, 47n12
Curtius, R. 68, 165–6

Davies, R.T. 28, 47n11
Davis, N. 176–7, 203n13, 204n24
desert 91, 112, 131n27, 134, 152, 158–60
Dinshaw, C. 42, 47n15
disconcertedness (as critical response) *see* unease
Doob, P. 129n7, 132n33, 166, 202n2
Dorigen 139–48, 151, 163n11, 163n12, 166, 167
see also Chaucer, G., Franklin's Tale
Douglass, R. 4–5, 18n4, 34
Duncan, T. 28, 32, 46n9

earth 21–47, 171, 190, 195
middle-earth 186, 192
as mother 23, 25–6, 46n6, 65
see also Gaia
ecocriticism (green reading) 2, 3–18, 33, 35, 36, 42–5, 53, 56, 67, 103, 106, 112, 142, 143, 145, 146, 157, 161, 170, 200
ecofeminism 9–10, 18n8, 60, 103, 130n17, 143, 146, 167, 202n4
ecology 3, 6, 7, 34, 43, 64, 125, 146, 155, 156, 158, 163n19
ecosystem 7, 8–10, 34, 145, 155
Elliott, R.W.V. 133, 135, 138, 148, 161n1, 194, 205n41

Emeleye 53, 55, 60, 166, 167
see also Chaucer, G., Knight's Tale
environmentalism 1, 6, 7, 10, 147
'erthe toc of erthe' 21–7, 43, 45, 64, 148
Eurydice 97, 99, 202n2
see also Henryson, R.; Heurodis; *Sir Orfeo*
Evernden, N. 89n13, 91–3

fairy 100–5, 107, 126
famine 14–15, 19n15, 33, 197, 199–200 205n41
fields 13–14, 53, 165, 172, 185, 198–201
Flood (Noah's) 135–8, 149, 150, 152, 161, 162n5, 163n16
flowers 63, 167, 170, 172, 174, 176
rose 178–9, 180–1, 184, 195, 201
forest 48–50, 59, 60–1, 63, 68, 71, 73–5, 79, 80–7, 88n11, 89n19, 91, 112, 131n31
see also trees; woods
'fowles in the frith' 38–40
Frank, R. W. Jnr. 199–200, 205n41, 205n46

Gaia 9, 10, 65, 89n18, 117, 141
see also earth, as mother
garden 59, 86, 146, 165–7, 169–70, 172–6, 181–5
of Eden (Paradise) 165–7, 177
see also parks
Gawain (Malory) 78, 80–2
see also Sir Gawain and the Green Knight
Glacken, C. 138, 162n8
Golden Age 12–16, 19n14, 86–7
Gordon, I. 173, 204n22
Graber, D. 128, 128n2
grafting 75–7, 90n31, 108, 130n22
Green Man 93, 109–14
Gros Louis, K. 93–4, 100, 104, 106, 129n5, 129n7
grove 53–4, 56, 58–9, 61–2, 67
see also trees; woods

Handleman, S. 185–6

Index

Harrison, R. 50, 64–5, 83, 87n1, 88n11, 89n19, 119, 125, 127, 132n35
Havely, N. 70, 89n21, 89n22
Henryson, R. 129n8
 Orpheus and Eurydice 97–100, 104, 126, 132n36
 Testament of Criseyde 31–2
Heurodis 93, 102–5, 107–9, 129, 131
 see also Eurydice; Henryson, R.; *Sir Orfeo*
Huffman, B. 22, 46n2
Hugh of St. Victor 6, 188–92, 195, 196, 201
hunt, 48–9, 55–60, 65, 71, 73, 74, 82, 90n24, 90n32, 101, 102, 103–6, 109, 128, 162n10

incorporation 52–3, 87, 113
 see also appropriation; assimilation; substitution
Ingham, P. 113, 131n29

Jacobs, N. 137, 152, 162n7
Jolly, K. 33–4
Jonah 134, 138, 148, 10, 156, 164n21
 see also *Patience*
Josipovici, G. 185, 186, 191

Kiser, L. 69, 89n21
Kroeber, K. 8

landscape 2, 5, 16, 18n1, 42, 50, 55, 59, 66, 71, 74, 76, 83, 92, 109, 115, 118, 119, 120, 122, 126, 150, 169, 173, 174, 177, 181, 183–4, 205n41
Langland, W. 198, 205n41, 205n44
 Piers Plowman 6, 15, 165, 179, 185–201, 204n27
Launcelot 78–80, 82, 84, 86, 93
Le Goff, J. 49, 87n1, 112, 131n28, 162n3
Lerer, S. 130n4
Lewis, C.S. 75–7, 90n27
Love, G. 5, 7, 18n5
Lovelock, J. 9–10, 19n8, 89n18, 117
 see also Gaia

Luria, M. and Hoffman, R. 28, 32, 46n2, 46n9
lyrics 21, 23, 27, 28, 35, 36, 40, 46n8, 50, 97–8, 147

madness 39, 73, 75, 85–6, 90n35, 93, 98, 103, 129n4
Malory, T. *Morte D'Arthur* 17, 59, 74–87
marvel(s) see wonder(s)
Marx, L. 17, 19n18
Merchant, C. 9–10, 18n8, 19n16, 46n6, 59, 88n13, 167, 202n4
metaphor see allegory
Minnis, A. J. 16
'Mirie it is' 35–6
mirror, (natural world as) 185–8, 198
Morgan le Fay 80, 112–13, 115
Morte D'Arthur see Malory, T.
Murray, H. 21, 22, 23, 46n1

nature (natural world) 1, 8, 16, 40–1, 65, 113, 115, 141
 control of 2–3, 138, 139, 143–4, 147, 152
 human construct 10, 59, 69, 88n13, 128
 personified 168–9, 188, 193
 vengeful 25–6, 64–5, 89n18
Nehamas, A. 34–5
Noah 135, 152
 see also *Cleanness*; Flood (Noah's)

ocean see sea
Oerlemans, O. 8, 18n6, 27, 40, 46n7
orchard 48, 77, 79
Orfeo 115, 125, 128
 see also *Sir Orfeo*

Palamoun see Chaucer, G., Knight's Tale
parks 69, 128, 128n2, 165, 174, 175, 177–8, 180–1
Patience 138, 148–61, 163n14
Pearl 165, 169–85, 193, 201
pearl (stone) 170–2, 176, 202n10, 203n12
Pearsall, D. 205n44

Salter, E. and 4–5, 89n14, 89n16, 131n30
Pepper, D. 89n13
personification 29, 37–8, 71, 118, 122–3
see also anthropomorphism
Phillips, D. 18n5
Piers Plowman see Langland, W.
Plumwood, V. 6, 9–10, 18n2, 18n8, 52, 60, 89n15, 87, 113, 130n16, 130n17, 146, 156, 157, 163n19, 164n22, 179, 201, 202n4

Raban, J. 133, 162n2, 163n12
Rackham, O. 87n1, 88n2, 88n4
rain 37–8, 47n12, 136–7, 120–1, 149
reason 18n2, 18n8, 61, 103, 103n16, 140, 145–6, 179–80, 187, 195–8, 204n26, 204n27
Reiss, E. 22, 28–9, 33, 41, 44, 46n2
resilience (also resistance) 27, 36–7, 40, 89n18, 109, 125, 181, 184
Riddy, F. 204n21
Roberston, D.W. 10–11, 19n10, 19n11
rocks (also cliffs) 120–1, 139–48, 175, 180
romance 5, 59, 74–5, 83, 141, 146, 162n10, 167, 173
Romance of the Rose 166, 201n1, 203n15, 203n17
rose *see* flowers
Rose, E. 167, 202n4
Ruether, R.R. 18n8, 46n4, 167, 202n4

St Colomba (Life of) 134, 162n3
St Winifred's Well 1–4
Salisbury, E. 17
Salter, D. 16–17
Saunders, J. 49, 65, 75, 81, 85, 87n1, 90n32, 129n4, 131n31
sea 112, 133–9, 147–57, 160–1, 195, 201
seasons 32, 35, 37, 38, 47n10, 109, 116–18, 147, 168
  autumn 174
  spring 37–8, 40, 42, 166, 174
  summer 35, 40, 41, 96

winter 31–2, 35–8, 71, 96, 111, 116, 119, 120–1, 176
Sikarski, W. 127, 129n2
Silverstein, J. 40, 42
Sir Gawain and the Green Knight 8n12, 92, 95, 109–26, 130n18, 130n19, 141, 162n1, 165, 194
Sir Orfeo 92–109, 118, 122, 125, 126, 162n10, 165, 198, 202n2
Smalley, B. 205n35, 205n37
Spiers, J. 33, 117
Stanbury, S. 92–3, 130n19, 131n30, 162n5, 163n17, 176, 204n22
stars 97–8, 176, 195, 201
storms 64, 136–9, 151–4, 160–1, 162n6, 162n7, 164n21
substitution 112–13, 115, 122–3, 127, 131n29, 147, 163n19
  see also appropriation; assimilation; incorporation
'summer is icomen in' 40
Sweeting, A. and Crochunis, T. 92, 94
symbol (ism) *see* allegory

trees 2, 41, 48–90, 106, 107, 108, 174–5
  apple 79–80, 90n31
  ash 51–3, 62, 67
  box 51–3, 62, 67
  oak 53–4, 58, 62, 66–7, 70–1, 73, 89n20, 89n22, 89n23
  see also forest; grafting; woods
Trevisa, J. 52, 88n7, 171–2, 178, 203n11, 204n25
Tristram 75, 79, 80, 85, 86, 90n32, 93
Tuve, R. 32, 37, 47n10, 116

unease (disconcerted) as critical response 3, 17–18, 21, 25, 26, 43–5, 51, 54, 56, 61, 83, 87, 92, 102, 108, 111, 117, 121, 123–4, 127, 148, 149, 155, 159, 160, 177, 182, 185, 191, 196

Vinaver, E. 75–6, 78, 90n27
vine 158–9

Index

weather 31–2, 38, 88n12, 98–9, 118, 119, 120, 139
  see also storms
'westron wind' 37
'when the turuf is thy tour' 43
wilderness 41, 48, 59, 91–109, 118–21, 125–8, 128n2, 131n27, 131n31
  see also desert; fields
wildmen 54, 88n12, 93, 96, 99, 106, 129n7
  see also wodwo
Winney, J. 118
Winter's Tale, The 75–6
'winter wakeneth all my care' 31, 32, 35
Wirral 116, 118, 120, 131n31, 150
wodwo 88n12, 93, 119, 120, 125, 126

wonder 6, 9, 101, 164n23, 186, 188, 190–8, 205n38
wonders 104, 109, 111, 165, 174, 195, 201
  see also marvel(s)
woods 13, 39, 41, 48-50, 53, 58, 60, 67, 68–70, 71, 74, 79, 86, 88n11, 94, 121, 176
Woolf, R. 22, 31, 34, 43, 46n2, 46n3
world *see* earth
wordly goods 15–16, 23, 25, 30–1, 43, 45
'wrecche mon, why artou proud' 30–1, 45
Wright, R. 156, 163n13

Ywain 78, 129n4

EU authorised representative for GPSR:
Easy Access System Europe, Mustamäe tee 50,
10621 Tallinn, Estonia
gpsr.requests@easproject.com